**Nevill Drury** is well known for his books on visionary consciousness and shamanism. Born in England in 1947 he has lived most of his life in Australia. He is the author of over forty books, including *The Dictionary of the Esoteric*, *Exploring the Labyrinth*, *Everyday Magic*, *The History of Magic in the Modern Age* and a work of mythic fiction titled *The Shaman's Quest*. His work has been published in fifteen languages.

**Other books by the same author**

*The Shaman's Quest*
*Everyday Magic*
*Inner Visions*
*The Dictionary of the Esoteric*
*Pan's Daughter*
*The History of Magic in the Modern Age*
*New Perspectives: Shamanism*
*The Visionary Human*
*Exploring the Labyrinth*
*The Occult Experience*
*Echoes From The Void*

# SACRED
# ENCOUNTERS

*Shamanism and Magical*
*Journeys of the Spirit*

NEVILL DRURY

Watkins Publishing
London

This edition published in the UK in 2003 by
Watkins Publishing, 20 Bloomsbury Street, London, WC1B 3QA

© Nevill Drury 2003

Nevill Drury has asserted his right under the Copyright, Designs
and Patents Act, 1988, to be identified as author of this work.

Cover design by Echelon Design, Wimborne
Cover photograph © GettyOne
Designed and typeset by Echelon Design, Wimborne
Printed and bound in Great Britain by NFF Production

British Library Cataloguing in Publication data available

Library of Congress Cataloging in Publication data available

ISBN 1 84293 055 9

www.watkinspublishing.com

# CONTENTS

# ACKNOWLEDGEMENTS

Over the years many people have assisted me along the magical path and I would like to thank them for contributing either directly, or indirectly, to the creation of this book. They include Stephen Skinner, who first introduced me to the study of the Kabbalah, John Cooper, Jonn Mumford, and Michael Harner, who taught me the technique of shamanic drumming. I have also been greatly influenced by key figures in the 'new consciousness' movement like Stanislav Grof, Timothy Leary, Jean Houston, John Lilly, Ralph Metzner and Joan Halifax – these people have helped define the new spiritual paradigms of our age. Influential thinkers like Mircea Eliade, the surrealist artists, Max Ernst and Wifredo Lam, and metaphysical writers like Arthur Machen, Lord Dunsany and Jorge Luis Borges have also had a great impact on my work.

With specific reference to the present book, I would like to thank Dolores Ashcroft-Nowicki for permission to reproduce passages from 'Highways of the Mind', first published in the journal *Round Merlin's Table*, and fellow magical practitioners Catherine Colefax, Cheryl Weeks and Moses Aaron for allowing me to publish extracts from their magical diaries.

# PREFACE

This book presents two magical traditions which share a common heart: shamanism and modern visionary magic. Shamanism and visionary magic help us enhance our sense of the sacred. They show us how to respect and revere the cyclic and spiritual forces of Nature, and they help us attune ourselves to our psychic and spiritual depths. They show us how we can encounter the gods and goddesses who collectively represent different and complementary aspects of our innate sacred potential.

*Sacred Encounters* is a fusion of two of my earlier books, *The Shaman and the Magician* and *Vision-Quest* – together with a considerable amount of additional material. And while I think it is useful to describe the remarkable parallels between traditional shamanism and the visionary magical practices which have emerged from the Golden Dawn and the work of Dion Fortune and her successors, this is not simply an academic exercise. I wanted to write this book because I have always been fascinated by visionary magic. For me, this type of magic leads directly to the potentials of greater self-awareness. Visionary magic shows us a way of exploring the archetypal forces of the creative imagination – a way of understanding the energies and images which have inspired art, music and cosmology throughout the ages.

Although visionary magic and shamanism offer us a path towards spiritual self-transformation, at the same time they remind us that as individual human beings we are all connected to the Universal Spirit. While we bring to this world our own sense of uniqueness, it is also our destiny to discover the sacred bonds which connect us with the Universe as a whole – to explore our place within the larger scheme of things. In my view, this is why shamanism and visionary magic are so important. Both involve powerful and profound encounters with the sacred. Both lead us towards the mystery which lies beyond appearances, the sacred mystery which defines and sustains the world we live in.

# Part One

# PATHWAYS IN SHAMANISM

# CHAPTER 1

# THE WORLD
# OF THE SHAMAN

Anthropological reports often provide fascinating insights into the role of the healer in indigenous societies. One such report describes how, in 1951, a legendary Iban healer named Manang Bungai performed a dramatic ritual which was believed to slay an incubus, or evil spirit, that had been blamed for the death of a seven-month-old baby girl. Bungai, clad in a loincloth and carrying a spear, entered a darkened room and began summoning the incubus by means of various invocations and also by tempting it with food. His audience was unable to clearly perceive what was happening and was in a state of heightened suggestibility.

Very soon there was a yelping sound and a noisy scuffle, after which Bungai emerged with a blood-smeared spear claiming he had inflicted mortal wounds on the incubus. Several experienced Iban hunters were aware that Bungai had in fact been doing battle with a monkey, and the anthropologist observing the event, Derek Freeman, was later able to verify this by means of blood tests. However the majority of the Iban present at the ceremony believed that their healing magician was engaged in a mystical encounter.[1]

The case of Manang Bungai represents the shaman-who-is-not. True shamanism is characterized by access to visionary realms of consciousness, rather than the theatrics of deception. The authentic shaman operates in a way which involves venturing forth on different planes of cosmic reality. As the distinguished scholar of comparative religion, Mircea Eliade, has written: '… the shaman specializes in a trance during which his soul is believed to leave his body and ascend to the sky or descend to the underworld.' [2]

# THE VISIONARY ORIGINS
# OF SHAMANISM

Shamanism is essentially a visionary tradition, an ancient practice of utilizing altered states of consciousness in order to contact the gods and spirits who hold sway over the forces of the natural world. When we think of the shaman, the enigmatic image of a mysterious medicine man or sorceress comes readily to mind – a figure who enters a trance state in order to undertake a vision-quest of the soul. This vision-quest involves journeying to sacred places and reporting back on matters of cosmic intent. It may be, within any given community, that the shaman is a healer able to conquer the spirits of disease, a sorcerer skilled in harnessing spirits as allies for magical purposes, or a type of psychic detective able to recover lost possessions. At other times the shaman may even seem to be priest-like – an authoritative figure who acts as a sanctioned intermediary between the gods of Creation and the more familiar realm of everyday domestic affairs.

Whatever the specific role within the community, the shaman commands awe and respect because he or she is able to journey to other worlds and return with revelations from the gods. However, in order to understand the essence of shamanism we must first consider the earliest forms of religious expression around the world, since we can then obtain a framework, or context, for the rise of shamanic beliefs and practices in different hunter-gatherer communities.

## BEGINNINGS

The earliest tangible manifestations of man's religious awareness have been found in prehistoric cave sites located in Europe and central Asia. A Neanderthal grave discovered in Uzbekistan revealed that a circle of ibex horns had been placed reverently around the body of a dead child, and in a cave at Le Moustier, in France, a dead youth was laid as if asleep with his head resting on his right arm, supported by a pillow of flint flakes. A selection of tools and bones of animals, left close to hand, suggested strongly that it was believed that such implements could serve the youth in some future life.

It is possible that even at this early stage of human development Neanderthal man believed in a world in which spirit beings inhabited animals, rocks and trees, and conceived of some sort of afterlife in which his role as a hunter continued. Although such a conclusion is, of course, speculative, with the advent of the Upper Palaeolithic Era there is a clear indication that man had begun to think magically. As the noted scholar Abbé Henri Breuil has written, referring to the prehistoric cave and mural art of western Europe:

> Animals are represented pierced with symbolical arrows (bison and ibexes at Niaux; horses at Lascaux), clay models are riddled with spear marks (at Montespan, a headless lion and bear, which seem to have received new skins at various times) – facts which evoke the idea of sympathetic magic. The numerous pregnant women, and men closely pursuing their women suggest the idea of fertility magic. The deliberate alteration of the essential features of certain animals seems to indicate taboos. Human figures dressed up in animal or grotesque masks evoke the dancing and initiation ceremonies of living peoples or represent the sorcerers or gods of the Upper Palaeolithic.[3]

One of the most characteristic examples of magical cave art was discovered in the Franco-Cantabrian cave of Les Trois-Frères. Some

15,000 years old, the cave drawing depicts a hunter-sorcerer armed with a bow and disguised as a bison, amidst a herd of wild beasts. Another drawing found at the same site shows a sorcerer wearing horned headgear to deceive his prey.

From earliest times, religion, art and magic have been intertwined. Traditionally the hunter-sorcerer has always been regarded as a master of wild animals – able to control their fate through his hunting magic, an adept at disguises, and a practitioner of animal sacrifice. Very early on, he learned to mimic the animals and based his dances on their movements. Quite possibly, he may also have felt some sort of psychic bond with them. In this way the Palaeolithic hunter-sorcerer can be seen as a precursor of the archetypal native shaman with his animal familiars and his clan totems. The powerful psychic connection between shamans and different animal species may also have led to the belief that some shamans could transform their human consciousness into an animal form.

## Animism and the Belief in Spirits

The pioneering English anthropologist Sir Edward Tylor (1832-1917) gave a name to the earliest phase of magical and religious thinking, calling it 'animism', after the Greek word meaning 'soul'. According to Tylor, the idea of a soul, or spirit, seemed already at this stage to be universal, and prehistoric man apparently believed that not only did he have a soul but animals and plants did also. In addition, stones, weapons, food and ornaments could also have souls, and a person's spirit could enter into the bodies of other people, animals or objects through an act of possession. Tylor believed that the origin of animism probably lay in the experience of dreams – which seemed to show that man could exist independently of his physical body. Today, certain native peoples still use a common word for 'shadows', 'spirits' and 'ghosts' reflecting the belief in our dual existence. The Algonquin Indians, for example, call a man's soul his *otahchuk*, or 'shadow'; the Quiché say *natub* to denote a 'shadow' or 'soul', and the Zulu use the term *tunzi* for a shadow, spirit or ghost.

Tylor considered that once prehistoric man had come to conceive of two selves – the waking self and the phantom – it was a logical progression to believe that one's soul could undertake spirit journeys beyond the body or into an afterlife. Early evidence for such beliefs could be found in the remains of funeral rites where low-ranking servants had been sacrificed so that they could continue to serve deceased high-ranking officials in the afterworld, thus perpetuating the social order in the realm beyond death. Tylor also believed that primitive tribesfolk – 'savages' or 'rude races' as he so disparagingly called them – continued to reflect such animism in their everyday behaviour. It was animism, the belief in spirits, which would lead native peoples to converse with wild beasts, seeking their pardon prior to slaying them in the hunt, or to form a conviction that animals could have souls which, in earlier lives, had occupied the bodies of other human beings – possibly deceased friends or ancestors.

Tylor's overall concept is still highly regarded today, although it has not gone unchallenged. The distinguished French sociologist Emile Durkheim (1858-1917) undertook a broad survey of cultural patterns and customs and believed that the earliest type of human society consisted of undifferentiated hordes. Later, the hordes became more independent and formed themselves into clans – a unit Durkheim believed to be more basic than the family. Durkheim was not impressed by Tylor's essentially psychological idea that magical and religious thinking originated from dreams. He believed that primitive man gradually came to conceive of the clan as the overriding social unit and that in due course it became 'sacred' simply because it represented a higher, more all-embracing reality than the individual. Indeed, he pointed out that, when the clans acquired totem animals as symbols of differentiation, such totems were even more sacred than the actual animals themselves. Durkheim believed he could find evidence of this development process among the ethnographic data from the Australian Aborigines – the best-documented of the hunter-gatherer tribal people still surviving in modern times.

According to Durkheim, among Australian hunter-gatherers the totem animal or plant not only identified the clan but helped define patterns of kinship, since all clan members considered that they were related to each other. Durkheim also noted that central Australian tribes like the Arunta, known also as the Aranda, had ritual instruments – *tjurunga* or *churinga* – which were sacred to the clan, and whose names were never revealed to strangers. Such was the potency of the clan as the basic social reality of the hunter-gatherer.

Today the distinction between Tylor's and Durkheim's ways of thinking continues. Anthropologists tend to be divided between those whose frameworks of explanation are primarily cognitive or psychological, and those who emphasize the functional aspect of social roles. As one would expect, this leads in turn to different types of approach. Anthropologists evaluating shamanism from a psychological perspective will tend to be more interested in the altered states of consciousness accessed through trance, in the visionary origins of the shaman's magical and religious beliefs, and in other factors such as epileptic seizures, schizophrenic behaviour patterns and the use of psychedelics, all of which are associated with shamanism. Functionalists, on the other hand, are more inclined to ignore the experiential side of the shaman and his metaphysical world, concentrating instead on the role the shaman plays in society by interpreting tribal customs and taboos, reinforcing the beliefs underpinning the social structure and providing guidelines for the tribe.

From my own viewpoint, there is no escaping the inner dimension, the awesome magical realm that, in the shaman's cosmological system, parallels the everyday world and fills it with meaning and significance. If we did not consider the role of familiar spirits, initiatory visions, the experience of magical dismemberment and rebirth, and the transformative projection of consciousness into other living forms like animals and birds, we would have a very one-sided understanding of shamanism. We could also hardly explain its mystique or account for the ongoing interest in shamanic states of consciousness within the modern personal growth movement.

With these factors in mind we can now ask: who exactly is the shaman, how does he or she become one, and what is 'the journey of the soul' which seems to be so central to the shamanic process? As we gain answers to these central questions we are then able to understand the actual nature of the shamanic experience.

# BECOMING A SHAMAN

Shamanism is really applied animism, or animism in practice. Because Nature is alive with gods and spirits, and because all aspects of the cosmos are perceived as interconnected – the universe consisting of a veritable network of energies, forms and vibrations – the shaman is required to operate as an intermediary between different planes of existence.

The idea of a universe alive with spirits is brought home in the journals of Danish explorer and anthropologist Knud Rasmussen (1879-1933), who undertook an epic three-year journey in the American Arctic regions. Rasmussen, whose own grandmother was part Eskimo, had a fine rapport with the polar Eskimos and was very interested when an Iglulik shaman told him:

> The greatest peril of life lies in the fact that human food consists entirely of souls. All the creatures that we have to kill and eat, all those that we have to strike down and destroy to make clothes for ourselves, have souls, souls that do not perish with the body and which must therefore be pacified lest they should revenge themselves on us for taking away their bodies.[4]

We can define a shaman as a person who is able to perceive this world of souls, spirits and gods, and who, in a state of ecstatic trance, is able to travel among them, gaining special knowledge of the supernatural realm. He or she is ever alert to the intrinsic perils of human existence, of the magical forces which lie waiting to trap the unwary, or which give rise to disease, famine or misfortune. But the shaman also takes the role of an active intermediary – a negotiator in both directions. As American anthropologist Joan Halifax points out: 'Only the shaman is able to behave as both a god and a human. The shaman then is an interspecies being, as well as a channel for the gods. He or she effects the interpenetration of diverse realms.' [5] How, then, does one become a shaman?

Shamans are called to their vocation in different ways. For some it is a matter of ancestral lineage or hereditary bonds establishing the person in that position or else a situation where a would-be shaman seeks initiation from one already established in this role. In other cases it seems almost as if the spirits have chosen the shaman, rather than the other way around. These are the 'greater shamans' – those who have been called spontaneously through dreams or mystical visions to embody supernatural power. Those who have simply inherited their role are regarded as 'lesser shamans' and hold a lower status in society, especially among the peoples of Siberia and Arctic North America.

To begin with, as children or young adults, shamans are often of nervous disposition and may seem strangely withdrawn from society. As anthropologist Ralph Linton notes:

> The shaman as a child usually shows marked introvert tendencies. When these inclinations become manifest they are encouraged by society. The budding shaman often wanders off and spends a long time by himself. He is rather anti-social in his attitudes and is frequently seized by mysterious illnesses of one sort or another. [6]

The Chukchee peoples of Siberia believe that a future shaman can be recognised by 'the look in the eyes which are not directed towards a listener during conversation but seemed fixed on something beyond. The eyes also have a strange quality of light, a peculiar brightness which allows them to see spirits and those things hidden from an ordinary person.' [7] Waldemar Bogoras, who studied the Chukchee at first hand, provides a context for this occurrence: 'The shamanistic call may come during some great misfortune, dangerous and protracted illness, sudden loss of family or property. Then the person, having no other services, turns to the spirits and claims their assistance.' [8]

Much has been made of the idea that shamanism is born of crisis and disease – it has even been compared with schizophrenia. Julian Silverman, a leading advocate of this view, feels that the main difference between schizophrenics and shamans is that shamans are 'institutionally supported' in their state of mental derangement while modern society, for the most part, regards schizophrenia as an aberration. He believes that there is a striking parallel between the two phenomena and quotes a psychiatric description of schizophrenic states to make his point:

> The experience which the patient undergoes is of the most awesome, universal character; he seems to be living in the midst of struggle between personified cosmic forces of good and evil, surrounded by animistically enlivened natural objects which are engaged in ominous performances that it is terribly necessary – and impossible – to understand. [9]

However, a clear distinction obviously needs to be made at this point. While shamans and schizophrenics share the ability to move in and out of different mental states, the shaman has gradually learned how to integrate the different realms of consciousness, thereby bringing matters firmly under control. As Mircea Eliade has observed:

> ... the primitive magician, the medicine man, or the shaman is not only a sick man; he is, above all, a sick man who has been cured, who has succeeded in curing himself. Often when the shaman's or medicine man's vocation is revealed through an illness or epileptoid attack, the initiation of the candidate is equivalent to a cure. [10]

11

Eliade also elaborates on this point in his book *Birth and Rebirth*:

> The shamans and mystics of primitive societies are considered
> – and rightly – to be superior beings; their magico-religious
> powers also find expression in an extension of their mental
> capacities. The shaman is the man who *knows* and *remembers*,
> that is, who understands the mysteries of life and death.[11]

Clearly, there is more involved here than just psychological aberration
or disease. Because epilepsy and schizophrenia are regarded in
primitive societies as manifestations of the spirit world, it is not
surprising that people suffering from these conditions could later
become worthwhile shamans. But it is because they are open to the
world of spirits and have learned to converse with them and manifest
their presence that they are special – not simply because they are sick.
It is only the person who has learned to master the inner worlds who
can become accepted as a true shaman. Harnessing the power is
everything – the crisis, or disease, thus becomes an initiation.

Shamans are very much expected to exhibit control of the supernatural powers which interfere with human life. This includes
procuring game animals at times when the hunt appears to be
failing, driving away evil spirits, obtaining good weather, and curing
the sick. The Eskimo shaman, for example, has to journey in trance
to the bottom of the sea to propitiate Sedna, the Goddess of the Sea.
Sedna controls the sea mammals which provide food, fuel and skins
for their clothing but she also unleashes most of the misfortunes that
the Eskimo experiences. As William Lessa and Evon Vogt explain:

> These misfortunes are due to misdeeds and offences committed
> by men and they gather in dirt and impurity over the body of
> the goddess. It is necessary for the shaman to go through a
> dangerous ordeal to reach the sea goddess at the bottom of the
> sea. He must then stroke her hair and report the difficulties of
> his people. The goddess replies that breaches of taboos have
> caused their misfortunes. Whereupon the shaman returns for

the mass confession from all the people who have committed misdeeds. Presumably when all sins are confessed, the sea goddess releases the game, returns lost souls, cures illnesses, and generally makes the world right with the Eskimos again. [12]

# MYTHIC DISMEMBERMENT AND REBIRTH

An initiatory theme of dismemberment and rebirth occurs in several forms of shamanism and sometimes distinguishes strong shamans from lesser shamans in their respective communities.

A typical tale describing mythic dismemberment is found among the Avam Samoyed. A neophyte who wished to be a shaman was told that he would receive his 'gift' from the Lords of the Water. The neophyte was sick from smallpox at the time and it was said that 'the sickness troubled the water of the sea'. The candidate came out and climbed a mountain. There he met a naked woman and began to suckle at her breast. She said he was her child and introduced him to her husband, the Lord of the Underworld, who provided him with animal guides to escort him to the subterranean region. There he encountered the inhabitants of the underworld, the evil shamans, and the lords of epidemics, who instructed him in the nature of the diseases plaguing mankind.

After having his heart ritually torn out and thrown into a pot, the candidate now travelled to the land of shamanesses where his throat and voice were strengthened, and then on to an island where the Tree of the Lord of Earth rose into the sky. The Lord gave him certain powers, among them the ability to cure the sick. He then continued, encountering magical stones that could speak, women covered with hair like a reindeer's and a naked blacksmith, working the bellows over a huge fire in the bowels of the earth. Again the novice was ritually slain and boiled over the fire in a cauldron 'for three years'. The blacksmith then forged the candidate's head on one of three anvils 'the one on which the best shamans were forged' and told him how to 'read inside his head', how to see mystically without his normal eyes and how to understand the language of plants. Having mastered these secrets, and having had his body constituted anew after immolation, the shaman awoke 'resurrected' as a revivified being.[13]

It is clear from this Avam Samoyed account that the shaman has both a social and an individual role to play in his shamanising function. His trance experiences reveal the source of illness and disease which affect everyone but he also gains for himself, via a spiritual rebirth process, impressive supernatural powers. The shaman becomes a special figure because he has been reconstituted by the god at the anvil; the shaman's gift of magical sight and communication are born of heaven and not of earth. Occasionally, in fact, the shaman demonstrates his ongoing relationship with the heavenly domain by taking spirit wives from that dimension. The Buryat believe that the offspring born by such unions are semi-divine.[14]

The dismemberment-rebirth theme is not exclusively associated with Siberian shamanism and also occurs, for example, among Australian Aboriginal 'men of high degree'. In western South Australia, for example, the would-be shaman is put into a waterhole where a mythical snake swallows him and then ejects him in the form of a baby – a sign perhaps that the shaman is still 'new' to the spirit world. The head medicine man now recovers him but treats him as if he were a corpse, by ritually breaking his neck, wrists and joints. Into each mark and cut he inserts *maban*, a life-giving shell which is believed to rejuvenate a person and fill them with power. In this way the formerly 'dead' Aborigine is reborn to the world of magical knowledge.[15]

Dr Petrie, who worked with the Aborigines of the Munja Cattle Station at Walcott Inlet, discovered similar initiatory patterns there. Dreams would reveal to a would-be 'doctor man' that the high god Unggud wished him to become a *banman* or shaman. Unggud would 'kill' him near a waterhole but his essence would rise up – visible only to medicine men. At the same time the Aborigine would observe a giant snake with arms, hands, and a crown of feathers. Unggud would then lead him to a subterranean cave where he would begin to transform him into a man of knowledge:

> Unggud gives him a new brain, puts in his body white quartz crystals which give secret strength, and reveals to him his future duties. He may remain unconscious for some time, but when he awakes he has a great feeling of inner light. He is certain of being equal to Unggud. Instruction, guidance and experience follow for many months, even years.[16]

The shaman now has special magical powers. With his inner eye he is able to see past and future events and also able to send his *ya-yari*, or dream familiar, out of his body in search of information. According to the late Professor A. P. Elkin, a specialist in Aboriginal supernaturalism:

> … the psychic element in these talents is clearly all pervasive. It is termed *miriru* and comes from Unggud. Fundamentally it is the capacity bestowed on the medicine man to go into a dream state or trance with its possibilities. Indeed, *miriru* makes him like a Wandjina, having the same abilities as the heroes of 'creation times'.[17]

One could be tempted to regard the death and rebirth theme in shamanism as being specific to particular cultures and characteristic of creation myth archetypes. However, on occasion western investigators, whose frameworks of reality derive from completely non-shamanic viewpoints, have found themselves engaged in parallel processes. Although the controversial accounts of Carlos Castaneda's initiatory experiences with the Yaqui sorcerer, don Juan, provide the best known examples of the western intellectual encounter with mystical shaman powers, there are other examples of similar occurrences in the literature. In 1976 American psychologist Stephen Larsen published details of an inner mythic journey undertaken by a 21-year-old Brooklyn poet named Joel with an aged Dogrib Indian shaman, near Great Slave Lake, in Canada.

Joel discovered that the Indian, whose name was Adamie, used *Amanita muscaria* mushrooms as a sacrament and was skilled in employing the trance condition for shamanic journeys. In a similar manner to Castaneda, Joel went through a rigorous apprenticeship during which he was beaten and whipped by his master, presumably to strengthen his character and sense of resolve. During his second psychedelic experience with Adamie, Joel encountered animal spirits who tore him apart in the same manner as the native shamans described earlier. In like fashion, the initiation culminated in a renewed sense of strength and illumination:

> In trance I had a vision, I saw a bear. And the bear motioned for me to follow it. This was the spirit, the force I was to follow, to take my journey with. As I was following the bear it turned into a woman. And then there was a whole series of sexual imagery, buttocks, thighs, breasts, a whole swirl of sexuality, of flesh.
>
> I was swirling and whirling, and I felt like I was falling to the centre of the earth. And as I was going down there were creatures on all sides of me. And they would rip and tear, take pieces from me as I went down.

After being subjected to this traumatic destructive process, Joel began to experience inner healing and a profound sense of renewal:

> My feelings were of high ecstasy, shock waves of energy travelling through me. I felt I could see through things, hearts, bones, souls. There was a sound and it was coming up from within me. I was singing a song, the song of my experience, and I felt the song gave me a new strength and power.[18]

Joel's account challenges the view that the shaman can experience rebirth only within the familiar archetypal frameworks of his own culture – an issue which will be considered in a later section of this book. However, in a general sense, it is clear that from a shamanic perspective the mystical restructuring process leads to new visionary insights, powers and abilities which are normally expressed in terms of the familiar cultural context.

# THE JOURNEY OF THE SOUL

As we have already noted, a distinguishing feature of shamanism in all cultures is the journey of the soul. Because the shaman can travel in his spirit-vision to other realms he is regarded as a 'technician of the sacred' or a 'master of ecstasy'. In his role as an intermediary between the physical and metaphysical worlds the shaman gains privileged and sacred knowledge from the gods or spirit beings with whom he interacts, and his capacity to return with sacred inform-ation for the benefit of society becomes all-important.

In a sense, the shamanic journey of the soul can be regarded as a controlled act of mental dissociation and this state of dissociation can come about in many ways. Sometimes sacred psychedelic plants provide the impetus for the shamanic journey – these sacred plants will be discussed in a subsequent chapter – but at other times the spirit quest is associated with periods of fasting or sensory depri-vation, with chanting and the beating of drums, or with a particular response to a powerful visionary dream.

The *dehar* shaman among the Kalash Kafirs of Pakistan, for example, enters a trance state by standing immovably, relaxing his posture and then focusing his attention on a ceremonial altar to such an extent that every external element in his vision is excluded from his gaze. He then begins to shiver, jerks spasmodically, and enters an altered state of consciousness.

Singaporean shamanic candidates – mostly recent arrivals from China – become a *dang-ki* by displaying spontaneous signs of possession during temple ceremonies and then meditating on well-known *shen* divinities until the dissociational state is fully developed.

Among the Menangkabau, in Indonesia, it is considered that the life force, or *sumangat*, leaves the body in dreams or during states of sickness, and that the task of the *dukun*, or shaman, is to counteract the hostile influence of evil spirits during the out-of-the-body state. Here the *dukun* summons friendly spirits through a smoke offering, lies down on the ground covered by a blanket, begins to tremble physically, and then projects his consciousness into the mystical realm of the spirit world.

In the Mentawei Islands near Sumatra, shamans dance until they fall into a state of trance. They are then borne up into the sky in a boat carried by eagles where they meet sky spirits and ask them for remedies to treat disease. Traditional Eskimo (or Inuit) shamans, meanwhile, work themselves into a state of ecstasy by utilizing the energy of a drumbeat and invoking helper spirits. Some Eskimos lace their arms and legs tightly to their bodies to hasten the release of the inner light-force on the 'spirit flight', or *ilimarneq*. The classic case of an Eskimo spirit-journey is provided by Knud Rasmussen, the Danish explorer referred to above, who has provided us with a definitive account of this type of metaphysical adventure. The particular incident described in his *Report of the Fifth Thule Expedition 1921–1924* involved breaches of taboos which had invoked the wrath of the Sea Goddess. Here the shaman's role was to intercede on the community's behalf, travelling in his spirit body to the bottom of the sea.

At the beginning of the ceremony, members of the adult community gather around the shaman and observe him while he sits in meditative silence. Soon, feeling he is surrounded by helper spirits, he declares that 'the way is open' for him to undertake his journey. Various members of the household now sing in chorus while the shaman undertakes his difficult task: carefully avoiding three large, rolling stones on the sea floor and slipping nimbly past the Goddess's snarling watchdog. Rasmussen provides us with some idea of the perceptual process experienced by the shaman in his spirit projection when he writes that 'He almost glides as if falling through a tube so fitted to his body that he can check his progress by pressing against the sides, and need not actually fall down with a rush. This tube is kept open for him by all the souls of his namesakes, until he returns on his way back to earth.'[19]

The shaman now meets the Sea Goddess who, he can see, is nearly suffocating from the impurities of the misdeeds enacted by mankind. As the shaman strokes her hair to placate her, the Sea Goddess communicates with him in spirit-language, telling him that on this occasion there have been secret miscarriages among the women, and boiled meat has also been eaten in breach of taboo. When the shaman returns in due course to his community, it is this message he will relay and the offenders are sought out to explain their wrongdoing.

We can see from this account that the spirit-journey is not undertaken purely as an indulgence. Always there is a clear task involved – to counteract sickness, to understand the nature of breached taboos, to recapture a lost or tormented soul, or to help restore harmony to the different planes of the cosmos, thereby easing the rift between the spirit world and members of the community. This, essentially, is the role of the shaman – to journey to other worlds and to use revealed knowledge for a positive outcome. In this way the shaman is an intermediary between the gods and mankind.

Shamanism is an extraordinarily far-ranging practice, occurring in many different regions of the world. The classical source literature on shamanism focuses especially on Siberia, and the term 'shaman' itself has entered our language, via the Russian, from the Tungusic world *saman*. However, forms of shamanism also occur in North and South America, among the Australian Aborigines, in Indonesia, South-East Asia, China, Tibet and Japan. The following areas of the world are the main places where traditional shamanism is found.

## SIBERIA

This vast region – stretching from the Urals in the west to the Altai Mountains in the south and the Arctic Ocean in the north – encompasses tundra, fertile plains and rugged, mineral-rich mountain systems. It is also the home of many diverse and exotic peoples, including the Buryat and Goldi, the nomadic reindeer-herding Chukchee of the north-east, the Turkic-speaking Kirghiz, Yakuts, Uighurs and Altaians, and the Evenks and other neighbouring tribes in the Tungus-speaking region near the Yenisey and Lena rivers.

Here in Siberia the shaman is both a healer and ecstatic who undertakes journeys to both the sky and the underworld in search of fugitive souls that are responsible for illness. Shamans in this region also utilize divination and clairvoyance, and are sometimes capable of handling fire-coals without being burned. Buryats distinguish between 'white' shamans who liaise with the gods, and 'black' shamans who summon spirits, while Yakuts contrast the gods 'above' – regarded as passive and comparatively powerless – with the gods 'below' who have closer ties with the earth. Yakuts believe they have obtained mastery of fire from Ulu-Toyan, who dwells in the west in the third heaven. This god also created birds, woodland animals and the forests.

The Altaian shaman sacrifices a horse, similarly addresses the Master of Fire, fumigates his ritual drum, invokes a multitude of spirits, and then calls to the Markut, the Birds of Heaven. After a complex ceremony of purification he then beats his drum violently, indicating that he is 'mounting' into the sky, accompanied by the spirit of the dead horse. After ascending through several heavens in his visionary consciousness, he converses with the creator god Yayutsi and also bows before the Moon and Sun in turn. Finally he arrives at the celestial abode of Bai Ulgan, where he learns details of future weather patterns and the outcome of the harvest. The shaman then collapses in a state of ecstatic release. Mircea Eliade notes that Bai Ulgan seems to be a god of the 'atmosphere' and it is not uncommon among Indo-European shamans to sacrifice horses to a god of the sky or storms.[20]

The Chukchee believe that spirits may be contacted in dreams and that a shaman can utilize them to recover the lost souls of sick patients. The shaman is said to 'open' the patient's skull and replace the soul, which he has just captured in the form of a fly or bee. Goldi shamans, on the other hand, specialize in funerary activities, guiding the deceased into the realms of the underworld. The Goldi shaman calls on his helper spirits for guidance as he accompanies the dead person, who is mounted on a sled together with food for the journey, toward the land of the departed. The Goldi subsequently locates relatives of the deceased in the underworld so that the newly departed soul is safely accepted in the nether realms. Only then does the shaman return.

Evenk shamans also accompany the souls of the dead to the underworld, where the deceased then lead a life substantially similar to the life they left behind – they continue to fish and hunt as before, although they are not visible to mortal eyes. Evenk shamans also use whirlpools to enter the cosmic river where they encounter the *khargi* spirits of the lower world. The *khargi* are able to assist the shaman to counteract the effects of evil spirits who are stealing the souls of the living or causing failures in the hunt.[21]

## NORTH AMERICA

In North America shamanism is found, as we have already seen, in Alaskan Eskimo society, among the Tlingit of the north-west coast, among the Paviotso hunters, fishers and gatherers from western Nevada, among the Mescalero and Chiricahua Apache hunters of Texas, Arizona and New Mexico, the Lakota Sioux of Dakota, and also the Nez Perce, Ojibwa (also known as Chippewa), Zuni and Twana. Shamanic traditions still survive among the Pacific Coast Indians like the Pomo and Salish, the Chumash, who formerly occupied the region around Ojai, and native tribes like the Yurok, Wintun and Karok of north-western California. However, in native North American societies it has become difficult to distinguish between shamans and other technicians of sacred knowledge, like priests, medicine men and women, and sorcerers.

The ecstatic movement known as the Ghost Dance Religion, which flourished throughout the nineteenth century, brought a messianic emphasis to the native American tradition by focusing on the end of the world and the future regeneration of the planet by Indians, both dead and alive. The Ghost Dance Religion did exhibit mystical tendencies – practitioners entered a state of trance and dancers would often become healers – but it differed from traditional shamanism by making it potentially a 'collective' experience for its members.

Nevertheless, there are clear instances of pure shamanism. Paviotso shamans enter trance states and fly in the spirit vision to retrieve lost souls and effect healing cures, and on occasion also hold shamanic ceremonies to control the weather – bringing rain when needed, halting clouds, or melting icy rivers. To this extent they are remarkably similar to their Siberian counterparts.

The Chumash medicine woman Chequeesh told researcher Will Noffke in 1985 that she had learned of her native heritage by utilizing the 'dream herb', mugwort. At Point Conception she presented herself to the local healer, fasted for four days and nights, then went to a nearby mountain alone to use the herb to obtain her 'vision'. Her dream came, provided her spiritual name, and showed her the path of healing she should follow.[22]

The Yurok, Wintun and Karok Indians also pay special regard to their dreams for signs of omens, portents and psychic attack. In these native cultures, for example, the appearance of an owl in a dream could be a sign that an evil shaman was endeavouring to cause harm, and such an event – imagined or otherwise – would cause considerable stress and often ensuing sickness to those who had the experience. Sometimes a hostile 'force' is also conveyed by *uma'a* – a type of psychic arrow fired at night towards the victims – and a healing shaman is then required to suck these arrows out of the victim's body to effect a healing.

Apache Indians express a strong fear of the dead, especially dead relatives, and also of illnesses which result from contact with certain animals like bears and snakes. As with the northern Californian Indians, they also fear owls because they believe that ghosts appear in this form, and they refer to the illness resulting from persecution by ghosts either as 'ghost sickness', 'owl sickness' or 'darkness sickness'. The Apache fearing attack of this kind may utilize the powers of a healer shaman who 'sings' over the patient to determine the nature of the bewitchment.[23]

The Paviotso Dick Mahwee, meanwhile, has described how he obtained his first shamanic visions during a dream in a cave near Dayton, when he was 50 years old. In a state of seemingly 'conscious sleep', Mahwee had a mystical encounter with a tall, thin Indian holding an eagle tail-feather, who taught him ways of curing sickness. Mahwee now utilizes trance states in his shamanising:

> I smoke before I go into the trance. While I am in the trance no one makes any noise. I go out to see what will happen to the patient. When I see a whirlwind I know that it caused the sickness. If I see the patient walking on grass and flowers it means that he will get well; he will soon be up and walking. When I see the patient among fresh flowers and he picks them it means that he will recover. If the flowers are withered or look as if the frost had killed them, I know that the patient will die. Sometimes in a trance I see the patient walking on the ground. If he leaves footprints I know that he will live, but if there are no tracks, I cannot cure him. When I am coming back from the trance I sing. I sing louder and louder until I am completely conscious. Then the men lift me to my feet and I go on with the doctoring.[24]

## MEXICO

Mexico is home to many shamanic cultures although, since this region of the western hemisphere is especially rich in hallucinogenic plants we tend to find an especially high incidence of psychedelic shamanism here. Examples include the Yaquis of northern Mexico who ritually smoke the yellow *Genista canariensis* flowers containing cytisine, and the Huichols who conduct their peyote pilgrimages in sacred country in the north-central Mexican desert. Also part of this psychedelic tradition are the Tarahumara Indians of Chihuahua who sometimes add *Datura inoxia* to the fermented maize drink *tesguino*.

A number of Mexican Indian tribes also consume sacred mushrooms as part of their vision-quest. These tribes include the Mazatecs, Chinantecs, Zapotecs, and Mixtecs, all of whom come from Oaxaca. The subject of shamanism and sacred plants is discussed in the following chapter.

## SOUTH AMERICA

This region is characterized by many exotic healing practices, not all of them shamanic. The distinction between a *curandero* and a shaman is not always clear and there are also various spiritist traditions which are unrelated to shamanism. For example, the practices of French spiritualist Allan Kardec have been very influential in Brazil, as has Macumba – a magical religion similar to Haitian Voudou, which combines native folk superstitions, African animism and aspects of Christianity.

As in Mexico, shamanism in South America tends to be psychedelic, making frequent use of tropical plants which contain hallucinogenic alkaloids. The Banisteriopsis vine is widely utilized by South American shamans in the forests of the Upper Amazon, because the visions it produces are believed to represent encounters with supernatural forces. This is the case with the Jivaro of Ecuador, the Shipibo-Conibo, Campa, Sharanahua and Cashinahua of eastern Peru, and the Sione Indians of eastern Colombia.

## AUSTRALIA

Among Australian Aborigines the shaman or medicine man is known as the *karadji*, or 'clever man'. Aboriginal culture extends back at least 40,000 years and it is thought that the Aborigines probably migrated to Australia from southern India, reaching Cape York via the Malay Peninsula and the East Indies. Today the principal regions where traditional Aboriginal religion is still found are Arnhem Land, in central North Australia and in the central Australian desert – although there are scattered communities in other regions.

For the Australian Aborigines, illness, death and accidents are caused by magical or animistic actions. Australian Aboriginal magicians also know how to 'sing' a person to death and 'point the bone' – a type of projective magic where a kangaroo bone or carefully prepared stick is pointed at the intended victim.

The shamanic aspect of Australian Aboriginal culture becomes more obvious when we consider the initiation of medicine men. Among the Arunta, or Aranda, the candidate goes to the mouth of a particular cave where he is 'noticed' by the spirits of the Dreamtime. They throw an invisible lance at him, which pierces his neck and tongue, and another which passes through his head from ear to ear. Dropping down 'dead' he is now carried by the spirits into the cave and his internal organs replaced with new ones, together with a supply of magical quartz crystals upon which his 'power' will later depend. When he rejoins his people as a person 'reborn', he has a new status as a healer-shaman, although he will not normally perform as a *karadji* for a year or so.

The power of the crystals stems from the fact that they are believed to embody the essence of Baiame, the All-Father or Great Sky-God of the Australian people. The Wiradjeri Aborigines of western New South Wales describe Baiame in reverent terms and one of their legends has a clearly shamanic perspective. For the Wiradjeri, Baiame is a very great old man, with a long beard, sitting in his camp with his legs under him. Two great quartz crystals extend from his shoulders to the sky above him. Baiame sometimes appears to the Aborigines in their dreams. He causes a sacred waterfall of liquid quartz to pour over their bodies, absorbing them totally. Then they grow wings which replace their arms. Later the dreamer learns to fly and Baiame sinks a piece of magical quartz into his forehead to enable him to see inside physical objects. Subsequently an inner flame and a heavenly cord are also incorporated into the body of the new shaman.

Crystals also feature in the tradition of the Chepara tribe in Queensland. Medicine men here are said to fly up to heaven after swallowing quartz crystals, and are also able to send rain through their contact with Targan, Lord of the Rainbow. Wurunjeri medicine men, meanwhile, maintain that their magical powers come from the sky-being Bunjil, to whom they were carried by spirits through a hole in the sky. The sky country is also the land of the dead.

As in Siberia and North America, Aboriginal shamans also learn of magical portents through dreams, and there are instances where initiates appear to use out-of-the-body states to perceive events at a distance.[25] It is likely that bull-roarers are also used by shamans to produce an altered state of consciousness which can be utilized magically. The bull-roarer is swung around in the air producing a unique sound which is said to be the voice of Baiame, and those present stare into the fire in the middle of the sacred circle. Visions then begin to appear in the flames. 'Clever men' are said to be able to roll in the fire and scatter hot coals without being burned, and shamans also employ an invisible cord of flame which links them with Baiame and helps them to travel up into the sky. In these respects, Australian Aboriginal beliefs and practices have all the hallmarks of classic shamanism.

## INDONESIA AND MALAYSIA

Shamans here exhibit many of the familiar characteristics found elsewhere in the world – including trance states, magical flight and contacts with spirits. Menangkabau shamans seek their visions by travelling deep into the jungle or to the top of high mountains, while among the Iban, shamans undertake a fast, sleep near a grave, or travel to a mountaintop until magical powers are obtained from a guardian spirit. The Iban also refer to the initiation of shamans through a metaphysical 'restructuring' process which has strong parallels with the Aboriginal account referred to above:

> … they cut his head open, take out his brains, wash and restore them, to give him a clear mind to penetrate into the mysteries of evil spirits and the intricacies of disease; they insert gold dust into his eyes to give him keenness and strength of sight powerful enough to see the soul wherever it may have wandered; they plant barbed hooks on the tips of his fingers to enable him to seize the soul and hold it fast; and lastly they pierce his heart with an arrow to make him tender-hearted and full of sympathy with the sick and suffering.[26]

Dyaks also refer in their legends to somewhat shamanic journeys to the sky. The god Tupa-Jing noticed that the Dyaks were on the verge of exterminating themselves because they had no remedies for sickness and were cremating ill people as their only solution. He therefore saved a woman from the funeral pyre as she ascended in clouds of smoke, took her to heaven, and instructed her in the skills of medicine. Then she was able to return to earth and pass on the precious knowledge she had obtained.

Notions of spirits and sickness also parallel those found in other shamanic cultures. The Sumatran Kubu believe that sickness arises when a person's soul is captured by a ghost. Shamans, known here as *malims*, are called in to effect an exorcism. During the seance the *malims* dance, fall into a trance, and the chief *malim* is then able to 'see' the patient's soul and retrieve it.

There are also instances, as in Siberia, where shamans journey to the nether regions. This is the case among the Dyaks, where the *manang*, or shaman-healer, falls into a trance state during a *belian*, or curing ceremony, and journeys to the underworld to retrieve a soul that has been captured by a spirit. Sometimes it is necessary for the *manang* to lure the evil demon back to the patient's house and kill it.

Meanwhile, among the Karo Bataks, when a person dies, a female shaman dances herself into a state of ecstasy and then explains to the soul that it has passed through the process of death. At a later ceremony she then sends the discarnate soul off to the land of the dead.[27]

## EASTERN ASIA AND THE ORIENT

Here shamanism and animism pre-date the more familiar mainstream religious philosophies like Buddhism and Confucianism.

In Tibet, Bon shamans speak of a sacred rope which in times past linked the priests with the celestial dwelling of the gods, and even today they are believed to use their drums to propel themselves through the air. As with other forms of shamanism, healers here similarly undertake the search for the patient's soul if this is perceived as a cause of sickness.

The Lolo of southern Yunnan also believe that in earlier times men moved more freely between heaven and earth. Among these people the shaman-priest also officiates in funerary rituals, 'opening the bridge to heaven' and helping the deceased find their way across various mountains and rivers to the Tree of Thought and other post-mortem regions beyond. Influenced by Chinese magic, the shamans of Yunnan also practise divination and undertake visionary journeys on horseback to retrieve lost souls.

In China, when Confucianism was established as the state religion in the first century, ecstatics, shamans and diviners were banished, and some were killed. However, some shamanic vestiges remain in the Taoist tradition which is still served by monasteries and temples throughout the country. Ch'u State, in particular, has been a stronghold of Chinese shamanism.

The most obvious link between Taoism and shamanism is found in the meditative practices. Taoists use incense to carry their prayers to heaven, strike pieces of wood together in a monotonous rhythm rather like Siberian shamans with their drums, and believe that they can discover a spirit guide in the 'cave' of the heart. As the meditative state becomes experientially more real with increasing skills of visualization and breath control, the Taoist then journeys with the spirit guide to distant mystic realms – perhaps communicating with the gods who live in the stars. In so doing, the Taoist meditator is behaving exactly like a shaman.[28]

According to Larry G. Peters, the Tamangs of Nepal also practise an authentic form of shamanism which, though drawing on elements of Hinduism and Buddhism, appears to pre-date them as a spiritual tradition. Peters' key informant, Bhirendra, was the son of a *bombo*, or shaman, and when he was 13 years old he experienced a spontaneous state of demonic possession which led to his initiatory calling. Under the guidance of his father, and also the spirit of his deceased grandfather, Bhirendra learned to enter trance states voluntarily and in due course to activate the spiritual light between the eyes – a condition leading to magical out-of-the-body flight. Bhirendra described to Peters a vision in which he journeyed to the highest heaven to meet the supreme shaman deity, Ghesar Gyalpo:

> I walked into a beautiful garden with flowers of many differ-
> ent colours. There was also a pond and golden glimmery trees.
> Next to the pond was a very tall building which reached up
> into the sky. It had a golden staircase of nine steps leading to
> the top. I climbed the nine steps and saw Ghesar Gyalpo at the
> top, sitting on his white throne which was covered with soul
> flowers. He was dressed in white and his face was all white. He
> had long hair and a white crown. He gave me milk to drink and
> told me that I would attain much shakti to be used for the
> good of my people.[29]

Shamanism is also found in isolated regions of Japan, which is not
surprising since it seems likely that Tungusic and Altaic-speaking
tribes exerted a cultural influence on Japan, prior to the advent of
Buddhism, in the third or fourth centuries. Shamanesses, or *miko* –
more common than male shamans – are still found in small villages
where they utilize trance, telepathy, mediumship and fortune telling
and communicate with guardian deities or spirits of the dead. In the
larger cities, however, the role of the shamaness has been absorbed
by Shinto ritual.

Nevertheless, it is clear that shamanic episodes can still occur in
modern times, as evidenced by the remarkable case of Deguchi
Onisaburo which gave rise to the Omoto religious movement in
Japan. In 1898, Deguchi, who was by all accounts a frail youth, was
beaten up by some gamblers and nearly died. A short while later he
sank into a comatose sleep and on recovering consciousness
declared that he had journeyed to a cave on Mount Takakura and
after fasting there had travelled through regions of heaven and hell.
On his journey he had been granted occult powers such as
clairvoyance and clairaudience and had seen back as far as the
creation of the world. His visionary experiences included a meeting
with the King of the Underworld who in a moment was able to
transform from a white-haired old man with a gentle face into a

frightening demonic monarch with a bright red face, eyes like mirrors and a tongue of flame. Deguchi was subsequently 'killed, split in half with a sharp blade like a spear, dashed to pieces on rocks, frozen, burnt, engulfed in avalanches of snow [and] turned into a goddess' and yet, despite all these bizarre occurrences, he then found himself at the centre of the world, at the summit of the huge axial mountain, Sumeru. Here he was granted a vision of the river leading towards paradise. Before him on a vast lotus stood a marvellous palace of gold, agate and jewels. All around him were blue mountains and the golden lapping waves of a lake, and golden doves flew above him in the air.[30]

Somewhat unfortunately, Deguchi's experiences led to messianic claims. During World War I he proclaimed that he was an incarnation of Maitreya – the future Buddha destined to descend from Tusita Heaven to save the human race – and he also advocated a form of spiritual healing which involved meditative union with the gods. In due course Deguchi's writings extended to over 80 volumes. His sect is still in existence and has a very active Internet website, even though Deguchi himself died in 1948 at the age of 78.

## SHAMANISM AND MEDIUMISM

Especially in Japan, but essentially wherever divinatory practices are also found, native shamanism has tended to blend somewhat with mediumism. Both practices involve trance states but the focus is clearly different. Essentially, shamanism tends to be active, while mediumism is more passive: shamanism involves a *going forth* of the spirit whereas mediumism involves a *coming in* of the sacred force. An example of the latter category is provided by the Pythian Oracle at Delphi, who made divinely inspired pronouncements in trance at the Temple of Apollo. Some of the more inspired forms of modern spiritualism – now referred to as 'channelling' – also belong in this category: here ancient discarnate sages are believed to communicate with the living through the body of the possessed trance medium. Also in this same mediumistic category, although quite different in terms of content and mythic imagery, is Haitian Voudou, where the

'Divine Horsemen', or *ba* divinities, are believed to 'descend' on the trance subjects during their ecstatic dance rituals and 'ride' them into a state of inspired frenzy. In all forms of mediumistic trance, however, subjects do not recall their visionary episodes, and act instead as passive channels for the received revelations. In the shamanic traditions, on the other hand, the ecstatic retains full consciousness during the altered state, and takes full responsibility for what transpires on the visionary journey. It is shamanism rather than mediumism which is the focus of this book.

## Notes

1 Derek Freeman, 'Shaman and incubus', 1964
2 Mircea Eliade, *Shamanism*, p.5
3 Abbé Henri Breuil, 'The Paleolithic Age', in René Huyghe, (ed.) *Larousse Encyclopedia of Prehistoric and Ancient Art*, 1962, p.30
4 Joan Halifax, *Shaman: the Wounded Healer*, 1982, p.6
5 ibid., p.14
6 Ralph Linton, *Culture and Mental Disorders*, 1956, p.124
7 Joan Halifax, op.cit., p.14
8 Waldemar Bogoras, *The Chukchee*, 1909, p.421
9 see H. S. Sullivan, *Conceptions of Modern Psychiatry*, Norton, New York 1953, pp.151-2
10 Mircea Eliade, *Shamanism*, op.cit., p.13
11 Mircea Eliade, *Birth and Rebirth*, 1964, p.102
12 W. A. Lessa and E. Z. Vogt, (ed.) *Reader in Comparative Religion*, 1972, p.388
13 Mircea Eliade, *Shamanism*, p.120
14 ibid., p.88
15 A. P. Elkin, *Aboriginal Men of High Degree*, 1977, p.20
16 ibid., pp.142-3
17 ibid., p.143
18 Stephen Larsen, *The Shaman's Doorway*, 1976, p.195
19 W. A. Lessa and E. Z. Vogt, op.cit., p.389
20 Mircea Eliade, *Shamanism*, p.198
21 G. M. Vasilevich, 'Early concepts about the Universe among the Evenks', 1963, p.58
22 Will Noffke, 'Living in a Sacred Way', 1985, pp.13-17

23  see W. A. Lessa and E. Z. Vogt, op.cit., Chapter 9

24  Joan Halifax, *Shamanic Voices*, 1979, p.183

25  A. P. Elkin, *Aboriginal Men of High Degree*, p.63

26  H. L. Roth, *The Natives of Sarawak and British North Borneo*, 1968, vol.1, p.281

27  Sue Ingram, 'Structures of Shamanism in Indonesia and Malaysia', 1972, p.127

28  Kenneth Cohen, 'Taoist Shamanism', in *The Laughing Man*, vol.2, no.4, p.49

29  Larry G. Peters, 'The Tamang Shamanism of Nepal', 1987, p.171

30  For an account of Deguchi Onisaburo's trance experiences see Carmen Blacker, *The Catalpa Bow*, 1975

CHAPTER 2

# SHAMANIC COSMOLOGIES AND RITUALS

Obviously mythologies, cultural heroes and deities differ around the world and the relationship between the gods and humankind is perceived in different ways. Some peoples view their gods as tyrannical overlords, others as helpful parental overseers. Still others view their deities as supernatural beings whose power can be usurped with appropriate chants or invocations. However, despite all these differences, when we eliminate the individual cultural variables there seems to be a remarkable consensus in shamanic societies about how the universe is structured.

As the noted scholar of comparative religion, Mircea Eliade, has indicated in his important work *Shamanism: Archaic Techniques of Ecstasy* – the shaman's universe consists basically of three levels. Human beings live on the earth in a type of middle zone between an upper world and a lower world, the latter two often associated with the sky and the underworld respectively. The three zones are usually linked by a central vertical axis, which is sometimes referred to as the *Axis Mundi*, or Axis of the World, and which is characterized in different mythologies as the World Tree, the Tree of Life and so on.

This axis passes upwards and downwards through 'holes' in the cosmic vault which lead to the upper and lower worlds, and it is through these that the shaman is able to pass from this level of existence to another, and back again.

As Eliade notes, different cultures employ different metaphors and symbols to describe these zones. The Turko-Tatars view the sky as a tent, with the stars as 'holes' for light, while the Yakuts describe stars as 'windows of the world'. The Pole Star is often considered to be the centre of the celestial vault and is variously labelled as the 'Sky Nail' by the Samoyed, the 'Golden Pillar' by the Mongols and Buryats and the 'Iron Pillar' by the Kirghiz.[1]

In those societies where the symbolism of a pillar or axis reaching to heaven is not utilized there are other variants like cosmic mountains, ziggurats, temples, palaces, bridges, stairs, ladders and rainbows or, as with the Evenks, a mighty river which joins the three levels of the cosmos. Always, the shaman has some means of ascending to the cosmic skies or journeying to the underworld.

# LINKING HEAVEN AND EARTH

World Trees feature extensively in different religious traditions. The Yakuts of Siberia, for example, believe a tree with eight branches rises from the 'golden navel of the earth' and reaches up to heaven. The first man was born here, and was suckled by a woman who half-emerged from the trunk. The Goldi and Dolgan peoples, meanwhile, believe that prior to being born, the souls of little children sit like birds on the branches of the World Tree and that shamans go there to find them.[2]

The World Tree also features in Indonesian Dyak mythology. Here the World Tree has seven branches and provides a 'road to the sky' for the spirits of the dead. Dyak shamans climb the cosmic tree to retrieve the lost souls of patients.

The World Tree is also a feature of Norse mythology: Yggdrasil was the sacred ash tree which overshadowed the entire universe, its roots, branches and trunk uniting heaven, earth and the nether regions. According to Norse cosmology, the roots of Yggdrasil lay in Hel, while the trunk ascended through Midgard, the earth. Rising through the mountain known as Asgard, the sacred tree branched high into the sky – its leaves being clouds in the sky, and its fruits the stars. The Osmanli Turks, meanwhile, talk of a Tree of Life which has a million leaves, each one containing a human fate. Every time a person dies, a leaf falls.[3]

The Tree of Life is also a central motif in the Jewish Kabbalah. Here it is a multi-faceted symbol for the different levels of mystical existence between the transcendent and infinite Hidden God in *Ain Soph Aur* – the Limitless Light – and the ten lower *sephiroth*, or sacred spheres of being, which reflect different aspects of God's divine nature in the manifested world of creation. For the Kabbalist, as for the shaman, the essential mystical purpose is to know God. It is also worth noting that the Kabbalistic Tree of Life continues to provide a central focus for modern Western magic, which in turn has evolved into a type of contemporary shamanism.

World Trees are a central motif in shamanism, but they are not the only way of maintaining contact with the gods. Sacred rivers can also provide these links, as we find among the Evenks, whose cosmology is characteristic of the Tungus-Manchu peoples of Siberia.

## EVENK COSMOLOGY – A CLASSIC SHAMANIC MODEL

The Evenks conceive of a universe consisting of the three characteristic levels identified by Mircea Eliade. This consists of the upper world called *ugu buga*, associated with the sky; the middle world called *dulugu buga*, where human beings live; and the lower world named *khergu-ergu buga*, which is the domain of deceased kinsmen and the spirits of illness. Linking each of these three worlds and providing the counterpart of the Cosmic Tree is the mythical Clan River whose headwaters originate in the upper world and which in turn flows through to an underground sea extending to the furthest reaches of the lower world.[4]

The upper world, to all intents and purposes, resembles the familiar world of everyday reality, but on a grander scale – the gods and spirits who dwell here are prototypes for man below. For example, *ugu buga* is the realm of the creator god Amaka, a very old man dressed in luxuriant fur clothing, who in earliest times taught humans how to use fire and tools, and how to domesticate reindeer. It is also the dwelling place of Eksheri, considered the master of animals, birds and fish, and who holds the 'threads' of their destiny in his hands, dictating when they live or die. Eksheri was very much a being to whom the shaman would appeal regarding the overall success of the hunt, for if Eksheri was not propitiated he could direct his spirit rulers to drive the animals away in different directions. Eksheri also represents the 'heavenly' counterpart of the Clan Mistress of the lower world, whom we shall meet later as the guardian of animal souls sought for the hunt.

Also residing in *ugu buga* is the thunder god Agdy, who upon awakening gives vent to peals of thunder and flashes of lightning which destroy evil spirits. Here too lives the old man Dylacha, who, as the master of heat and light, toils unceasingly to provide warmth for mankind – an effort very much appreciated during the Siberian winter. It is he who lights the heavenly fire, collects its heat in his huge leather bag, and then, when the spring comes, disperses it to middle earth with the assistance of his sons, helping to warm the land and melt the icy rivers.

All of these beings, as one would expect, are considered benevolent, but this is not the case with the dwellers in the lower world, who are much more formidable. In *khergu-ergu buga* the world is turned on its heels so that what has been living becomes dead, and what was dead comes alive. It is a domain that on one particular level, called *buni*, is inhabited by dead clansmen whose bodies are cold and who live there without breathing, but who nevertheless continue to hunt and fish like the living. However, *khergu-ergu buga* is also the realm of the spirits of illness and disease, and of the Clan Mistress who watches for breaches of tribal taboos. The rulers of the lower world, known collectively as the *khargi*, cannot be ignored for they govern the ancestor-spirits and must be respected as overlords of the dead. The Evenks say that the *khargi*, including the Clan Mistress who rules the hunt, are themselves half-animal and half-human, so ironically, despite the dangers, the lower world provides the possibility for totemic clan unity. The shaman is special because he has a sacred link with the totem animal, can conquer the domain of death, and is then 'reborn', alive, into the familiar world of middle earth.

The unique role of the shaman is also represented in hero myths. The Evenks have a legend about a figure called Main, who is a master of destiny, a hunter in the heavens, and an archetypal cosmic shaman. One day Kheglen, the heavenly elk, steals the sun from the sky by impaling it on its antlers. This plunges the world into seemingly eternal night and humankind is at a loss what to do. Main, the hero shaman, then comes forth, donning his skis and heading off to the opening in the heavenly vault. Once in *ugu buga*, Main is able to track down the elk and strike it with an arrow from his bow. He then returns the sun – and all its light and warmth – to Middle Earth, while in turn becoming recognised as a guardian of life itself.

However, if a shaman like Main has to learn to be effective in the upper world – and in the above myth he is really a counterpart of Dylacha, the god of warmth – he also has to negotiate with the special figure of the Clan Mistress, who dwells in the lower world. Having announced in a song that he will confirm how many animals can be caught in the hunt, he journeys through a whirlpool and along a river to the subterranean clan territories, overcomes various obstacles in his path, and meets the Clan Mistress face to face. She appears before him in a forbidding form that is half-animal and half-human, but undaunted by her appearance he knows he must persuade her to release the animal souls under her command. Finally, after pleading with her at length, he is granted permission to capture a certain number of animals – these he turns into silken threads and hides inside his shaman drum. When he returns to middle earth he takes his drum to the clan's hunting grounds and shakes the threads forth. They then transform into real animals which will provide the future catch for his fellow hunters.

Nevertheless, if appeasing the gods of both the upper and lower worlds is the central task of the shaman, usually he does not act alone. Often he is accompanied by helper guides who assist him in wending his way from one realm to the next, and invariably he has various allies – spirits or familiars – which can help him perform his task successfully.

# SPIRIT GUIDES

In the shaman's world, spirit allies have many functions – they can detect the origins of illness, be sent by the shaman to recover lost souls, be summoned in acts of aggression, or be called upon to find a clear path past the various obstacles which might arise on the shaman's spirit quest. As we have already seen, spirit helpers may appear to shamans in dreams, in visions, and spontaneously after initiations. In some societies shamans also exchange or inherit their magical allies. In all cases, however, spirit guides are perceived as crucial to the shaman's resolve and power – literal embodiments of his psychic and magical strength.

There are two basic types of spirit guide. Firstly there are spirits which are substantially under the shaman's control and which serve as his familiars. But there are also other spirits – thought of more as guardians or helpers – who are available when the shaman needs to call on their aid. These may be minor deities or the spirits of deceased shamans: entities who maintain a certain independence in their particular realm and who are not automatically subject to the control of the shaman.

Siberian shamans generally have animal familiars like bears, wolves and hares, or birds like geese, eagles or owls. Yakuts, for example, view bulls, eagles and bears as their strongest allies, preferring them to wolves or dogs – who are considered to be the spirits of lesser shamans. The guardian spirit, however, is on a different level. Our earlier example of Tamang shamanism in Nepal is a case in point. Here Bhirendra was guided by the spirit of his dead grandfather, and it was through him, as well as through the tutelage of his father, that he was able to acquire shamanic visionary consciousness.

On occasion, as Mircea Eliade has pointed out, the guardian spirit also becomes a type of alter ego of the shaman – his psychic counterpart on the inner planes. To this extent we can understand the magical claims of human-animal transformation, for on these occasions the shaman projects his consciousness into an animal form on an imaginal level and it is in this 'energy body' that he goes forth on his spirit journey. Chukchee and Eskimo shamans maintain that they can change themselves into wolves, while Lapps can become bears or reindeer. The Semang shamans of the Malay Peninsula, on the other hand, believe they can transform themselves into tigers. Not that this type of magical transformation is without its dangers, however. Sometimes shamans fight each other on the inner planes in their magical bodies. If a shaman 'dies' during this encounter, it is often said that he will die in real life as well, for his 'essence' will have been destroyed.

On the more basic level of animal familiars, a good example of their role is provided by the Netsilik Eskimos of the Arctic coast of Canada. Here established shamans, or *angakoks*, recruit young prospective male shamans and put them through a magical apprenticeship. They join the household of a shaman-teacher, are instructed in observing ritual taboos, and then move to a special igloo where they learn shamanic techniques. The teacher provides his novice with a *tunraq* – a helper spirit, or familiar – and in the beginning it is clear that the *tunraq* has more power than its new owner. However, with time the young Eskimo shaman will learn to tame it. As the shaman grows in experience and confidence he may later acquire further *tunraqs* and can keep doing so throughout his life. The famous shaman Iksivalitaq, whom anthropologist Asen Balikci calls 'the last Netsilik shaman of importance', and who was still alive in the 1940s, had seven *tunraqs* – including the spirit of Big Mountain; the ghosts of three dead men, one of them his grandfather; and the spirits of a sea scorpion, a killer whale and a black dog without ears.

According to Asen Balikci, who studied Netsilik culture in some detail, *tunraqs* like to be 'frequently called and used', thus reinforcing the notion that ideally there should be a strong personal bond between the shaman and his helper spirits. But it is also possible for *tunraqs* to unleash their potency against their owners if things go wrong. Perhaps a shaman has sent his *tunraq* on a difficult mission and the spirit has failed to achieve its task. It can then become a 'reversed spirit' or *tunraq kigdloretto* – angry, bloodthirsty and out of control – wreaking havoc on its former owner and relatives, and bringing with it sickness and death.

Even at the best of times in Netsilik Eskimo society *tunraqs* have an uneasy relationship with their irascible owners. Balikci quotes two cases where aggressive shamanising was the result of jealous rivalry:

> Kaormik was a better bear hunter than Amaoligardjuk's son, so Amaoligardjuk, a shaman, became jealous and sent his *tunraq* polar bear against Kaormik. The bear scratched the left side of his face severely but failed to kill him. Amaoligardjuk added after: 'This man is hard to kill!'

And, on another occasion:

> Tavoq, a shaman, grew jealous of Angutitak, an excellent hunter, and scolded him repeatedly. Angutitak, a quiet and fearful man, never answered, until one day he accused Tavoq of being a mediocre and lazy hunter. Tavoq avenged himself by dispatching his *tunraq* to raise a snow storm just at the moment when Angutitak was stalking caribou.[5]

Another remarkable instance of the sometimes precarious relationship between a shaman and his spirit guide is provided by an unnamed Goldi shaman who had lengthy discussions with Russian anthropologist Lev Shternberg in the early 1900s. He explained to Shternberg that he had been drawn to shamanism initially by having bad headaches which other shamans were unable to cure, and he yearned to be a shaman himself.

One night while he was asleep in his bed he was visited by a very beautiful woman who resembled other Goldi women but was much smaller (around 70 cm in height). She told him that she was one of his spirit ancestors – an *ayami* – and had taught shamanic healing to other shamans. Now she was going to teach him.

The *ayami* also said that she would now regard the man as her husband and would provide him with assistant spirits that could help him to heal. She was also somewhat threatening. 'If you will not obey,' she told him sternly, 'so much the worse for you. I shall kill you.'[6]

The shaman told Shternberg how his spirit wife could change form at will – sometimes appearing like an old woman, sometimes as a wolf or winged tiger – and that she had taken him on aerial journeys to other locations. She had likewise bequeathed him three assistant familiar spirits – a panther, a bear and a tiger – to help out during his shamanising. It was they who provided the source of his shamanic power: 'When I am [shamanising] the *ayami* and the assistant spirits are possessing me,' he told Shternberg, '… whether big or small, they penetrate me, as smoke or vapour would. When the *ayami* is within me, it is she who speaks through my mouth.'[7]

We see here a blurring of the distinction made earlier between shamans and mediums – in a sense this shaman has become possessed by his spirit guides. However, it is really a case of the shaman consciously tapping his inner resources – in this case his multiple spirit helpers – to perform the act of magical healing. To this extent he is still exercising his will, rather than responding passively to the situation and channelling an unknown force from realms beyond his mind.

Overall, as we have said, the relationship between the shaman and his allies is a vital but sometimes precarious one, and the latter may, for a time, dictate the state of play. The relationship may on occasions take the form of a spiritual 'marriage' – as in the Goldi case above – or else it might involve the shaman honouring his helper spirits through song, dance and ritual. It might entail making offerings to fetishes linked to his spirit guides, actively respecting taboos – for example, not eating the meat of the animal concerned – or simply agreeing to keep the existence of the spirit-ally a secret from others. Whatever the situation, it is clear that in the final analysis the shaman depends very much on his helper spirits, whether they are animal familiars under his control or cosmic denizens who hold the key to realms beyond, in the upper and lower worlds. The shaman's unique role, after all, is as an intermediary: the shaman is special because he is effective on more than one plane of reality and it is up to him to maintain that special access by mustering *all* the assistance he can obtain.

# SHAMANIC RITUALS AND THE INNER WORLD

Ceremonial ritual is the outer enactment of an internal event. In all religions, and also in shamanism and ceremonial magic, those performing a ritual believe that what they are doing is not simply theatrical but accords with some sort of sacred, inner reality – that for a time they are caught up in a mystical drama, perhaps involving union with a god, identification with a source of spiritual healing, or the act of embodying some sort of transcendent power. In such a way the shaman, priest or magician believes he is tapping into a dimension which is much larger and more awesome than the world of familiar reality. It is very much a case of participating in a mystery – of leaving the everyday realm and, for a sacred and special period of time, entering the magical cosmos.

Many anthropologists and sociologists have a problem with this. Because they are trained to record external events in detail, to monitor behaviour patterns and the ways in which such behaviour proves meaningful in the social matrix, they are often inclined to believe that this is *all* that is happening.

Shamanism is no exception. To many observers the shaman is little more than an exotic performer, a person who, through evocative and stimulating ritual is able to induce a state of hysteria which deludes both himself and his audience. A case in point is provided by Weston La Barre's commentary on shamanism in his epic work on the origins of religion, *The Ghost Dance*. La Barre makes the valid point that from earliest times shamans learned to imitate the movements and sounds of birds and animals. This was natural because animal shamans would wish to identify with forces in the underworld responsible for the success of the hunt, while bird shamans would wish to identify with spirits of the weather and the sky. Noting that the Yakuts of Siberia, for example, are skilled in imitating the calls of such birds as the lapwing, the falcon, the eagle and the cuckoo, La Barre emphazises that:

> ... to become like animals and birds, one must not only dress in their skins and masks but also imitate their behaviours. In addition to birds' mastery of the air, which shamans achieve in trance and in their flying dreams, the major attribute of birds is their song ... bird shamans [borrow] song from their sources of power.[8]

However, when it comes to the crunch, La Barre, like other anthropologists concerned primarily with social explanations, is inclined to view the shaman simply as an imitator and manipulator, and his ritual as a deception. He quotes Diamond Jenness's description of a Copper Eskimo shamanic ritual observed in the 1920s:

> The shaman is not conscious of acting a part; he becomes in his own mind the animal or the shade of the dead man who is deemed to possess him. To the audience, too, this strange figure, with its wild and frenzied appearance, its ventriloquistic cries and its unearthly falsetto gabble, with only a broken word here and there of intelligible speech, is no longer a human being, but the thing it personifies. Their minds become receptive to the wildest imaginings, and they see the strangest and most fantastic happenings.[9]

La Barre, who follows this quote with the observation that 'the resemblance to stage illusion is striking', also emphazises that shamans can often be downright dishonest in their rituals, and recalls the case of the Kiowa shaman Lone Bear, who was so 'incompetent' that the ethnographer watching him, William Bascom, could see him fumble red clay from his pouch and chew it in his mouth – later spitting it out as his own 'blood'.

But is this interpretation a 'true' representation of what really took place? Whether this particular deception occurred or not, in general what seems more likely is that on such occasions the shaman is resorting to ceremonial activities, and using ritual objects, which on a physical level reflect his inner, psychic processes. If we consider rituals in this light, it is quite reasonable that red clay can become blood and that the Kirghiz shaman who imitates the sound of bird wings experiences the sensation of actually flying.

This is a conclusion also reached by American anthropologist Dr Michael Harner in evaluating the dance of the Beast Gods as performed by the Zuni Pueblo:

The Beast Gods are summoned by dancing, rattling and drumming, and the dancers work themselves into a frenzied condition in which they imitate the actions and cries of animals. Those dancers assuming the personality of the bear may even wear actual bear paws over their hands. But this dance of the Beast Gods is more than simple imitation, since the Zuni dancer, like a North American Plains Indian doing an Eagle or Buffalo Dance, is striving to go beyond imitation to become one with the animal … Likewise, a Zuni dancer wearing the mask of one of the *kachina* gods is doing more than impersonating the *kachina*. Transported into an altered state of consciousness by the dancing, drumming, rattling and whirr of bull roarers he 'becomes for the time being the actual embodiment of the spirit which is believed to reside in the mask'. [10]

Another example of the transformational nature of ritual is provided by the Australian Aborigines of Forrest River, who undertake ceremonial initiations which feature the symbolic death and resurrection of the candidate and his ascent to the sky:

> The usual method is as follows: The master assumes the form of a skeleton and equips himself with a small bag, in which he puts the candidate, whom his magic has reduced to the size of an infant. Then seating himself astride the Rainbow-Serpent, he begins to pull himself up by his arms, as if climbing a rope. When near the top, he throws the candidate into the sky, 'killing' him. Once they are in the sky, the master inserts into the candidate's body small rainbow-serpents, brimures [small fresh-water snakes], and quartz crystals (which have the same name as the mythical Rainbow-Serpent). After this operation the candidate is brought back to earth, still on the Rainbow-Serpent's back. The master again introduces magical objects into his body, this time through the navel, and wakens him by touching him with a magical stone. The candidate returns to normal size. On the following day the ascent by the Rainbow-Serpent is repeated in the same way.[11]

Clearly in such rituals there are physical activities – things one can see externally – and symbolic, mythic processes that are represented by the ceremonial sequence of events. Unlike the scientifically trained Western observer, who no doubt would miss much of the import of such a ritual as that described above, the shaman does not distinguish between 'real' and 'unreal' worlds. The entire magical domain explored during the shamanising is an integrated expression of both 'natural' and 'magical' events, for the shaman is 'breaking through in plane' from the everyday reality to the upper or lower worlds. For him, the magic is real.

## SHAMANIC COSTUMES

When we look at shamanic costumes we also see evidence of the mythic processes involved. The Japanese shamans observed by Carmen Blacker wore caps of eagle and owl feathers and cloaks adorned with stuffed snakes, intended to facilitate 'the passage from one world to another'. Emphasizing this point, Blacker notes that '… the magic clothes and instruments, of which the drum is the most important, embody in their shape, in the materials of which they are made, in the patterns and figures engraved upon them, symbolic links with the other world.' [12]

Likewise, a Yakut shaman wears a kaftan decorated with a solar disc – representing the opening of the underworld – while the Goldi shaman dons a coat depicting the Cosmic Tree and 'power animals' like bears and wild cats, which are part of his mythic experience. Teleut shamans often wear winged owl caps to symbolize magical flight, while the Buryat shaman costume is heavily laden with iron ornaments which portray the iron bones of immortality. The bears, leopards, serpents and lizards which appear on it are the shaman's helping spirits.

To some extent, then, one is obliged to heed the shaman's own perceptions of his universe, expressed in his own terms. For many anthropologists, especially those not attuned to the mindset of the shaman, this is especially difficult. However, the apparently formidable gap between scientific anthropology and mythic experiential shamanism is capable of being narrowed. More psychologists are now taking note of such phenomena as near-death and out-of-the-body experiences, which strongly suggest that human consciousness can operate functionally at a distance from the body. Here, ordinary citizens in an urban Western environment report aerial sensations not so far removed from the shamanic experience. The following account from Winnebago shaman Thunder Cloud is much more believable than it first seems, when considered in this context.

Thunder Cloud was a member of the Medicine Dance Secret Society and a highly respected shaman. He maintained that he was able to consciously recall two previous incarnations, in the second actually watching the people burying him after his death. He then journeyed towards the Setting Sun, arriving at a village where there were other dead people:

I was told that I would have to stop there for four nights, but, in reality, I stayed there for four years. The people enjoy themselves here. They have all sorts of dances of a lively kind. From that place we went up to where Earthmaker lives and I saw him and talked to him, face to face, even as I am talking to you now. I saw the spirits too and, indeed, I was like one of them. Thence I came to this earth for the third time and here I am. I am going through the same that I knew before.[13]

One can only conclude that the world of the shaman, bizarre as it must sometimes seem to outsiders, is nevertheless totally real to the person experiencing it. Thunder Cloud also describes shamanic dancing and healing from the view of the spirit vision associated with it:

… at Blue Clay Bank [St Paul] there lives one who is a dancing grizzly-bear spirit. Whenever I am in great trouble I was to pour tobacco, as much as I thought necessary, and he would help me. This grizzly bear gave me songs and the power of beholding a holy thing: he gave me his claws, claws that are holy. Then the grizzly bear danced and performed while he danced. He tore his abdomen open and, making himself holy, healed himself again. This he repeated. One grizzly bear shot claws at the other and the wounded one became badly choked with blood. Then both made themselves holy again and cured themselves.[14]

Clearly, in this instance Thunder Cloud is speaking both literally and metaphysically. Although the grizzly-bear spirit is associated with a specific location (Blue Clay Bank), the descriptions provided are of magical events – Thunder Cloud has seen the miraculous healing not on a physical level but in his spirit vision. Nevertheless, the two levels of perception have begun to merge. The demonstration of healing has provided what the shaman himself calls 'holy' revelations. The shamanising is occurring in sacred space.

Having explored aspects of the shaman's experiential realm we should now also consider two of the specifics of shamanic technique – the shaman's drum and his use of song. Both are of central importance since they offer a means of entering the shamanic state of consciousness and attracting helper spirits. Without skills of this sort, a shaman can hardly hope to be successful.

# THE SHAMAN'S DRUM

The drum has a special role in shamanism for it is literally the vehicle that 'carries' the shaman to the other world. Often it is closely identified with a horse, or some other sort of animal. Soyots call their shaman drums *khamu-at*, meaning 'shaman horse' and Altaic shamans embellish their drums with horse symbols. Interestingly, the anthropologist L. P. Potapov discovered that the Altaian people name their drum not after the animals whose skin is used in its manufacture (camel or dappled horse) but after the domestic horses actually used as steeds. This confirms the idea that the drum is a mode of transport: it is the monotonous rhythm of the drum which the shaman 'rides' into the upper and lower worlds. A Soyot poem also makes this clear:

> *Skin-covered drum,*
> *Fulfil my wishes,*
> *Like flitting clouds, carry me*
> *Through the lands of dusk*
> *And below the leaden sky,*
> *Sweep along like wind*
> *Over the mountain peaks!* [15]

The sound of the drum acts as a focusing device for the shaman. It creates an atmosphere of concentration and resolve, enabling him to sink deep into trance as he shifts his attention to the inner journey of the spirit. It is not uncommon, either, for the drum to have a symbolic link with the Centre of the World, or the World Tree. The Evenks fashion the rims of their drums from the wood of the sacred larch, and Lapp shamans decorate their drums with mythic symbols like the Cosmic Tree, the sun, moon or rainbow.[16]

So, the crucial point which emerges from this is that the shaman's drum not only produces an altered state of consciousness, but confirms the shift in perception, which results from the drumming, as the basis for a mythic encounter.

Recent research among the Salish Indians, undertaken by Wolfgang G. Jilek, found that rhythmic shamanic drumming produced a drumbeat frequency in the theta wave EEG frequency (4–7 cycles per second) – the brainwave range associated with dreams, hypnotic imagery and trance.[17] This is hardly surprising, for shamanism is a type of mythic 'lucid dreaming'. In the latter category of dreaming one is 'aware' that one is dreaming and likewise, in shamanism, one is conscious within the altered state and able to act purposefully within it. Shamans invariably report their encounters not as hallucinations or fanciful imagination but as experientially valid: what happens during the spirit journey is *real* in that dimension.

# SHAMAN SONG

Song is another vital aspect of shamanism. It is through songs and chants that the shaman expresses both his power and his intent. Songs are the sounds of the gods and spirits and, like the sacred drum, can help the shaman feel propelled by their energy. As the Apache shaman-chief Geronimo once proclaimed: 'As I sing, I go through the air to a holy place where Yusun [the Supreme Being] will give me power to do wonderful things. I am surrounded by little clouds, and as I go through the air I change, becoming spirit only.'[18]

The Australian Aborigines also provide an excellent example of the link between musical sounds and the gods. Some Aborigines, for example, believe that their creator gods dwell in bull-roarers which may be whirled in the air to restore energy and vibrancy to both tribe and totem. They also believe that the songs they continue to sing today are the same as those sung by their ancestors in the Dream-time, when the gods brought the world into being. The most sacred songs are chanted at the special sites where the gods were thought to roam: these songs are considered to have a special magic which helps to produce abundant food and water supplies.

When the explorers Baldwin Spencer and F. J. Gillen visited the Warraminga Aborigines and neighbouring tribes in 1901 they saw a marvellous fire ceremony where torches five metres long blazed to the wild music of the *Kingilli* singers. They listened to legends about Wollungua, the great serpent whose head reached up to the sky, and when visiting the Kaitish Aborigines observed a rainmaking cere-mony which included imitations of the plover's call.

The central Australian Ljaba Aranda Aborigines, meanwhile, have a Honey Ant Song which describes the insects nestling under the roots of native mulga trees. But these honey ants are also thought to be ancestor spirits with elaborate decorations on their bodies. When the song is sung, the Aborigines performing the ceremony sweep brushes of mulga over themselves, allowing the honey ant spirits to come forth – for they believe themselves to be magically possessed at this time by the ancestors. Such a song is typical of the sacred music which links Aborigines of the Dreamtime to their forefathers.[19]

Sometimes, as a bridge to sacred reality, song may also be evoked from the shaman's own being. As anthropologist Joan Halifax elo-quently observes:

As the World Tree stands at the centre of the vast planes of the cosmos, song stands at the intimate centre of the cosmos of the individual. At that moment when the shaman song emerges, when the sacred breath rises up from the depths of the heart, the centre is found, and the source of all that is divine has been tapped.[20]

A wonderful description of this process is provided by the North

American Gitksan Indian, Isaac Tens. At the age of 30, Tens began to fall continually into trance states and experienced dramatic, and often terrifying, visions. On one occasion animal spirits and snake-like trees seemed to be chasing him and an owl took hold of him, catching his face and trying to lift him up. Later, while Tens was on a hunting trip, an owl appeared to him again, high up in a cedar tree. Tens shot the owl and went to retrieve it in the bushes, but found to his amazement that it had disappeared. He then hastened back towards his village, puzzled and alarmed, but on the way again fell into a trance:

> When I came to, my head was buried in a snowbank. I got up and walked on the ice up the river to the village. There I met my father who had just come out to look for me, for he had missed me. We went back together to my house. Then my heart started to beat fast, and I began to tremble, just as had happened a while before, when the *halaaits* [medicine-men] were trying to fix me up. My flesh seemed to be boiling ... my body was quivering. While I remained in this state, I began to sing. A chant was coming out of me without my being able to do anything to stop it. Many things appeared to me presently: huge birds and other animals. They were calling me. I saw a *meskyawawderh* [a kind of bird] and a *mesqagweeuk* [bullhead fish]. These were visible only to me, not to the others in my house. Such visions happen when a man is about to become a *halaait*; they occur of their own accord. The songs force themselves out, complete, without any attempt to compose them. But I learned and memorised these songs by repeating them.[21]

While such visions may seem to belong solely to the exotic world of the primitive shaman, it is interesting that urban Westerners who find themselves in a shamanic context sometimes report comparable initiations. An impressive account is provided by the distinguished American anthropologist Michael Harner, formerly an Associate

Professor at the New School for Social Research, New York. In 1959, Harner was invited by the American Museum of Natural History to study the Conibo Indians of the Peruvian Amazon. He set off the following year for the Ucayali River and found the Indians friendly and receptive on his arrival. Harner, however, wished to be more than an anthropologist: he hoped to be initiated as a shaman. He was told that to tap the magical reality he would have to drink the sacred potion *ayahuasca*, made from the Banisteriopsis vine. *Ayahuasca* contains the alkaloids harmine and harmaline and produces out-of-the-body experiences, telepathic and psychic impressions and spectacular visions. Among the Conibo the sacred drink was also known as 'the little death' and its powers were regarded with awe.

Harner took the shamanic potion at night, accompanied by an elder of the village. Soon the sound of a waterfall filled his ears and his body became numb. As he began to hallucinate he became aware of a giant crocodile, from whose jaws rushed a torrent of water. These waters formed an ocean and Harner saw a dragon-headed ship sailing towards him. Several hundred oars propelled the vessel, producing a rhythmic, swishing sound as it moved along. Harner now experienced the music of the inner worlds:

I became conscious … of the most beautiful singing I have ever heard in my life, high-pitched and ethereal, emanating from myriad voices on board the galley. As I looked more closely at the deck, I could make out large numbers of people with the heads of blue jays and the bodies of humans, not unlike the bird-headed gods of ancient Egyptian tomb paintings. At the same time, some energy-essence began to float from my chest up into the boat.[22]

Harner's mind now seemed to function on several levels as he was granted sacred visions by the spirit creatures – secrets, they told him, which would normally be given only to those about to die. These visions included a survey of the birth of the earth, aeons before the advent of man, and an explanation of how human consciousness had evolved.

In traditional shamanism, irrespective of its cultural context, it is not uncommon for the shaman to be shown by the gods how society came into existence, how the worlds were formed, and how man has a privileged and special relationship with the gods. What is so interesting about Michael Harner's account is that he was able to enter the shaman's exotic world so totally, despite his Western intellectual background. As we will see, the shamanic approach appears to have no conceptual boundaries and opens doorways to a potentially infinite universe.

### Notes

1   Mircea Eliade, *Shamanism*, p.261
2   ibid., p.272
3   ibid., p.273
4   G. M. Vasilevich, 'Early concepts about the Universe among the Evenks', 1963
5   Asen Balikci, 'Shamanistic Behavior Among the Netsilik Eskimos', 1967, p.200
6   Joan Halifax, *Shamanic Voices*, 1979, p.121
7   ibid., p.122
8   Weston La Barre, *The Ghost Dance*, 1972, p.421
9   ibid., p.320
10  Michael Harner, *The Way of the Shaman*, 1980, p.62
11  Mircea Eliade, *Shamanism*, 1972, p.132
12  Carmen Blacker, *The Catalpa Bow*, 1975, p.25
13  Joan Halifax, *Shamanic Voices*, 1979, p.176
14  ibid., p.177
15  Michael Harner, op.cit., p.51
16  Mircea Eliade, op.cit., p.172
17  Michael Harner, op cit., p.52
18  Joan Halifax, op.cit., p.30
19  Nevill Drury, *Music and Musicians*, Nelson, Melbourne 1980, p.51
20  Joan Halifax, op.cit., p.30
21  ibid., p.185
22  Michael Harner, op.cit., p.3

CHAPTER 3

# SACRED PLANTS

Sacred plants – plants which cause visions and hallucinations – are a central feature of shamanism in many regions of the world. To modern urban Westerners the idea of visions induced by psychotropic means may seem like an aberration, perhaps even a type of decadence. Indeed, during the late 1960s, when the youthful exploration of psychedelics was rampant, one would often read in the press about mystical episodes being 'artificially' produced by drugs like LSD and psilocybin. The perception was that such drugs invariably produced a distortion, a wavering from 'reality'.

In the preliterate world of the shaman the exact opposite is true. Here the sacred plants are believed to open the doors to the heavens, to allow contact with the gods and spirits, and to permit access to a greater reality beyond. The Jivaro of Ecuador, for example, describe the familiar world as 'a lie'. There is only one reality – the world of the supernatural.

Our attitude to such matters in modern Western society is mirrored by our language. The word 'drug' itself is a highly coloured term and is frequently associated with acts that are disapproved of in the mainstream. As a consequence, the 'drug experience' – if one can call it that – is not something valued in modern Western culture as a whole. Little distinction exists in the popular mind between sacred or psychedelic drugs, like those which feature in shamanism and the recreational, addictive or analgesic drugs which are part of contemporary urban life.

A revealing anecdote which throws light on modern attitudes from a shamanic point of view is provided by anthropologist Peter Furst in his book *Hallucinogens and Culture*. Furst was present when a newspaper reporter referred to peyote as a 'drug' in front of a Huichol shaman. The shaman replied succinctly: 'Aspirina is a drug, peyote is sacred.'[1]

Hallucinogenic plants of the type used in shamanism thus require some sort of clarification. While by definition such plants are toxic – if we mean by that something which has a distinct biodynamic effect on the body – this does not mean that such plants are invariably poisonous, though some are in certain dosages (e.g. datura or *Sophora secundiflora*). As far as we know, none of the hallucinogenic plants utilized in shamanism is addictive. Also it is important that we make the distinction that these plants do not simply modify moods but are capable of producing a dramatic and often profound change in perception. Colours are enhanced, spirits may appear, the sacramental plant appears godlike to the shaman who has invoked it ceremonially, and perhaps a cosmic bridge or smoke tunnel appears in the shaman's vision, allowing him to ascend to the heavens. In every way the sacred plant is a doorway to a realm that is awesome and wondrous, and the undertaking is not one which is taken lightly. To this extent, then, the ritual use of hallucinogenic plants is not recreational but *transformative* – one undertakes the vision-quest to 'learn' or to 'see', not to 'escape' into a world of 'fantasy'.

Psychologists have produced various terms to describe the substances which produce such radical shifts in consciousness. The psychiatrist Dr Humphry Osmond coined the term 'psychedelic', meaning 'mind-revealing' or 'mind-manifesting', but a term preferred by many is 'psychotomimetic': substances within this category are capable of inducing temporary psychotic states of such intensity that the 'visionary' or 'dream' world appears profoundly real. In shamanic societies experiences like this are highly valued. Sacred plants remove the barriers between humankind and the realm of gods and spirits, and from them one receives wisdom and learning. The gods *know*; the sacred plant *speaks.*

Generally, the psychotropic components of sacred plants are contained in the alkaloids, resins, glucosides and essential oils found in the leaves, bark, stem, flowers, sap, roots or seeds of the plants. The regions richest in naturally occurring hallucinogenic plants are Mexico and South America. On the other hand, with the exception of *Amanita muscaria* (apparently deified by the Aryans of Vedic India as the god Soma), datura and marijuana, Asia is comparatively lacking in such plant species. And they appear not to be used shamanically to any great extent in Africa and Australasia.

In Mexico the most important plants in shamanic usage are peyote, psilocybe mushrooms and morning glory, while in South America the most prevalent hallucinogen is a drink made from the Banisteriopsis vine, and known variously as *ayahuasca, caapi, natema* or *yaje*. Other plant species used in that region are San Pedro cactus, native tobacco, the Brugmansias, a hallucinogenic snuff known as *yopo*, and virola.

The use of such plants extends back for hundreds, and in some cases many thousands, of years. Peyote, for example, was known to the Toltecs some 1,900 years prior to the arrival of the Europeans, while the ritual use of San Pedro cactus – established through its association with jaguar motifs and spirit beings on ceremonial pottery – appears to date back at least 3,000 years. The ritual use of psychotropic mushrooms in Mexico certainly predates the conquests by many centuries, as evidenced by surviving Mayan, 'mushroom stones', while an Aztec mural at Teotihuacan depicting a Mother Goddess who personifies the morning glory or *ololiuhqui* – sacred to the Aztecs – dates from c.500.

## PEYOTE

Deriving its name from the Aztec *peyotl*, the famous peyote cactus (*Lophophora williamsii*) was the first hallucinogenic plant discovered by the Europeans in the Americas. It is associated primarily with the

Huichol Indians of the Sierra Madre in Mexico, although it is also used by the Cora and Tarahumara Indians, the Amerindian Kiowa and Comanche, and in the more recently established Native American Church which now has around 250,000 members.

Peyote is a complex hallucinogenic plant capable of producing a wide range of effects. Its main alkaloid constituent is mescaline but it also contains around 30 other psychoactive agents. Users may experience vividly coloured images, shimmering auras around objects, feelings of weightlessness and also unusual auditory and tactile sensations.

The first detailed description of the cactus was provided by Dr Francisco Hernandez, physician to King Philip II of Spain, who studied Aztec medicine quite thoroughly. He writes:

> The root is of nearly medium size, sending forth no branches or leaves above the ground, but with a certain woolliness adhering to it on account of which it could not aptly be figured by me. Both men and women are said to be harmed by it. It appears to be of a sweetish taste and moderately hot. Ground up and applied to painful joints, it is said to give relief. Wonderful properties are attributed to this root, if any faith can be given to what is commonly said among them on this point. It causes those devouring it to be able to foresee and predict things.[2]

Not surprisingly, the cactus was fiercely suppressed in Mexico by Christian missionaries because of its 'pagan' associations. A priest, Padre Nicholas de Leon, asked potential converts to Christianity:

> Art thou a soothsayer? Dost thou foretell events by reading omens, interpreting dreams or by tracing circles and figures on water? Dost thou garnish with flower garlands the places where idols are kept? Dost thou suck the blood of others? Dost thou wander about at night, calling upon demons to help thee? Hast thou drunk Peyote or given it to others to

drink, in order to discover secrets or to discover where stolen or lost articles were?[3]

Fortunately the Huichol Indians managed to escape the proselytizing influence of the Christian missionaries even though the Sierra Madre came under Spanish influence in 1722. Today the Indians continue to regard the peyote cactus as divine, associating the region where it grows with Paradise (*Wirikuta*) and the plant itself with the Divine Deer, or Master of the Deer species.

Each year groups of Huichols – usually numbering 10-15 people – make a pilgrimage to gather the peyote, which they call *Hikuri*. They are led by a shaman who is in contact with Tatewari, the peyote god: Tatewari is the archetypal 'first shaman' who led the first peyote pilgrimage and subsequent shamans seek to emulate his example.

The distance between the Sierra Madre and the high desert of San Luis Potosi where the cactus grows, is around 300 miles, and although in the past this pilgrimage was always undertaken on foot, it is now considered permissible to travel by car, bus or train provided that offerings, prayers and acts of ritual cleansing are made en route. The desert destination, Wirikuta, is regarded as the 'mythic place of Origin' of the Huichols. As Peter Furst notes:

> The pattern was established long ago, in mythic times, when the Great Shaman, Fire, addressed as Tatewari, Our Grandfather, led the ancestral gods on the first peyote quest. It is told that the fire god came upon them as they sat in a circle in the Huichol temple, each complaining of a different ailment. Asked to divine the cause of their ills, the Great Shaman, Fire, said they were suffering because they had not gone to hunt the divine Deer [Peyote] in Wirikuta, as their own ancestors had done, and so had been deprived of the healing powers of its miraculous flesh. It was decided to take up bow and arrow and to follow Tatewari to 'find their lives' in the distant land of the Deer-Peyote.[4]

At Wirikuta dwell the divine ancestors, Kakauyarixi, and the Divine Deer, which is personified by the sacred cactus of the region and is believed to represent life itself. When the shaman leading the pilgrimage finds the peyote he declares that he has 'seen the deer tracks'. He then 'shoots' the cactus with his bow and arrow as if it were a deer pursued in the hunt.

The peyote cactus is subsequently collected and shared out to those participating in the pilgrimage. The cactus is either consumed direct in small pieces, or macerated and mixed with water (symbolizing the dry and wet seasons). Huichols say the sacred Deer is a mount to the upper levels of the Cosmos and a spirit helper who can be called upon during healing ceremonies.

A Western observer, Prem Das, has described the feelings which come from partaking of peyote with the Huichols:

> When I looked down to the ground I saw peyote cacti every-where about me, and they seemed to glow with a special luminescence of their own. The two richly embroidered Huichol peyote bags I was wearing were easily filled and held at least a hundred peyote cacti of various sizes. I ate several more, continuing to watch the luminous and constantly changing cloud formations in the awesome and penetrating silence of Wirikuta.
>
> I began to cry as I thought of my own people, my own race, with its atomic bombs and missiles sitting ready to destroy everyone and everything at any moment. Why, I wondered, why had we become so isolated and estranged from the harmony and beauty of our wonderful planet?
>
> I heard an answer that seemed to come from all around me, and it rose in my mind's eye like a great time-lapse vision. I saw a human being rise from the earth, stand for a moment, and then dissolve back into it. It was only a brief moment, and in that moment our whole lives passed. Then I saw a huge city rise out of the desert floor beneath me, exist for a second, and then vanish back into the vastness of the desert. The plants,

rocks, and the earth under me were saying, 'Yes, this is how it really is, your life, the city you live in.' It was as if in my peyotized state I was able to perceive and communicate with a resonance or vibration that surrounded me. Those inner barriers which defined 'me' as a separate identity from 'that' – my environment – had dissolved. An overwhelming realisation poured through me – that the human race and all technology formed by it are nothing other than flowers of the earth. The painful problem that had confronted me disappeared entirely, to be replaced with a vision of people and their technology as temporary forms through which Mother Earth was expressing herself. I felt a surge of happiness and ecstasy which flowed out to dance with all forms of the earth about me; I cried with joy and thanked Wirikuta, don José and the Huichols for such a profound blessing.[5]

## PSILOCYBE MUSHROOMS

For a long time, the existence of the 'sacred mushrooms' of Mexico was doubted by expert botanists. In 1915 William Safford addressed the Botanical Society in Washington, arguing that sacred inebriating mushrooms did not exist – they had been confused with peyote. It took Richard Evans Schultes, Professor of Natural Sciences at Harvard University and Director of the Harvard Botanical Museum, to correct this mistaken impression.

In 1938 Schultes visited the little town of Huautla de Jimenez in the Sierra Mazateca mountains, obtaining specimens of the sacred mushrooms and returning with them to Harvard. A Protestant missionary and linguist, Eunice V. Pike, who had worked among the Mazatecs, also knew about them, and it was as a result of her letters, and Schultes' field study articles that the retired banker R. Gordon Wasson and his wife Valentina, embarked on their celebrated 'pilgrimage' to experience sacred mushrooms at first hand. It was Wasson who brought the issue to prominence in 1957 with an article in *Life* magazine describing, as he writes in his own words, 'the awe and reverence ... of a shamanic mushroom agape'.[6] For those unfamiliar with Gordon Wasson's remarkable adventure, a brief summary is provided later in this chapter.

The most important of the shamanic mushrooms in Mexico is the species *Psilocybe mexicana*, which grows in wet pasturelands, although other, related types of mushrooms are also consumed. Psilocybe mushrooms provide a state of intoxication characterized by vivid and colourful hallucinations and also unusual auditory effects. It is for the latter reason that the Mazatecs say, respectfully, that 'the mushrooms speak'.

We are extremely fortunate to have a poetic account of native mushroom practices from Henry Munn, a Westerner who has lived for many years among the Mazatecs of Oaxaca, and who married the niece of a shaman and shamaness in that society. As Munn writes in his article 'The Mushrooms of Language': 'The shamans who eat them, their function is to speak, they are the speakers who chant and sing the truth, they are the oral poets of their people, the doctors of the word, they who tell what is wrong and how to remedy it, the seers and oracles, the ones possessed by the voice.'

There is also an intriguing tendency among the Mazatecs to blend native folk traditions and mythology with Christian beliefs. According to Munn the Mazatecs say that 'Through their miraculous mountains of light and rain ... Christ once walked – it is a transformation of the legend of Quetzalcoatl – and from where dropped his blood, the essence of his life, from there the holy mushrooms grew, the awakeners of the spirit, the food of the luminous one.'[8] Mazatec shamans only utilize the sacred mushrooms to diagnose disease – to contact the spirits causing illness. If there is nothing wrong, there is no reason to eat them, and the mushrooms are certainly not taken recreationally.

The Aztecs were in such awe of them that they called the mushrooms *teonanacatl*, which translates as 'divine flesh'. Today they are used ritually not only by the Mazatecs, but also by the Nahua Indians of Puebla and the Tarascana of Michoacan – specifically in religious and divinatory rites. In all cases the mushrooms are taken at night in rituals accompanied by chants and invocations. Interestingly, although psychoactive mushrooms also grow in South America, they appear not to enjoy the same ritual usage there as they do in Mexico.

## MORNING GLORY

The morning glory species *Rivea corymbosa* was known to the Aztecs as *ololiuhqui*, and they regarded the plant as a divinity. The seeds of this well-known flowering vine contain ergot alkaloids related to d-lysergic acid diethylamide – better known as LSD. However, the effects of morning glory seeds are generally of shorter duration than the LSD experience, lasting only six hours. Often associated with nausea, intake of the seeds can produce a sensation of bright lights and colour patterns, feelings of euphoria, and often profound states of peace and relaxation.

Employed these days especially by Zapotec shamans to treat sickness or to acquire powers of divination, the morning glory seeds are carefully prepared for ritual use. They have to be ground on a stone to produce a type of flour which is added to cold water. The beverage is then strained through cloth and consumed. If the seeds are taken whole they have no effect, passing through the body without producing hallucinations.

As with peyote, we have an early, if somewhat biased, description of *ololiuhqui* from the Spanish physician Francisco Hernandez who, in 1651, wrote of the Aztecs that 'when the priests wanted to commune with the gods and to receive a message from them, they ate this plant to induce a delirium. A thousand visions and satanic hallucinations appeared to them. In its manner of action, this plant can be compared with *Solanum maniacum* of Dioscorides. It grows in warm places in the fields.'⁹

Predictably, the ritual use of morning glory among the Aztecs was suppressed after the Spanish conquest although the Aztecs continued to hide the seeds in secret locations to avoid detection and persecution. Of interest in this regard is the Aztec mural at Teotihuacan, referred to earlier. Thought previously to be a representation of the male rain god Tlaloc, it is now considered to be a Mother Goddess akin to the fertility deity Xochiquetzal, an embodiment of the morning glory. Gordon Wasson believed that the Aztec God of Flowers, Xochipilli, also had a link with *ololiuhqui*, being a 'patron deity of sacred hallucinogenic plants' and the 'flowery dream'. [10]

Ironically, as if to redeem their 'Satanic' associations in the minds of the Spanish conquerors, the Zapotecs of Oaxaca now refer to the morning glory seeds in Christian terms, calling them 'Mary's Herb' or 'The Seed of the Virgin'.

## BANISTERIOPSIS

The tree-climbing forest vine known botanically as *Banisteriopsis caapi* is the pre-eminent sacred plant of South America. Its bark is brewed to make a beverage which allows direct contact with the super-natural realm, enabling shamans to contact ancestors or helper spirits and have initiatory visions. Among the Jivaro of Ecuador the Banisteriopsis drink is called *natema*; elsewhere it is called *caapi, yaje* or *ayahuasca* – a term which translates as 'vine of the soul'.

The hallucinogenic qualities of Banisteriopsis derive from the presence of the alkaloids, harmaline and harmine – formerly known collectively as 'telepathine' because of their apparent capacity to stimulate extrasensory perception. The drug certainly produces in many subjects – both native and Western – the sensation of the 'flight of the soul' and intensely coloured and dramatic visions. Shamans utilizing *ayahuasca* report encounters with supernatural beings – the Conibo say it helps them to see demons in the air and Jivaro shamans have visions of giant anacondas and jaguars rolling over and over through the rainforest. The claims of enhanced telepathic faculties also appear to have some foundation. The South American anthropologist Tomas Roessner reported that members of a tribe located near the Ucayali River in eastern Peru were genuinely surprised at the objects they 'observed' clairvoyantly in modern cities they had never visited physically:

[The Indians] who frequently practise the use of ayahuasca sit at times together and, drinking it, propose that they all see something of the same subject, for example: 'Let's see cities!' It so happens that Indians have asked white men what those strange things (*aparatos*) are which run so swiftly along the street: they had seen automobiles, which, of course, they were not acquainted with.[11]

On the whole, the Banisteriopsis beverage is used to recover the souls of sick patients, to ask the spirits about the cause of bewitchment, or – in the case of sorcery – to allow the black magician to change his form into that of a bird or some other animal in order to cause harm to someone. However, the sacred drug also has the role of allowing the shaman to participate in his own cosmology, to 'become one with the mythic world of the Creation'. Gerardo Reichel-Dolmatoff provides these details of shamanic visions experienced by the Tukano Indians of Colombia:

According to the Tukano, after a stage of undefined luminosity of moving forms and colours, the vision begins to clear up and significant details present themselves. The Milky Way appears and the distant fertilising reflection of the Sun. The first woman surges forth from the waters of the river, and first pair of ancestors is formed. The supernatural Master of the Animals of the jungle and waters is perceived, as are the gigantic prototypes of the game animals, and the origins of plants – indeed, the origins of life itself. The origins of Evil also manifest themselves, jaguars and serpents, the representatives of illness, and the spirits of the jungle that lie in ambush for the solitary hunter. At the same time their voices are heard, the music of the mythic epoch is perceived, and the ancestors are seen, dancing at the dawn of Creation. The origin of the ornaments used in dances, the feather crowns, necklaces, armlets, and musical instruments, are all seen. The division into phratries is witnessed, and the *yurupari* flutes promulgate the laws of exogamy. Beyond these visions new 'doors' are opening, and through the apertures glimmer yet other dimensions, which are even more profound ... For the Indian the hallucinatory experience is essentially a sexual one. To make it sublime, to pass from the erotic, the sensual, to a mystical union with the mythic era, the intra-uterine stage, is the ultimate goal, attained by a mere handful, but coveted by all. We find the most cogent expression of this objective in the words of an Indian educated by missionaries, who said: 'To take *yaje* is a spiritual coitus; it is the spiritual communion which the priests speak of.'[12]

On a more basic level, Banisteriopsis is considered simply as a powerful medicine, as a means of healing, and a way of acquiring special knowledge. The Cashinahua regard the visions they experience as portents of things to come and view the sacrament as 'a fearsome thing' – something regarded with awe and very much respected. The Jivaro, meanwhile, consider that their helper spirits, *tsentsak*, can only be seen in *natema*-induced visions and since disease is caused primarily by witchcraft, the sacred drug allows access to the sources of the trouble. Some *tsentsak* spirits also provide a type of psychic shield against magical attack.

## Tobacco

Strictly speaking, tobacco is an intoxicant rather than a hallucinogen, although it is used shamanically in some parts of South America. The Campa Indians of the eastern Peruvian rainforest combine tobacco and *ayahuasca* as a shamanic sacrament but regard the tobacco in itself as a source of power. Used in nocturnal rituals, the combination of tobacco and Banisteriopsis produces an altered state of consciousness in which the shaman's voice takes on an eerie quality. As he begins to sing, the shaman's soul may go to some distant place, but the words themselves are those of the spirits – the trance allowing direct communication. 'When the shaman sings he is only repeating what he hears the spirits sing,' writes Gerald Weiss; 'he is merely singing along with them. At no time is he possessed by a spirit, since Campa culture does not include a belief in spirit possession.'[13]

The following shaman song indicates that tobacco is revered in its own right:

*Tobacco, tobacco, pure tobacco,*
*It comes from River's Beginning*
*Kaokiti, the hawk, brings it to you*
*Its flowers are flying, tobacco*
*It comes to your [or our] aid, tobacco*
*Tobacco, tobacco, pure tobacco*
*Kaokiti, the hawk, is its owner*

The Warao Indian shamans of Venezuela, meanwhile, undertake periods of fasting and then smoke large cigars made of strong, native tobacco to induce a state of narcotic trance. The Warao believe that the earth is surrounded by water and that both the earth and ocean in turn are covered by a celestial vault. At the cardinal and inter-cardinal points, the vault rests on a series of mountains, and Supreme Spirits (*Kanobos*) dwell in these mountains at the edge of the world.

The priest-shaman, or *wishiratu*, is able to visit these spirits during tobacco-induced trance journeys, even though the journeys are themselves fraught with such an assortment of obstacles and perils that one would hardly think the journeys worthwhile! To begin with, the shaman journeys towards the *manaca* palm— the shamanic tree of all *wishiratus* – and then travels to a series of waterholes where he can drink and purify himself. He then has to clear an abyss where jaguars, alligators, sharks and spear-bearing demons threaten to destroy him. He is also likely to encounter sexually provocative women, whom he must resist, and also a giant hawk with a savage beak and flapping wings. These the shaman must pass by without temptation or fear – only then is he nearing his goal:

Finally the candidate shaman has to pass through a hole in an enormous tree trunk with rapidly opening and closing doors. He hears the voice of his guide and companion from the other side of the trunk, for this spirit has already cleared the dangerous passage and now encourages the fearful novice to follow his example. The candidate jumps through the clashing doors and looks around inside the hollow tree. There he beholds a huge serpent with four colourful horns and a fiery-red luminous ball on the tip of her protruding tongue. This serpent has a servant with reptilean body and human head whom the candidate sees carrying away the bones of novices who failed to clear the clashing doors.

The novice hurries outside and finds himself at the end of the cosmos. His patron *Kanobo's* mountain rises before him. Here he will be given a small house of his own, where he may sojourn in his future trances to consult with the *Kanobo* and where eventually he will come to live forever upon successful completion of his shaman's life on earth.[14]

## SAN PEDRO CACTUS

Dating back at least three thousand years as a ritual sacrament, San Pedro cactus (*Trichocereus pachanoi*) is one of the most ancient magical plants of South America. The Spanish noticed shamans in Peru drinking a beverage made from its sap and, essentially, this process still continues today. The cactus is cut into slices, boiled for around seven hours in water, and then consumed to bring on the visions. In Peru it is known simply as San Pedro, in Bolivia, *Achuma*. Purchased by shamans at the markets, the cactus contains mescaline and initially produces drowsiness and a state of dreamy lethargy. However, this is followed by a remarkable lucidity of mental faculties. Finally, one may experience 'a telepathic sense of transmitting oneself across time and matter'. Shamans in Peru and Bolivia utilize the cactus to contact spirits, to treat illness, to counteract the dangers of witchcraft, and for purposes of divination.

## THE STORY OF GORDON WASSON

For R. Gordon Wasson the shamanic pilgrimage came late in life. Born in 1898, Wasson had had a career in newspapers and banking, rising to the position of vice-president with J. P. Morgan & Co. in

New York. Wasson and his Russian-born wife Valentina had read the Mexican field reports of Richard Evans Schultes and had communicated with Eunice V. Pike about the secret mushroom ceremonies of the Mazatec Indians. So it was, that on three occasions between 1953 and 1955 they went to Mexico 'as Pilgrims seeking the Grail' – to use their own phrase – to see if they could uncover first-hand evidence of the use of sacred mushrooms.

The Wassons had as a guide an Austrian, Robert Weitlaner, who had studied the Mazatecs for many years and who accompanied them on their first mule-ride to the Sierra Mazateca. He would also travel with them on subsequent trips.

In June 1955 the Wassons arrived in the town of Huautla, together with their daughter Masha, and Allan Richardson – a friend and photographer. After pondering for some time how he would actually contact the shamans – who presumably worked in secret and shunned strangers – Wasson approached a town official, Cayetano Garcia, to ask if he knew anyone who could help him learn the secrets of the sacred mushrooms, or *ntixitjo* – as they were known to the Mazatecs. Fortunately, Garcia was receptive and invited Wasson to come to his home during the siesta, late in the afternoon.

When Wasson and Allan Richardson arrived they were subsequently taken to a place in a nearby gully where the sacred mushrooms were growing on a bed of refuse from a cane-mill. They gathered some mushrooms in a box and returned to Garcia's house. Garcia then directed Wasson, with his brother Emilio acting as interpreter, to seek out a renowned shamaness, Maria Sabina, to provide help that night. Fortunately she agreed to participate, and said she would come to Cayetano's after dark.

At the time, Maria Sabina was a woman in her fifties, and was highly regarded by the Mazatec community as *una Senora sin mancha* – a lady without blemish. This first night was to be one of several all-night vigils, or *veladas*, that she, Gordon Wasson, Allan Richardson and other local residents, would undertake together.

That night, after Maria Sabina had arrived, they all ate the sacred mushrooms together. Since the Mazatecs regard the mushrooms with reverence, they were eaten in respectful silence near a small altar table. Cayetano's father, don Emilio, intended to consult the sacred mushrooms about his left forearm, which was infected, but for Wasson it would be a much more all-encompassing initiatory experience. He did not especially enjoy the acrid taste of the mushrooms, but shortly before midnight it was apparent that the effects were coming on. Eventually, as Wasson writes, they took 'full and sweeping possession' of him:

> There is no better way to describe the sensation than to say that it was as though my very soul had been scooped out of my body and translated to a point floating in space, leaving behind the husk of clay, my body. Our bodies lay there while our souls soared ...
>
> At first we saw geometric patterns, angular not circular, in richest colours, such as might adorn textiles or carpets. Then the patterns grew into architectural structures, with colonnades and architraves, patios of regal splendour, the stone-work all in brilliant colours, gold and onyx and ebony, all most harmoniously and ingeniously contrived, in richest magnificence extending beyond the reach of sight. For some reason these architectural visions seemed oriental, though at every stage I pointed out to myself that they could not be identified with any specific oriental country. They were neither Japanese nor Chinese nor Indian nor Moslem. They seemed to belong rather to the imaginary architecture described by the visionaries of the Bible. In the aesthetics of this discovered world Attic simplicity had no place: everything was resplendently rich.
>
> At one point in the faint moonlight the bouquet on the table assumed the dimensions and shape of an imperial conveyance, a triumphal car, drawn by zoological creatures conceivable only in an imaginary mythology, bearing a woman clothed in regal splendour. With our eyes wide open, the visions came in endless succession, each growing out of

the preceding one. We had the sensation that the walls of our humble house had vanished, that our untrammelled souls were floating in the empyrean, stroked by divine breezes, possessed of a divine mobility that would transport us anywhere on the wings of a thought. Now it was clear why don Aurelio in 1953 and others too had told us that the mushrooms *le Ilevan ahi donde Dios esta* – would take you there where God is. Only when by an act of conscious effort I touched the wall of Cayetano's house would I be brought back to the confines of the room where we all were. [15]

During each *velada* – Wasson attended two during his 1955 visit to Huautla – Maria Sabina would take thirteen pairs of mushrooms while the visiting participants took five or six pairs each. Maria Sabina explained to Gordon Wasson that the purpose of a *velada* was to enable the patient to consult with the shaman about something that was worrying them – an illness, a theft, a loss of some kind, or the causes of an accident. During the *velada* the mushrooms would then speak through the voice of the shaman – the mushrooms literally 'uttering the word'. The pronouncements would then be conveyed to the patient.

To achieve this divinely inspired communication, Maria Sabina – and also her daughter, who took a similar number of mushrooms, and acted as an assistant – would initially hum and chant, both in Mazatec and Spanish. They would then invoke the spirits of the sacred mushroom. Maria has herself explained the effect of the sacred inebriation: 'I see the Word fall, come down from above, as though they were little luminous objects falling from heaven. The Word falls on the Holy Table, on my body: with my hand I catch them, Word by Word.' [16]

Maria Sabina's emphasis on 'the Word' is also confirmed by Henry Munn who, as we mentioned earlier, similarly refers to 'the mushrooms of language' among the Mazatecs. But it is important to remember that it is a sacred language we are talking about here. It is the God who is speaking. The mushrooms are an embodiment of the divine Logos. Through the sacred mushroom, the Word has become flesh. For the Mazatec shamans it is the sacred mushroom which provides access to the wisdom of the Cosmos.

## Psychedelic Shamanism comes to the West

As a phenomenon, shamanism first attracted widespread attention in the West during the late 1960s and early 1970s. However this interest was not aroused initially by the research of Gordon Wasson – he would gain more widespread recognition later in his life. Instead the fascination with shamanism was aroused through the writings of Carlos Castaneda (1925–98), who similarly described the magical, visionary world accessed through psychedelic plants.

For many devotees of the new spiritual perspectives then surfacing in the American psychedelic counterculture, Castaneda and his 'teacher' – Yaqui shaman don Juan Matus – were the first point of contact with the figure of the shaman. Even after his recent death, Castaneda's influence and fame continue to spread, alongside that of his equally controversial female counterpart, Lynn Andrews.[17] And while Casteneda's later works are now regarded substantially as 'fiction', his early writings did appear to be grounded in more solid shamanic research and had a core authenticity, even if – as now seems likely – some of the material may have been taken from other sources.

Castaneda was always a highly private person and only sketchy details of his personal history are known. However it has been established that between 1959 and 1973 he undertook a series of degree courses in anthropology at the University of California, Los Angeles. Although his real name was Carlos Arana, or Carlos Aranha, and he came from either Lima, Sao Paulo or Buenos Aires, he adopted the name Carlos Castaneda when he acquired United States citizenship in 1959. The following year, having commenced his studies, he apparently travelled to the American southwest to explore the Indian use of medicinal plants. As the story goes, a friend introduced him to an old Yaqui Indian who was said to be an expert on the hallucinogen peyote.

The Indian, don Juan Matus, said he was a *brujo*, a term which connotes a sorcerer, or one who cures by means of magical techniques. Born in Sonora, Mexico, in 1891, he spoke Spanish 'remarkably well' but appeared at the first meeting to be unimpressed with Castaneda's self-confidence. He indicated, however, that Castaneda could come to see him subsequently, and an increasingly warm relationship developed as the young academic entered into an 'apprenticeship' in shamanic magic.

Carlos Castaneda found many of don Juan's ideas and techniques strange and irrational. The world of the sorcerer contained mysterious, inexplicable forces that he was obliged not to question, but had to accept as a fact of life. The apprentice sorcerer would begin to 'see' whereas previously he had merely 'looked'. Eventually he would become a 'man of knowledge'.

According to Castaneda's exposition of don Juan's ideas, the familiar world we perceive is only one of a number of worlds. It is in reality a description of the relationship between objects that we have learned to recognise as significant from birth, and which has been reinforced by language and the communication of mutually acceptable concepts. This world is not the same as the world of the sorcerer, for while ours tends to be based on the confidence of perception, the *brujo's* involves many intangibles. His universe is a vast and continuing mystery which cannot be contained within rational categories and frameworks.

In order to transform one's perception from ordinary to magical reality, an 'unlearning' process has to occur. The apprentice must learn how to 'not do' what he has previously 'done'. He must learn how to transcend his previous frameworks and conceptual categories and for a moment freeze himself between the two universes, the 'real' and the 'magically real'. To use don Juan's expression, he must 'stop the world'. From this point onwards, he may begin to *see*, to acquire a knowledge and mastery of the mysterious forces operating in the environment which most people close off from their everyday perception.

'Seeing' said don Juan, was a means of perception which could be brought about often, although not necessarily, by using sacred plants

– among them *mescalito* (peyote), *yerba del diablo* (Jimson weed, or datura) and *humito* (psilocybe mushrooms). Through these, the *brujo* could acquire a magical ally, who could in turn grant further power and the ability to enter more readily into 'states of non-ordinary reality'. The *brujo* would become able to see the 'fibres of light' and energy patterns emanating from people and other living organisms, encounter the forces within the wind and sacred waterhole, and isolate as visionary experiences – as if on film – the incidents of one's earlier life and their influence on the development of the personality. Such knowledge would enable the *brujo* to tighten his defences as a 'warrior'. He would know himself, and have complete command over his physical vehicle. He would also be able to project his consciousness from his body into images of birds and animals, thereby transforming into a myriad of magical forms and shapes while travelling in the spirit vision.

While Castaneda's books have been attacked by critics like Weston La Barre and Richard de Mille for containing fanciful and possibly concocted elements, it is likely that the early volumes in particular are based substantially on shamanic tradition – even if some of the material has been borrowed from elsewhere. For example there are parallels between the shamanic figure don Genaro, a friend of don Juan, and the famous Huichol shaman Ramon Medina.

One of Castaneda's friends, the anthropologist Barbara Myerhoff, was studying the Huichol Indians at the same time that Castaneda was claiming to be studying Yaqui sorcery, and Myerhoff introduced Ramon Medina to Castaneda. It may be that Castaneda borrowed an incident in *A Separate Reality* – where don Genaro leaps across a precipitous waterfall clinging to it by magical 'tentacles of power' – from an actual Huichol occurrence.

Myerhoff and another noted anthropologist, Peter Furst, watched Ramon Medina leaping like a bird across a waterfall which cascaded 300 metres below over slippery rocks. Medina was exhibiting the balance of the shaman in 'crossing the narrow bridge to the other world'. Myerhoff told Richard de Mille how pleased she felt, in terms of validation, when Castaneda related to her how the sorcerer don

Genaro could also do similar things. It now seems, she feels, that Castaneda was like a mirror – his own accounts reflecting borrowed data from all sorts of sources, including her own. The rapid mystical running known as 'the gait of power', for example, was likely to have come from accounts of Tibetan mysticism and there were definite parallels between don Juan's abilities and statements in other anthropological, psychedelic and occult sources.

Even in death, Castaneda remains controversial. However while Castaneda's brand of shamanic sorcery was always elusive – no one ever knew for sure whether don Juan really existed – another, more accessible approach to practical shamanism was being introduced to the personal growth movement by an American anthropologist who really did have impeccable academic credentials – Dr Michael Harner.

A former visiting professor at Columbia, Yale and the University of California, Harner is now Director of the Foundation for Shamanic Studies in Mill Valley, California. Born in Washington D.C. in 1929, Harner spent the early years of his childhood in South America. In 1956 he returned to undertake fieldwork among the Jivaro Indians of the Ecuadorian Andes and between 1960 and 1961 visited the Conibo Indians of the Upper Amazon in Peru. His first period of fieldwork was conducted as 'an outside observer of the world of the shaman', but his second endeavour – which included his psychedelic initiation among the Conibo – led him to pursue shamanism first-hand. In 1964 he returned to Ecuador to experience the supernatural world of the Jivaro in a more complete way.

After arriving at the former Spanish settlement of Macas, Harner made contact with his Jivaro guide, Akachu. Two days later he ventured with him northwards, crossing the Rio Upano and entering the forest. It was here that he told his Indian friend that he wished to acquire spirit-helpers, known to the Jivaro as *tsentsak*. Harner offered gifts to Akachu and was told that the first preparatory task was to bathe in the sacred waterfall. Later he was presented with a magical pole to ward off demons. Then, after an arduous journey to the waterfall, Harner was led into a dark recess behind the wall of spray – a cave known as 'the house of the Grandfathers' – and here he had to call out, attracting the attention of the ancestor spirits. He now had his first magical experiences: the wall of falling water became iridescent, a torrent of liquid prisms. 'As they went by,' says Harner, 'I had the continuous sensation of floating upward, as though they were stable and I was the one in motion … It was like flying inside a mountain.'

Deeper in the jungle, Akachu squeezed the juice of some psyche-delic datura plants he had brought with him and asked Harner to drink it that night. Reassuring him, Akachu told him he was not to fear anything he might see, and if anything frightening did appear, he should run up and touch it!

That night was especially dramatic anyway – with intense rain, thunder and flashes of lightning – but after a while the effects of the datura became apparent and it was clear that something quite specific was going to happen.

Suddenly Harner became aware of a luminous, multi-coloured serpent writhing towards him. Remembering Akachu's advice, Harner charged at the visionary serpent with a stick. Suddenly the forest was empty and silent and the monster had gone. Akachu later explained to Harner that this supernatural encounter was an important precursor to acquiring spirit helpers. And his triumph over the serpent had confirmed that he was now an acceptable candidate for the path of the shaman.

Harner believes, as the Jivaro do, that the energizing force within any human being can be represented by what the Indians call a 'power animal'. One of the most important tasks of the shaman is to summon the power animal while in trance, and undertake visionary journeys with the animal as an ally. It is in such a way that one is able to explore the 'upper' and 'lower' worlds of the magical universe. The shaman also learns techniques of healing which usually entail journeys to the spirit world to obtain sources of 'magical energy'. This energy can then be transferred to sick or dis-spirited people in a ceremonial healing rite. When a person is 'dis-spirited', their animating force, or spirit, has departed and it is the shaman's role to retrieve it.

After living with the Conibo and Jivaro, Michael Harner under-took further fieldwork among the Wintun and Pomo Indians in California, the Lakota Sioux of South Dakota and the Coast Salish in Washington State. The techniques of applied shamanism which he now teaches in his workshops, and which are outlined in his important and influential book *The Way of the Shaman*, are a synthesis from many cultures, but they are true to the core essence of the tradition. 'Shamanism,' says Harner, 'takes us into the realms of myth and the Dreamtime ... and in these experiences we are able to contact sources of power and use them in daily life.'[18]

Michael Harner remains one of the major figures in international shamanic research and the Foundation for Shamanic Studies, which he helped establish, continues to help create a bridge between modern Western society and the world of indigenous spirituality. It is becoming increasingly apparent that shamanic practices around the world offer us a profound source of visionary insights into the human condition, and this material is being steadily absorbed into modern western consciousness as a valuable contribution to the world's wisdom traditions.

### Notes
1   Peter T. Furst, Hallucinogens and Culture, p.112
2   Quoted in R. E. Schultes and A. Hofmann, Plants of the Gods, 1979, p.134
3   ibid., p.135
4   Peter T. Furst, op.cit., pp.113-4
5   Prem Das, 'Initiation by a Huichol Shaman', pp.18-19
6   R. G. Wasson, *The Wondrous Mushroom*, 1980, p.*xvi*
7   Henry Munn, 'The Mushrooms of Language' in Michael Harner (ed.)
     *Hallucinogens and Shamanism*, 1973, p.88
8   ibid., p.90
9   R. E. Schultes and A. Hofmann, op.cit., p.159
10  Peter T. Furst, op.cit., p.72
11  Michael Harner, op.cit., p.169
12  Peter T. Furst, op cit., p.48
13  Michael Harner, op.cit., p.44

14  Peter T. Furst (ed.) *Flesh of the Gods*, 1972, p.64

15  R. G. Wasson, op.cit., pp.15-16

16  ibid., p.21

17  See 'Two Controversies' in Nevill Drury, *The Elements of Shamanism*, 1989
    pp.81-92

18  Personal communication to the author.

Part Two

# PATHWAYS IN MAGIC

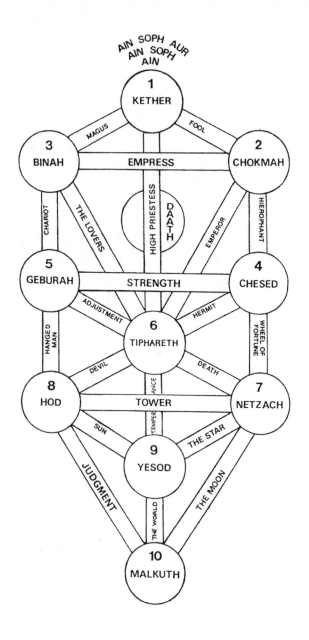

*The Cosmic Tree of modern magic –*
*the Tree of Life with interconnecting tarot paths*

# CHAPTER 4

# THE MYTHOLOGY
# AND SYMBOLS
# OF MAGIC

Shamanism and modern western magic may seem at first glance to be poles apart – shamanism has its roots in the Paleolithic era while modern magic draws substantially on Gnostic and medieval esoteric traditions. However, as we shall see, at a fundamental level both shamanism and magic share much in common. Both traditions have an operative model of the universe involving different levels of spiritual reality and in both traditions the gods and goddesses become accessible through a Cosmic Tree, which is itself conceived of as the very axis of the universe – the *Axis Mundi*. Shamans and magicians enter their respective visionary universes through an act of will or intent, and by undertaking magical journeys to the higher planes of the mystical cosmos they are granted sacred knowledge and special insights into the workings of the universe as a whole.

While it is true that in the past magical thought has been commonly identified with superstition and regarded as a form of pre-science – an earlier and less sophisticated phase of human intellectual development – contemporary magic has an altogether different thrust. Modern western magic is substantially about developing greater spiritual awareness and here the concept of magical consciousness itself is very much associated with individual *will* or *intent* – with the idea that one can bring about specific effects or changes within one's individual sphere of consciousness. This form of magic is substantially about personal transformation – or more specifically, about the transformation of one's perception or state of awareness.

# MAGICAL WILL

It is in relation to the issue of *will* that magic differs from mysticism and the more mainstream forms of religion. The magician, unlike the mystic or religious devotee, draws not so much upon the concept of grace bestowed by God as on the idea that one may alter one's state of consciousness magically at will – that the gods will respond if one undertakes certain ritual or visualisation procedures. It may be that the magician dresses ceremonially to capture their likeness and in so doing invokes their sacred and symbolic energy. Perhaps sacred god names are uttered or intoned – like those found in the Kabbalah and in certain Gnostic formulations. Here the core idea is that the name of the god or goddess embodies the very *essence* of the deity and that by invoking that sacred vibration one is not only tuning in to the archetypal level of awareness associated with these sacred beings but actually attaining *mastery* of them.

As will become evident later in this book, the idea of *will* is vital to the magical attitude. We find it in the magic of the Hermetic Order of the Golden Dawn, where focused intent enables the magician to rise through the planes of 'inner space' – through the symbolic and mythological realms of the Tree of Life. We find it in the quest for the Higher Self – anthropomorphised in Aleister Crowley's writings as the Holy Guardian Angel. And we find it in the shamanic accounts of Carlos Castaneda, where the magical apprentice has to whirl his spirit catcher near the sacred waterhole and concentrate on the 'spaces' within the conjured sounds, in order to will a magical 'ally' to appear. In all of these instances the idea of magical will is central to the activity in question. And often magic of this sort has a spiritual or metaphysical intent. Indeed, Gareth Knight, in his *History of White Magic*, has defined magic as a means of assisting the 'evolution of spiritual will'.[1]

All of this, of course, is quite foreign to most established religious traditions. Prayer and supplication, offerings of thanks to a Saviour god, and acts of worship in a church, are in no way intended to *capture* the god. Quite the reverse, in fact. Western religious devotion is an attitude of mind where one humbly submits oneself before God in the hope that He will bestow grace and salvation. One waits, passively, until grace is received.

The magical attitude, on the other hand, is clearly more active – and often more assertive. Magicians are at the centre of their own particular universe. With their sacred formulae, ritual invocations and concentrated willpower, they believe they can bring certain forces to bear. The magician believes that he or she can *will* to effect.

In one sense the 'primitivism' of this approach has been legiti-mized by existential philosophy and the rise of the contemporary human potential or 'personal growth' movement. It has become common for recent interpreters of the western magical tradition to regard the gods of High Magic as emanations of the creative imagination, as forces of the transcendent psyche.

The noted authority on western magic, the late Dr Israel Regardie – who was also a psychotherapist – employed a substantially Jungian model of the archetypes of the collective unconscious to explain to his contemporary audience what he meant by invoking a god. For him it was nothing other than a ritual means of channelling into conscious awareness a specific archetypal energy-form from the universal or 'collective' psyche. Occult writer Colin Wilson has similarly related his long involvement with the European existentialist tradition to a study of western magic in order to show that such an approach offers both a transcendental and an optimistic goal – that human beings can overcome their feelings of isolation by engaging with universal aspects of consciousness and being.

It is only fair to point out, however, that many magicians and occultists view their pantheon of gods and goddesses as existing in their own right – as beings beyond the human psyche, as entities belonging intrinsically to another plane of existence. For these devotees magic becomes a vital means of communication. The gods provide knowledge of these esoteric domains to the enquiring magician and thereby allow the devotee to grow in awareness.

Nevertheless, most modern magicians – irrespective of the tradition they follow – do tend to share one feature in common and that is the notion of a hierarchy of supernatural beings or 'powers' with whom they can interrelate. These powers in turn provide sacred knowledge and wisdom – wisdom which allows the magical devotee special insights into the dynamics of the universe and the sacred potentials of humanity. Considered in this light, magic is essentially about growth and renewal on an archetypal level of being. In its most profound and spiritual expressions it is about transforming our perception of the world from one which is profane and devalued to one which is sacred. This type of magic is about vision, and deep, insightful spiritual knowledge. This is High Magic, or gnosis.

We can now consider the core frameworks of the western magical tradition, with a special focus on the symbolic and experiential connections between shamanism and modern magic. These connections arise in the first instance through a visionary approach to the Jewish mystical Kabbalah and the ten spheres of consciousness on the Tree of Life.

# THE KABBALAH

The Kabbalah is the name given to the sacred tradition of Jewish mysticism. The word 'Kabbalah' itself translates as 'from mouth to ear' and refers to a secret, oral tradition. The Kabbalah is generally regarded as a mystical interpretation of the Torah, the first five books of the Old Testament, although the principal text of the Kabbalah – the *Zohar* – was not written down until the 13th century, when it was compiled by a Spanish mystic named Moses de Leon. Nevertheless, the Kabbalah is probably as ancient as the Old Testament Jewish tradition itself. Many scholars believe that the book of Genesis and the account of the Seven Days of Creation cannot be truly understood without an awareness of the spiritual themes of the Kabbalah, for it is in the Kabbalistic teachings that an effort is made to explain the symbolic process of divine Creation and the cosmological origins of the universe.

The Kabbalistic explanation of the Creation of the universe is based on a wonderful and very profound theme – the idea of Spirit, or infinite formlessness, gradually becoming more manifest, producing a succession of different levels of mystical reality before finally giving rise to the physical world as we know it.

In a sense this is not so different from the quantum concept of the universe we mentioned earlier – the idea that physical matter appears to contain the potentials for consciousness within its very structure even though matter itself consists mostly of space. Expressed another way we can say that, according to the Kabbalah, before the world was formed the universe consisted basically of infinite sacred energy (known variously in the Kabbalah as *En Sof*, *Ain Soph* or *Ain Soph Aur*) and this sacred energy gradually acquired a more tangible outer form by manifesting through different levels of being. This process happened phase by phase – in the Kabbalah it is said that a bolt of lightning, representing the sacred life-force, descended through ten different levels on the Tree of Life.

In the Kabbalah these ten levels on the Tree are known as 'sephiroth', or 'spheres'. They are symbolic, and are not meant to be taken literally. The first three sephiroth represent the Trinity and remain pure and transcendent – unsullied by the descent of Infinite Spirit into the finite world of physical matter. The next seven sephiroth represent the Seven Days of Creation. Between the Trinity and the manifested world of Creation lies the Abyss – a level clearly demarcated on the Tree to convey the idea of the 'Fall of Spirit' from infinite to finite awareness.

According to the Kabbalah, the mystical universe is sustained by the utterance of the Holy Names of God, and the ten spheres upon the Tree of Life are none other than 'the creative names which God called into the world, the names which He gave to Himself'.[2]

In the *Zohar* we read:

> In the Beginning, when the will of the King began to take effect, he engraved signs into the divine aura. A dark flame sprang forth from the innermost recess of the mystery of the Infinite, *En-Sof* [*Ain Soph*] like a fog which forms out of the formless, enclosed in the ring of this aura, neither white nor black, neither red nor green, and of no colour whatever. But when this flame began to assume size and extension it produced radiant colours. For in the innermost centre of the flame a well sprang forth from which flames poured upon everything below, hidden in the mysterious secrets of *En-Sof*. The well broke through, and yet did not entirely break through, the ethereal aura which surrounded it. It was entirely unrecognisable until under the impact of its breakthrough a hidden supernal point shone forth. Beyond this point nothing may be known or understood, and therefore it is called *Reshith*, that is 'Beginning', the first word of Creation.[3]

These wonderful words are endeavouring to describe a process which in the ultimate sense cannot really be described, for we are dealing here with the Great Mystery – the creation of the world out of formlessness. Nevertheless, as this text describes, with the manifestation of the first spark of Creation the universe gradually came into existence. In the Kabbalah the ten levels of Creation are as follows:

|  |  |
|---|---|
| *Kether* | The Crown, or first point of Creation |
| *Chokmah* | Wisdom (The Father) |
| *Binah* | Understanding (The Mother) |
| *Chesed* | Mercy |

| | |
|---|---|
| *Geburah* | Severity, or Strength |
| *Tiphareth* | Beauty, or Harmony (The Son) |
| *Netzach* | Victory |
| *Hod* | Splendour |
| *Yesod* | The Foundation |
| *Malkuth* | Kingdom, or Earth  (The Daughter) |

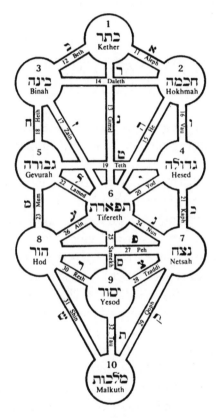

*The Jewish Tree of Life*

Another interesting idea in the Kabbalah is the concept that these ten spheres of consciousness also reside as spheres or spiritual centres within the body of the archetypal human being, known by the Jews as Adam Kadmon. Diagrams depicting these spheres position them in the body in a rather similar way to the chakras of Indian yoga. And the symbolic concept of these archetypal spheres conveys the idea that by knowing ourselves in the fullest mystical sense, we also come to know God – because ultimately there is only one supreme reality in the universe. This same concept later entered the western mystical tradition through the expression 'As above, so below' – meaning that in a very real way, every human being contains the sacred potentials and divine life force of the whole universe.

# MYTHIC AND MAGICAL CONSCIOUSNESS

Brief mention has already been made of the Hermetic Order of the Golden Dawn, an organisation which has substantially influenced contemporary western magical beliefs and practices up to the present day. Founded by a group of Victorian Freemasons, including Samuel MacGregor Mathers, Dr Wynn Westcott and Dr William Woodman, the first Golden Dawn temple was opened in London in 1888. By 1896 there were also ritual temples in Weston-Super-Mare, Bradford, Edinburgh and Paris. In the period up till the end of the First World War the Golden Dawn attracted many notable occultists, among them the distinguished poet William Butler Yeats, the well-known scholar A. E. Waite, spirited female visionaries like Florence Farr and Dion Fortune, and the influential, and later notorious, ceremonial magician, Aleister Crowley.

The magic of the Golden Dawn was essentially a fusion of Kabbalah, Rosicrucianism and ceremonial visualisation in which the ultimate mythic attainment was to come forth ritually into the Light. This in itself was considered a form of spiritual rebirth. In order to attain this state of transcendence and spiritual wholeness, the magician had to venture into the higher realms of the Tree of Life. Ascending the Tree through sacred ceremonial involved a powerful act of creative imagination – the magician had to feel fully engaged with each sphere of sacred consciousness in turn.

However Judaism and the Kabbalah are monotheistic: each *sephirah* is an aspect of the Godhead, a face of the Divine – not an individual deity in itself – and in the Jewish mystical tradition there is finally only the Unity Consciousness of *Ain Soph Aur*. This presented the Golden Dawn occultists with a paradox, for while they acknowledged the sacred unity of the Tree of Life in all its emanations they also believed that they had to focus their creative awareness upon specific archetypal images if they were to ascend to the Light. The solution to this was to regard the Kabbalistic Tree of Life as a type of unifying matrix upon which the archetypes of the great western mythologies could be charted. It then became possible to correlate the major deities from the pantheons of ancient Egypt, Greece, Rome and Celtic Europe in what amounted to a cumulative approach to the western mythological imagination. In due course other aspects of magical symbolism would also be charted upon the Tree so that various precious stones, perfumes, minerals and sacred plants could also be assigned to specific gods and goddesses in a ceremonial context. These charted mythological images were known to the Golden Dawn magicians as 'magical correspondences'.

Guided in this particular task by their principal founding figure, Samuel MacGregor Mathers, the Golden Dawn cosmology became a very elaborate one indeed. Despite his modest social origins Mathers himself was nevertheless a self-taught scholar with a sound knowledge of French, Latin and Greek, as well as some Coptic and Hebrew. He had translated Knorr von Rosenroth's Latin text of *Kabbala Denudata* (*The Kabbalah Unveiled*) into English – the specialist esoteric publisher George Redway issued it in 1887 – and one of his major interests was to translate key magical documents which might otherwise have been doomed to obscurity in museum archives. It was primarily through Mathers' initiative that the magical rituals of the Golden Dawn, in whose shaping and formation he had assumed a major role, would come to draw on every significant mythology in Western culture.

As we have seen, the Tree of Life can be regarded as a cosmological metaphor which describes the hierarchy of energy levels in the manifested universe. Mathers' vision for the Golden Dawn was that the magicians in his Order could follow the mythic pathways on the Tree of Life and grow in spiritual awareness as they ascended through each level. Several methods were open to them. They could simulate each of the levels imaginatively through ritual, they could meditate upon each sphere of consciousness, or they could 'rise on the inner planes' in a state of magical trance. The latter techniques will be discussed subsequently, but the essence of Mathers' approach was to list the deities from the different pantheons and cross-correlate them as important magical archetypes.

In due course this work was published in 1909 under the title *777* – not by Mathers himself but by his friend and fellow Golden Dawn occultist Aleister Crowley, who appears to have added a number of oriental listings to Mathers' original table of magical correspondences as well as including some individual elements of his own.[4]

The listings in *777* are complex and extend beyond classical Graeco-Roman and Egyptian mythology to include Scandinavian gods, western astrology, Buddhist meditations, magical weapons and the letters of the Greek, Arabic and Coptic alphabets. However when we sample some of the core data included in *777* we find listings like the following:

### Magical Correspondences

|    | *Kabbalah* | *Astrology* | *Egyptian* | *Greek* |
|----|-----------|-------------|------------|---------|
| 1  | Kether    | Primum Mobile | Harpocrates | Zeus |
| 2  | Chokmah   | Zodiac/Fixed Stars | Ptah | Uranus |
| 3  | Binah     | Saturn | Isis | Demeter |
| 4  | Chesed    | Jupiter | Amoun | Poseidon |
| 5  | Geburah   | Mars | Horus | Ares |
| 6  | Tiphareth | Sol (Sun) | Ra | Apollo |
| 7  | Netzach   | Venus | Hathor | Aphrodite |
| 8  | Hod       | Mercury | Anubis | Hermes |
| 9  | Yesod     | Luna | Shu | Diana |
| 10 | Malkuth   | The Elements | Seb | Persephone |

The perfumes and precious stones listed below were considered appropriate in rituals corresponding to the invoked god or goddess:

| Level | Precious Stones | Perfumes |
|---|---|---|
| 1 | diamond | ambergris |
| 2 | star ruby, turquoise | musk |
| 3 | star sapphire, pearl | myrrh, civet |
| 4 | amethyst | cedar |
| 5 | ruby | tobacco |
| 6 | topaz | olibanum |
| 7 | emerald | benzoin, rose, sandalwood |
| 8 | opal | storax |
| 9 | quartz | jasmine |
| 10 | rock crystal | dittany of Crete |

As a document, *777* represents the parameters of the modern magical imagination, and its historic significance lies in the fact that it was an early attempt to systematise the various images associated with different levels of spiritual awareness – predating Jung's concept of archetypes and the collective unconscious.

From a psychological perspective one can see clearly that the magicians of the Golden Dawn regarded the Tree of Life as a complex symbol of the spiritual world within, a world containing sacred potentialities. To simulate the gods and goddesses was to *become like them*. The challenge was to engage oneself in the mythological processes of the psyche through methods of direct encounter.

The magicians in the Golden Dawn had therefore to imagine that they were partaking of the nature of each of the gods in turn, embodying within themselves the very essence of the deity. The rituals were designed to control all the circumstances which might assist them in their journey through the subconscious mind and mythic imagination. They included all the symbols and colours of the god, the utterance of *magical names of power*, and the burning of incense or perfume appropriate to the deity concerned.

In the Golden Dawn tradition – an approach to archetypal magic which remains   influential a century later – the ritual magician imagines that he has become the deity whose forms he imitates in ritual. The process of the gods ruling humanity is thus reversed so that the magician now controls the gods – he has seized the fire from heaven. It is now the magician himself and not the gods of Creation who utters the sacred names which sustain the universe. In the approach employed by the Golden Dawn magicians one entered the underworld of the subconscious mind through Malkuth at the base of the Tree, and then proceeded along various pathways culminating in the solar vision of Tiphareth, at the very heart of the Tree of Life.

The most 'direct' route upon the Tree was the vertical path from Malkuth through Yesod to Tiphareth, upon the so-called 'Middle Pillar'. The Golden Dawn grades, however, also encompassed the other sephiroth Hod and Netzach on the outer extremities of the Tree and the process here was one of following the so-called 'zig-zag lightning flash' of sacred manifestation – retracing the path of the Divine Energy of Creation through each of the sephiroth in turn.

# MYTHOLOGICAL LEVELS ON THE TREE OF LIFE

In the Golden Dawn, and in modern magic generally, the Tree of Life has  been used as a type of universal framework of 'mythic' cons-ciousness. It became possible – although orthodox Jewish Kabbalists would no doubt frown at the idea – to map other mythologies upon the Tree of Life by assigning them to the different spiritual 'spheres'. Here we also encounter the idea that the gods and goddesses of different spiritual traditions are somehow equivalent to each other – cultural variables on an archetypal theme. For example, many practising magicians locate the gods and goddesses from ancient Greece and Rome upon the Tree, as well as those from ancient Egypt and other early civilisations. When we consider the Tree of Life in this 'mythological' way – and this is certainly the way it is now represented in the western esoteric tradition – the ten spheres of consciousness are as follows:

## MALKUTH

Associated with the earth, crops, the immediate environment, living things, this sphere of consciousness represents the beginning of the inner journey. In Roman mythology the entrance to the underworld was through a cave near Naples, and symbolically Malkuth is the entrance through the earth – the totality of the four elements – leading to what in psychological terms is the subconscious mind. Malkuth in itself represents familiar everyday consciousness.

## YESOD

Associated with the Moon, Yesod – like Malkuth – is a predominantly female sphere. It is both the recipient of impulses and fluxes from the higher realms upon the Tree of Life and the transmitter of these energies into a more tangible physical form in Malkuth. Consequently it abounds in an ocean of astral imagery, and is appropriately associated with water. Yesod is also the seat of the sexual instinct, corresponding to the genital area when 'mapped' upon the figure of Adam Kadmon, the archetypal human being. Yesod is the sphere of subconscious activity immediately entered through sexual magic and is the level of awareness activated through basic forms of witchcraft. The ancient rites of Wicca were primarily a form of lunar worship; the traditional dance around the maypole derived from the worship of an enlarged artificial phallus worn by the coven leader who assumed the role of the goat-headed god. Yesod is thus regarded as a transitional sephirah in which the individual's animal nature is resolved.

## HOD

Associated with the planet Mercury – representing intellect and rational thinking – Hod is a lower aspect of the Great Father (Chokmah: Wisdom) for Mercury is the messenger of the gods. As the next stage beyond Yesod, Hod represents in some measure the conquest of the animal instincts, albeit at an intellectual rather than an emotional level. Hod symbolizes the structuring principle in the manifested universe and is considered a levelling and balancing sephirah which embodies a sense of order. It is in this capacity that we perceive 'God the Architect' manifesting in a world of myriad forms and structures.

## NETZACH

Associated with the planet Venus, Netzach complements Hod because whereas Hod is to some extent clinical and rational, this sephirah represents the arts, creativity, subjectivity and the emotions. In the same way that Hod lies on the Pillar of Form (the left-hand pillar) on the Tree of Life, Netzach resides on the Pillar of Force (the right-hand pillar). It is outward-going in its emphasis, with an element of instinctual drive as opposed to intellect, and is the sphere of love and spiritual passion. A fine balance exists between Hod and Netzach upon the Tree of Life as the process of Creation weaves a fine web of love energy between the polarities of force and form. These potencies flow through the uniting sephirah of the Moon, lower on the Tree, and in turn are channelled through to the earth – where they are perceived as the beauty innate within living forms.

## TIPHARETH

Just as Hod and Netzach are opposites, so too are Yesod and Tiphareth for they are embodiments of the Moon (feminine) and Sun (masculine) respectively. If Yesod represents the animal instincts, Tiphareth is the mediating stage between humanity and the Godhead on the journey of mystical ascent. It is here that the individual experiences spiritual rebirth. The personality has acquired a sense of true and authentic balance and one's aspirations are now oriented towards higher states of being. Tiphareth is associated with deities of rebirth and resurrection and in a planetary sense with the Sun as a giver of life and light. Tiphareth is also the sphere of sacrifice, for the old limited and restricted persona is now offered in place of new understanding and insight. The individual now begins to function in a spiritual way.

## GEBURAH

Associated with Mars, traditionally a god of war, Geburah represents severity and justice. The energies of Geburah are absolutely impartial, since there can be no flaw of self-pity or sentiment in the eye of a wise ruler. The destructive forces of this sphere are intended as a purging, cleansing force and are positive in their application. Geburah thus embodies a spiritual vision of power operating in the universe to destroy unwanted and unnecessary elements after their usefulness has passed. As an aspect of the Ruler, Demiurge, or 'Father of the Gods' below the Abyss, Geburah shows discipline and precision in his destructiveness. His mission in the battlefield of the cosmos is to inculcate a rational economy of form which, at a lower level upon the Tree, is reflected in Hod.

## CHESED

Associated with Jupiter, Chesed is the other face of the destructive Ruler, and represents divine mercy and majesty. In the same way that Geburah breaks down forms, Chesed is protective and tends to reinforce and consolidate. Whereas Mars rides in his chariot, Chesed is seated upon his throne, where he oversees his kingdom – the entire manifested universe. Through his stabilizing influence the sacred potencies which originate in the transcendent spheres above the Abyss (i.e. at the level of the Trinity) are channelled down the Tree into various forms of being. Within Chesed all the ideas are archetypal for he is mythologically located at the highest level of the collective unconscious.

## BINAH

At the first of the three levels known collectively as the Trinity we find the Great Mother in all her mythological aspects. She is the Womb of Forthcoming, the source of all the great images and forms which will enter the manifested universe as archetypes. She is also the supreme Female principle in the process of Creation, and as such is invariably the mother of the god-man or messiah who in turn provides the bridge between humanity and the gods (or God). Binah is thus associated with the Virgin Mary, mother of Christ in Tiphareth, but she is also associated with Rhea and Isis. Because she is also so intimately connected with the archetypal world as the Mother of Creation she is often the wife of the ruler of the manifested universe. In this way Demeter, mother of Persephone, is the wife of Zeus.

## CHOKMAH

The next of the Trinitarian god-images is the Great Father. He provides the seminal spark of life which is potency only, until it enters the womb of the Great Mother. From the union of the Great Father and the Great Mother come forth all the images of Creation. Associated with those transcendent male gods whose realm lies beyond time and the manifested universe, Chokmah is associated with deities who sustain existence itself.

## KETHER

This stage of consciousness represents the first spark of Creation which emanates from beyond the veils of non-Existence (*Ain Soph Aur* – the Limitless Light). Kether is located on the Middle Pillar of the Tree of Life and thus transcends the duality of male and female polarities. Sometimes represented as the Heavenly Androgyne for this reason, Kether represents a level of sublime spiritual transcendence.

# MAGIC AND THE SENSES

Most of the Golden Dawn magicians focused their attention on mythic levels associated with the lower sephiroth of the Tree of Life. They nevertheless developed specific techniques for the expansion of spiritual awareness. These included a rich application of magical symbols and mythic imagery in their ritual adornments, ceremonial procedures and invocations, all of which were intended to focus the imagination during the the performance of a given magical ritual. In one of his most important books, Israel Regardie described magical ritual as 'a deliberate exhilaration of the Will and the exaltation of the Imagination, the end being the purification of the personality and the attainment of a spiritual state of consciousness, in which the ego enters into a union with either its own Higher Self or a God'.[5] MacGregor Mathers would surely have agreed with this definition.

Because the consciousness of the ceremonial magician is to be transformed in its entirety, any given ritual must enhance each of the senses to a fine degree – and with a specific purpose in mind. The way in which this is done can be summarized as follows:

*Sight*   The ritual robes, actions and implements are a visual repre-sentation relevant to the specific end which is sought (for example the invoking of a particular deity). In this drama carefully chosen colours and symbols play a para-mount role. The ritual magician's vestments, and also the motifs mounted upon the wall of the Temple, are intended to stimulate the mythic imagination and help consolidate the spiritual connection with the gods and goddesses to whom the ritual is addressed.

*Sound*   This involves the vibration of sacred god-names, chants or invocations (predominantly derived from the Kabbalah) whose auditory rhythms have a profound impact on one's consciousness.

*Taste*   This may take the form of a sacrament which relates symbolically to the nature of the god or goddess in the ritual.

*Smell*   Incense and perfumes may be used to increase the sense of rapport with a specific deity or being from the magical cosmology.

*Touch*    The magician endeavours to develop a sense of tactile awareness beyond the normal functions of the organism since assimilation with 'god-forms' takes place in a trance state. The magician's imaginal 'soul body' performs functions parallel to those undertaken in a physical context although here they are in a sacred ritual setting.

# THE POWER OF
# THE SACRED WORD

In the western esoteric tradition, sound – and more particularly the power of the magical utterance – have been traditionally emphasized as being of central importance. According to the Kabbalistic *Zohar*, the world was formed by the utterance of the Sacred Name of God, a forty-two letter extension of the Tetragrammaton JHVH (*Yod, He, Vau, He*, usually transposed as Jehovah, or Yahweh). The Word, or Logos, therefore permeates the entire mystical act of Creation. Ritual magicians both within the Golden Dawn and also in other magical orders have held a similar view. According to the late Franz Bardon, 'the divine names are symbolic designations of divine qualities and powers.'[6] And the 19th century occultist Eliphas Lévi stated in his seminal text *The Key of the Mysteries* that 'all magic is in a word, and that word pronounced Kabbalistically is stronger than all the powers of Heaven, Earth and Hell. With the name of *Yod, He, Vau, He*, one commands Nature …'[7]

In many ancient traditions the name was regarded as the very essence of *being*. The Ethiopian Gnostics, in their sacred book *Lefefa Sedek*, argued that God had created Himself and the Universe through the utterance of His own name and therefore 'the Name of God was the essence of God [and] was not only the source of His power but also the seat of His very Life, and was to all intents and purposes His Soul'.[8] In the apocryphal Gnostic-Christian literature we find the Virgin Mary beseeching Jesus for his secret names since, as a source of power, they were regarded as a protection for the deceased against all manner of harmful devils.

Similarly in the *Egyptian Book of the Dead* the deceased new-comer to the Hall of Maat (Hall of Judgement) says to the deity Osiris: 'I know thee. I know thy name. I know the names of the two-and-forty gods who are with thee.'[9] For it follows that he who knows the secret name strikes home to the very heart of the matter, and has the ability to liberate his soul: he is in control, for the essence of the god is within his very grasp. According to the distinguished Egyptol-ogist Sir Wallis Budge, in ancient Egypt 'the knowledge of the name of a god enabled a man not only to free himself from the power of that god, but to use that name as a means of obtaining what he himself wanted without considering the god's will'.[10]

In the Golden Dawn and elsewhere, magical ritual has invariably involved the invocation of beings or archetypal forces through the potency of the spoken word, and this also relates strongly to the idea of will, which distinguishes magic from passive forms of mysticism. As an initiated member of the Golden Dawn, Aleister Crowley took the magical name *Perdurabo* – 'I will endure to the end' – and he himself noted: 'Words should express will; hence the Mystic Name of the Probationer is the expression of his highest Will.'[11]

The Golden Dawn magicians believed that one of their most important goals was to communicate through the magical will with their Higher Self – often referred to as the Holy Guardian Angel – and this required a level of mystical awareness associated with the most transcendent levels of the Tree of Life. Sometimes too, it involved techniques of magical trance and 'rising in the planes' – which we will discuss later. However it is of interest here that Dion Fortune, who was a member of the Alpha and Omega Temple of the Golden Dawn, found it more easy to project her 'body of light' when she uttered her magical name. In her book *Applied Magic* she writes:

In my own experience of the operation, the utterance to myself of my Magical name led to the picturing of myself in an idealised form, not differing in type, but upon an altogether grander scale, superhuman in fact, but recognisable as myself, as a statue more than life-size may yet be a good likeness. Once perceived, I could re-picture this idealised version of my body and personality at will, but I could not identify myself with it unless I uttered my Magical name. Upon my affirming it as my own, identification was immediate.[12]

# THE SYMBOLS OF
# RITUAL MAGIC

We can now consider the central symbols in the ritual magic practised in the Golden Dawn and also within derivative magical orders following the Golden Dawn tradition. The first of these symbols is the place of the sacred working itself – the Temple.

The **Temple** contains all magical activities ; it therefore represents the entire Universe and, by inference, the magician himself, because of the relationship of the microcosm to the macrocosm. Upon the walls are mounted banners emblazoned with sacred symbols and colours appropriate to the mythic imagery of the ritual, and on the floor of the Temple are certain inscriptions, the most important of which is the Circle. The **Circle** incorporates many symbolic meanings but most significantly it represents the Infinite Godhead – the Alpha and Omega – the divine self-knowledge which the magician aspires to. As a symbol of what the magician may become, the Circle symbolizes the process of invocation – which in turn is essentially an act of reaching towards a higher spiritual reality. By standing in the centre of the Circle, the magician is able to identify with the sacred source of Creation and consequently his magical will ensures that the 'ego-devils' of his lower self remain outside this sphere of higher aspiration.

The magician now takes on a role of authority in the sense that he intends to subject the invoked deity to his will. The **God-names**, which have already been mentioned, are of vital importance in this respect. Inscribed around the periphery of the Circle, these holy names stipulate the exact nature of the symbolic working. In addition, the Circle may be circumscribed by an equal-sided geometric figure the number of sides of which corresponds to the pertinent sephirah upon the Tree of Life. For example, a hexagram would be employed to invoke Osiris because as a god of rebirth Osiris is symbolically associated with Tiphareth – the sixth emanation upon the Tree.

The Circle also contains a Tau cross which, as an assertive masculine symbol, balances the receptive role of the Circle itself – the two together producing an appropriate balance of opposites. The Tau is made up of ten squares, one for each sephirah, and is vermilion in colour – as are the inscribed god-names. The Circle area is complementary green. Nine equidistant pentagrams, each containing a small glowing lamp, surround the Circle, and a tenth – the most important – hangs above the centre as a symbol of mystical aspiration. The Circle must of course be large enough for the ritual magician to move around in. He must not leave it during the invocation for to do so would destroy its power as a focus for the magical will.

In terms of construction, where the Circle is not a permanent fixture of the Temple floor, it may be chalked in colour, or alternatively sewn or printed on cloth. Whenever the Circle is already in existence its sacred nature must be ritually reaffirmed in the mind of the magician, for otherwise the Circle remains a purely profane, or secular symbol. The magician thus traces over its inscribed form with his ritual sword or outstretched hand, at the same time carefully reflecting upon the symbolic meaning of his action. If conditions for a Temple working do not exist, the Circle may be inscribed upon the ground – as in the case of workings outdoors – or held within the imagination. The effectiveness of this latter type of Circle naturally depends upon the magician's powers of visualization.

Some magical rituals utilize the **Triangle**, but this symbol has an essentially opposite role. Unlike the Circle, which symbolizes the Infinite, the Triangle represents finite manifestation, a focus for that which already exists. Symbolic of the triadic nature of Creation and the union of spiritual, mental and physical levels, the Triangle represents 'evocation' – a magical term for calling forth specific spirit beings by means of spells or words of power.[13]

Like the Circle, the Triangle must be carefully constructed or mentally reinforced to impress the mind of the magician. In like fashion, the Triangle must restrain the evoked entity, for otherwise the magician could lose control of the manifestation and might even find himself mentally conquered by it – that is to say, 'possessed'. The magical talisman placed in the centre of the Triangle incorporates the seal, or sign, of the spirit and provides the focus of the ritual. Some ritual magicians have regarded evoked spirits as their 'spirit familiars' or 'astral guardians'. Evocation is more often than not associated with low magic rather than with the high magic of spiritual transformation, and it was not a central feature of the magic of the Golden Dawn temples. However MacGregor Mathers was fascinated by medieval tracts on the evocation of spirits and several such documents gained currency through his translations.[14] Aleister Crowley was also an enthusiastic practitioner of magical evocation.

Returning to the nature of invocation, certain magical imple-ments are also employed by the magician within the Circle. Most of these objects are placed upon the central **Altar**, which symbolizes the foundation of the ritual itself. Consisting of a double cube of wood – usually made of acacia or oak – the Altar has ten exposed faces, corresponding with the ten sephiroth upon the Tree of Life. The lowest face is Malkuth – the World – which represents things as they are in the manifested universe. The upper face represents Kether, the Crown – the First-Manifest – and Aleister Crowley recommended it be plated with gold, the metal of perfection. Upon the sides of the Altar, wrote Crowley, one could inscribe 'the sigils of the holy Elemental Kings'.[15]

Placed upon the Altar are certain symbolic implements designed to channel the imagination of the ritual magician towards transcendence:

**The Holy Oil:**

This golden fluid is ideally contained in a vessel of rock-crystal. In using it, the magician anoints the Four Points of the Microcosm (Kether, Chesed, Geburah and Malkuth) upon his forehead, left and right shoulders and solar plexus respectively, at the same time reflecting on the sacred task ahead. The holy ointment consists of the oils of olive, myrrh, cinnamon and galangual, these corresponding in turn to Chokmah (Wisdom), Binah (Understanding), Tiphareth (Harmony/Spiritual Awakening) and Kether-Malkuth (the so-called Greater and Lesser Countenance, the Union of Being and Creation upon the Tree of Life).

**The Wand:**

This implement symbolises the pursuit of Higher Wisdom (Chokmah), achieved through the Will. Symbolically the tip of the wand is in Kether, the first sephirah of the Tree of Life which contains the Union of Opposites and represents the transcendence of duality in all its forms. In the Golden Dawn a Lotus Wand was used which was multi-coloured, with its upper end white and its lower end black. In between were twelve bands of colour corresponding to the different signs of the zodiac:

| | |
|---|---|
| white | |
| red | Aries |
| red-orange | Taurus |
| orange | Gemini |
| amber | Cancer |
| lemon-yellow | Leo |
| yellow-green | Virgo |
| emerald | Libra |
| green-blue | Scorpio |
| blue | Sagittarius |
| indigo | Capricorn |
| violet | Aquarius |
| purple | Pisces |
| black | |

A lotus flower, with three whorls of petals, was placed upon the tip of the wand, the white end being used for magical invocation, the black end for 'banishing', or removing malevolent forces.

The Wand represents the first letter, Yod, of the Tetragrammaton JHVH and also the element Fire. The other ritual magical implements described here – the Cup, Sword and Disc (also known as the Pentacle) complete the Sacred Name of God and represent the elements Water, Air and Earth respectively.

**The Cup:**
As a feminine, receptive symbol, the Cup aligns with Binah, the Mother of Understanding. The magician believes he must fill his cup of consciousness with an understanding and knowledge of his Higher Self. As a symbol of *containment* rather than of *becoming*, the Cup is not used in rituals of invocation, but in ceremonies related to acts of manifestation.

**The Sword:**
Indicative of the magician's mastery over evoked and invoked powers, the Sword – which symbolizes human force – parallels the Wand, which represents divine power. Suggestive of control and order, the Sword is the 'offspring' of Wisdom and Understanding (Chokmah and Binah) and is therefore attributed to Tiphareth, the sphere of harmony. The symmetry of the Sword is correspondingly appropriate. According to Aleister Crowley, the guard should consist of two moons waxing and waning, affixed to the back (Yesod) and the blade should be made of steel (corresponding to Mars). The hilt should be constructed of copper (the metal symbolically associated with Venus), indicating that ultimately the Sword is subject to the rule of Love. When the Sword is placed symbolically upon the Tree of Life, the pommel rests in Daath – the 'sphere' associated with the Abyss beneath the Trinity – and the points of the guard lie in Chesed and Geburah. The tip rests in Malkuth. Crowley makes the observation that 'the Magician cannot wield the Sword unless the Crown is on his head'. That is to say, force and aspiration without inspiration are of no avail.

**The Disc (Pentacle):**

In the same way that the Sword is paired with the Wand – both being symbolically masculine – the Disc is paired with the Cup as a feminine symbol. Symbolic of Malkuth, the Heavenly Daughter and Goddess of the Manifest Universe, the Disc is said traditionally to 'induce awe' in the consciousness of the magician. Malkuth represents the first step upon the mystical journey back to the Source of All Being. It is also representative of the body of the magician which he would wish to be filled with the Holy Ghost, and symbolizes the state of one's personal being prior to spiritual transformation.

The ceremonial magician wears upon his head the **Crown**, or headband, representative of Kether. Golden in colour, it is a symbol of aspiration towards the Divine. Over his body falls the **Robe**, the function of which is to protect the magician from adverse 'astral' influences. Hooded, and normally black in colour, the Robe symbolizes anonymity and silence and is the dark vessel into which Light will be poured. Attached to it, or sewn across the chest is the **Lamen**, or breastplate, which protects the heart (Tiphareth). And in the same way that Tiphareth is the focal point of all the sephiroth because of its central position upon the Tree of Life, the Lamen has inscribed upon it symbols which relate to all aspects of the magical purpose. Considered an 'active' form of the passive Disc, the Lamen indicates strength. So too does the **Magical Book**, which the magician holds in his hands. This book contains all the details of one's ritual aims and practice and in a sense represents the unfolding 'history' of the effects of the Magical Will. As such, the Magical Book constitutes a steadfast symbol of power and resolve.

In addition, the ceremonial magician sometimes employs the use of a **Bell**, worn on a chain around the neck. Representative of a state of alertness it is said to be the Bell which sounds 'at the elevation of the Host' and thus alludes to the sublime music of the higher spheres. In this respect the symbolism of the Bell parallels that of the **Sacred Lamp**, which as 'the light of the pure soul' is positioned above the ritual implements on the altar and represents the descent of Spirit into Form,

Light into Darkness, God into Man. It stands for all that is eternal and unchanging and also represents the first swirlings of the Primal Energy in the Universe. ('Let there be Light …'). 'Without this Light', notes Aleister Crowley in one of his more insightful moments, 'the magicians could not work at all; yet few indeed are the magicians that have known of it, and far fewer they that have beheld its brilliance.'[16]

### Notes

1 Gareth Knight, *A History of White Magic*, Mowbray, London and Oxford 1978, p.15

2 see Gershom Scholem, *Major Trends in Jewish Mysticism*, Schocken, New York 1961, pp.215-16

3 ibid. pp.218-19

4 Mathers' manuscript *The Book of Correspondences* was circulated among senior Golden Dawn students in the 1890s. Ithell Colquhoun, author of a biography of Samuel Mathers, *Sword of Wisdom*, believes that Crowley and another Golden Dawn member, Allan Bennett, borrowed a substantial portion of the material in *777* from their teacher. The Tarot listings in *777*, for example, are conventional, whereas Crowley derived his own symbolic meanings and rearranged the correspondences to fit in with his own magical philosophy after leaving the Golden Dawn in 1900. Had the material in *777* belonged entirely to Crowley this would not have been the case.

5 Israel Regardie, *The Tree of Life*, 1932, p.106

6 Franz Bardon, *The Practice of Magical Evocation*, 1967, p.20

7 Eliphas Levi, *The Key of the Mysteries*, 1959, p.174

8 E. A. Wallis Budge, (ed.) *Lefefa Sedek: The Bandlet of Righteousness*, 1929, p.3

9 ibid., p.4

10 ibid., p.5

11 Aleister Crowley, *Book Four*, 1972, p.42

12 Dion Fortune, *Applied Magic*, Aquarian Press, London 1962, pp.56-57

13 For further information on magical evocation see Franz Bardon, *The Practice of Magical Evocation*, 1967

14 MacGregor Mathers translated such works as *The Greater Key of Solomon* and *Goetia: The Book of Evil Spirits*, as well as *The Grimoire of Armadel*, and these are available in various editions – see Bibliography.

15 Aleister Crowley, *Book Four*, op.cit., p.23

16 ibid., p.112

CHAPTER 5

# TECHNIQUES OF MAGICAL TRANCE

When occultists describe the inner journey of the psyche they commonly refer to such terms as 'astral projection', 'pathworkings' and 'the Body of Light'. Essentially, all techniques of magical trance involve a transfer of consciousness to the visionary world of symbols through an act of willed imagination.

Trance in a contemporary occult context is brought about initially by a technique combining bodily relaxation with mental acuity, in which the magician focuses increasingly on his inner psychic processes. He may conjure specific images to mind and endeavour to activate energy centres in his spiritual body which are equivalent to the 'chakras' of yoga, while at the same time relaxing his body and restricting his outer vision. Usually visualizations like this take place in the dark: most occultists believe it is easier to 'project' the astral body in the dark than in the light. In this sense the magician, like the traditional shaman, applies a technique of sensory deprivation by shifting attention away from outer visual stimuli to an inner perspective. He then attempts to develop and reinforce the sense of the 'alternative reality' provided by the mythological images or visionary landscapes which arise in his mind as a result of his willed concentration. The following summary is taken from the magical record of Frater Sub Spe (J. W. Brodie-Innes), a leading member of the Golden Dawn:

> Gradually the attention is withdrawn from all surrounding sights and sounds, a grey mist seems to swathe everything, on which, as though thrown from a magic lantern on steam, the form of the symbol is projected. The Consciousness then seems to pass through the symbol to realms beyond ... the sensation is as if one looked at a series of moving pictures ... When this sensitiveness of brain and power of perception is once established there seems to grow out of it a power of actually going to the scenes so visionary and seeing them as solid, indeed of actually doing things *and producing effects there.*[1]

The shaman's journey of the soul translates in occult terms as an astral projection upon the 'inner planes' and these in turn frequently relate to the levels of consciousness delineated upon the Tree of Life. Like the shaman, the occultist uses his cosmology to define his trance wanderings and the gods upon the Tree similarly represent higher causality and a return to the source of primal being and creation. Because the occultist believes, following the Hermetic axiom 'as above so below', that his inner body is a microcosm reflecting the macrocosm of the Creation, his inner journey is potentially revelatory and may lead to the experience of spiritual rebirth.

The exercise described below involves a magical world view in which man is regarded as both the microcosm and the macrocosm. The trance-inducing technique known as the 'Middle Pillar' transposes the Kabbalistic Tree onto the body of man. The magician equates the Axis of the World, as it were, with his own central nervous system, which he tries to activate by a western equivalent of yogic Kundalini arousal.

The Middle Pillar exercise may be summarized as follows:

*Seated in a chair, or standing erect, the magician imagines radiant white light descending from above his head. This light equates with the first light of Creation which manifests itself in the first sephirah Kether upon the Kabbalistic Tree of Life. The magician vibrates the sacred Hebrew god name Ehieh (pronounced Eee Hee Yeh) as his magical formula.*

*The light is now imagined coursing down the central nervous system in a similar fashion to the primal energy flash which descended through the sephiroth in the creation process. It descends to the throat and is imagined to radiate forth in the form of mauve light: (Sephirah: Daath, god-name Jehovah Elohim – 'Ye-ho-waa Eloheem').*

*Descending further, it reaches the region of the heart and solar plexus. It now transforms to golden-yellow light: (Sephirah: Tiphareth, god-name Jehovah Aloah Va Daath – 'Ye-ho-waaa Aloaaa Vaaa Daaath').*

*From the heart it descends to the region of the genitals and the colour of the imagined light changes from yellow into deep, radiant purple: (Sephirah: Yesod, god-name Shaddai El Chai – 'Sha-Dai El-Hai').*

*Finally the light reaches the magician's feet and he visualizes the colours of autumnal earth: russet, citrine, black and olive: (Sephirah: Malkuth, god-name Adonai Ha Aretz – 'Aadohnaiii Haaa Aaaretz').*

*The magician now imagines white light streaming down his left side, beneath his feet and up his right side to the top of his head. He then visualizes a similar band of light-energy travelling from his head along his nose, down the chest, once again beneath his feet, and up past the back of his legs to the head. In his mind he has now completely surrounded his body with white light. His breathing is deep and regular. He imagines that the boundaries of light define a translucent container which is in reality his field of conscious awareness. He now visualizes the container filling up, perhaps with liquid, the amount of unoccupied space left in the container representing the extent of his awareness. At first his legs 'fill' and he is aware of his body only above the knees. Then the level rises and he remains 'aware' of only his chest. Soon the only conscious part of his body remaining is his head, for the rest of his body has fallen into a state of trance and is to all intents and purposes 'inert'.*

The magician uses this technique and variations of it to shift his range of visual alertness from his outer waking domain to an inner contemplative range of images. Within the magical context he now combines the act of 'consciousness transfer' with the magical act of willing an image to appear. Usually this image is a form in which the magician will travel upon the inner planes. Frequently it is a stylized form of the occultist himself, usually in a cloak but, as with traditional shamans, it may take animal and other forms appropriate to the plane of magical encounter. While the body of the occultist appears to have sunk into a deep trance, he wills his consciousness, as it were, to occupy an inner plane image or 'god-form'. The magician may simulate, for example, Horus's venture into the Egyptian underworld in search of Osiris, by imagining that he now occupies the body of Horus and to all intents and purposes acts, perceives and looks like him. Magical records indicate that such transfer techniques lead to visual experiences with a strong existential authenticity. They resemble the consciousness states enhanced by the techniques of 'active imagination' pioneered by psychotherapists like Desoille, Caslant and others, and also the hallucinatory experiences of subjects using such psychedelics as LSD, mescaline and datura. The occultist believes that his focus of conscious awareness has now transferred to an area of the psyche which would normally be unconscious, rather like entering a waking dream. Fantasy and mythological components which arise, as in the 'dream of the shaman', are existentially perceived as real and have the same perceptual status as 'normal' waking reality.

Some magical projectionists claim that a silver cord can be seen connecting the physical and 'astral' bodies although according to parapsychologists Dr Celia Green and Dr Peter Bicknell, who have made extensive surveys of the out-of-the-body experience in Britain and Australia respectively, the appearance of a connecting cord is rarely reported.[2]

As in the case of the epileptic shaman, it is not merely the altered state of consciousness which confers magical status. The occultist has to make use of his dissociated mental state to travel along the magical paths which he visualizes stretching out ahead of him, and which in turn lead to archetypal or mythological regions. In the out-of-the-body state the magician visualizes an entire Tree of Life extending above him and may choose which of the paths he will explore. Invariably he will be guided by his knowledge of the associated images which are likely to arise – images like those we discussed earlier in the section on mythological correspondences – and he will also make use of magical formulae and gestures to dispel these archetypal images if they become hostile or aggressive.

Most occultists travel on one visionary path at a time as they ascend the Tree of Life, although there are exceptions to this. As in the case of Golden Dawn ceremonial workings, the essential aim upon the Kabbalistic Tree is to reach Tiphareth, the mythological domain of spiritual renewal and rebirth. Astral flights up the Middle Pillar beyond this level bring the occultist towards the Abyss, the region of the Tree which cosmologically divides the created universe from the Trinity. With the notable exception of Aleister Crowley, few magicians have ever claimed to cross the Abyss. By definition this entails extraordinary spiritual purity and an extremely exalted level of spiritual consciousness, and it is much more usual for occultists to explore more limited mythic domains while in a state of trance. Magical records of these experiences show that the visual stimulus used to induce the initial state of magical dissociation has a strong link with the contents of the visionary experience.

# GOLDEN DAWN
# TRANCE TECHNIQUES

Several accounts of magical trance journeys are contained in a series of papers prepared by senior occultists within the Order of the Golden Dawn. These papers were known as 'Flying Rolls' and have been republished in an anthology of magical documents. Several of these magical journeys involved the so-called Tattva colour symbols, which constitute one of the few Eastern influences to enter into modern magical practice and represent the five primal elements of Hindu mythology. In their basic form they are:

| | |
|---|---|
| *Tejas* | a red equilateral triangle representing Fire |
| *Apas* | a silver crescent representing Water |
| *Vayu* | a blue circle representing Air |
| *Prithivi* | a yellow square representing Earth |
| *Akasha* | a black, indigo or violet egg representing Spirit |

Golden Dawn *Flying Roll XI* describes a Tattva vision by Mrs Moina Mathers as she sat meditating in her ceremonial robes, contemplating a Tattva card combining Tejas and Akasha, a violet egg within a red triangle (Spirit within Fire). The symbol seemed to grow before her gaze 'filling the place [so] that she seemed to pass into it, or into a vast triangle of flame'. She felt herself to be in a harsh desert of sand. Vibrating the god-name 'Elohim' she perceived a small pyramid in the distance and drawing closer noticed a small door on each face. She then vibrated the formula 'Sephariel' and a warrior appeared, leading behind him a procession of guards. After a series of tests involving ritual grade signs, the guards knelt before her and she passed in:

> ... dazzling light, as in a Temple. An altar in the midst – kneeling figures surround it, there is a dais beyond, and many figures upon it – they seem to be Elementals of a fiery nature ... She sees a pentagram, puts a Leo into it (i.e. a Fire sign),

thanks the figure who conducts her – wills to pass through the pyramid, finds herself out amid the sand. Wills her return – returns – perceiving her body in robes.[3]

In this account and others like it, it is clear that the visionary landscape derives specifically from the focusing symbol. The intangible aspect of the vision – Spirit – seems to be incorporated into the mysterious and sanctified nature of the inner temple which, in this case, the magician is privileged to enter. The beings she perceives, however, are fire elementals, which within the order of occult hierarchy are far beneath the level of the gods. From a magical viewpoint we can see that this experience, while interesting, provided no insights of a self-transforming nature. Tattva visions often tend to be limiting, or containing, since by their nature they flow from a specific focusing motif.

On another occasion Mrs Mathers made use of the Tattva combinations Water and Spirit. Her account shows not only the link between the magical symbol and the visionary beings which appear, but also indicates the role of the controlled imagination. Like the shaman the occultist is required to be a master of such visions:

A wide expanse of water with many reflections of bright light, and occasionally glimpses of rainbow colours appearing. When divine and other names were pronounced, elementals of the mermaid and merman type [would] appear, but few of the other elemental forms. These water forms were extremely changeable, one moment appearing as solid mermaids and mermen, the next melting into foam.

Raising myself by means of the highest symbol I had been taught, and vibrating the names of Water, I rose until the Water vanished, and instead I beheld a mighty world or globe, with its dimensions and divisions of Gods, Angels, elementals and demons – the whole Universe of Water.

I called on HCOMA and there appeared standing before me a mighty Archangel, with four wings, robed in glistening white and crowned. In one hand, the right, he held a species of trident, and in the left a Cup filled to the brim with an essence which he poured down below on either side.[4]

In this example the perception of a hierarchy of beings and symbols actually produces a change in consciousness. Mrs Mathers uses her range of magical names to invoke beyond the level of the focusing elements until the archangel himself appears. Also present in the account is a reference to a magical name HCOMA derived from the so-called Enochian language (see below). Enochian patterns continue to be used by contemporary occultists to precipitate trance journeys, both in their pure form and in conjunction with the Tattvas.

# ENOCHIAN TRANCE

The so-called Enochian system derives from the work of Elizabethan occultists John Dee and Edward Kelley, who met in 1581. Dee had already established his reputation as a classical scholar at Cambridge and was also a noted astrologer; he was invited to calculate the most beneficial date for Queen Elizabeth I's Coronation. Kelley possessed an alchemical manuscript which was of considerable interest to Dee, and Kelley also claimed to be able to undertake journeys in the spirit vision. Dee and Kelley made use of wax tablets called 'almadels' engraved with magical symbols, and also a large number of squares measuring 49 x 49 inches, filled with letters of the alphabet. Nearby on his table Kelley had a large crystal stone upon which he would focus his concentration until he saw 'angels' appear. They would point to various letters on the squares in turn and these were written down by Dee as Kelley called them out. When these invocations were completely transcribed, Kelley would reverse their order for he believed that the angels communicated them backwards to avoid unleashing the magical power which they contained.

Dee and Kelley considered that the communications formed the basis of a new language – Enochian – and these magical conjurations were subsequently incorporated into magical practice by the Golden Dawn magicians who used them as focusing stimuli to precipitate trance visions.

Each square was ruled by an Enochian god-name and was bound by the four elements in different combinations. The technique of entry was to imagine the square as a three-dimensional truncated pyramid with the god-name superimposed on top. The magician imagined himself rising through the pyramid on a beam of white light which streamed down through the apex.[5]

For example, the Enochian square ruled by 'Amesheth' has a large elemental ingredient of water and fire. In the following vision, which the Golden Dawn magician Soror Fortiter Et Recte (Miss Annie Horniman) regarded as initiatory, a dominant figure appeared with characteristics pertaining to these two elements: an angel with a lunar crescent upon her head and carrying a cup (symbols of water) but with a fire pentagram upon her breast. In her hand were symbols of each element:

I made the Signs and called on the Names and begged to be allowed to see the Angel. She appeared with a blue lunar crescent on her head and brown hair which was very long. Her robe was pale blue with a black border, and a pentagram in red on her breast: her wings were blue also, and so was the Cup in her left hand, in her right hand she bore a red torch. Around her was a diamond of red yods.[6] She told me her office was 'Change and purification through suffering such as spiritualises the material nature'. I told her that her pale face and blue eyes had a sad and tender expression as she spoke. The elementals were like blue maids, bearing flames and their robes were black bordered. Some wore blue winged helmets and cloaks, red breastplates and Swords and black leg-armour. I was told that only through my Knowledge of Amesheth was all this shown unto me.

The magician then perceived the links between visionary causality and her own context on the Earth:

> On this World the effect is that of the floods of water mingling with submarine volcanoes and so disturbing the Earth under the Sea. The animal life is that represented by the fish who rest hidden among the rocks in warm climates. I seemed to see them, blue with black or red specks. The plants are water-lilies, a root in the black mud, the leaves resting on the surface of the water, living in the Sun. In regard to minerals I saw a great blueish opal with red lights playing in it; it rested in a black marble basin, and from all sides radiated a lovely light.
>
> On man the effect of the Square is restlessness, like waves of the sea, carrying him on with enthusiasm to some completed work. I seemed to see a nervous [highly strung] person with a pale face, dark deep-set eyes, and thin white hands, making a great effort, willing to pass through fire to reach his goal, a solid black pedestal from which I knew that he could begin to rise to the Higher. But hot clouds of steam and great water tried to hinder him from even reaching the fire. The lesson seemed to me that severe criticism, social difficulties, and heredity must all be overcome before we can reach the purifying fire of Initiation and, through that, the solid ground of spiritual knowledge.[7]

These visionary Enochian experiences were not confined to members of the Golden Dawn. Some time after breaking his link with the Order, Aleister Crowley and his disciple Victor Neuberg conducted a series of initiatory experiments which involved Enochian forms of magic. They made use specifically of a series of conjurations written by Dee and Kelley to invoke a series of 30 so-called 'Aethyrs' or 'Aires'.

According to Israel Regardie, Crowley carried with him a large golden topaz set in a wooden cross decorated with ritual symbols.[8] He recited the Enochian conjuration in a place of solitude and then used his topaz as a focusing glass to concentrate his attention. As a result of his meditations, Crowley had a number of visionary experiences which were then transcribed by Neuberg, who wrote down his trance utterances in sequence. Although Crowley had invoked two of the Aethyrs in Mexico in 1900 the bulk of his Enochian workings were made in 1909 in the isolation of the Algerian desert at locations such as Aumale, Am El Hajel, Bou-Saada, Benshrur, Tolga and Biskra.

Crowley's Enochian entries have pronounced shamanic characteristics. The Aethyr called NIA involves magical flight through the aeons in a chariot, a theme familiar in several ecstatic traditions as well as in early Kabbalistic Merkabah texts like *The Book of Enoch*. Another Aethyr, LIT, transports Crowley to a magical mountain beyond which is a sacred shrine where the worshippers of God are depicted. The following are excerpts from these records:

## NIA (*AETHYR 24*)

An angel comes forward into the stone like a warrior clad in chain-armour. Upon his head are plumes of gray, spread out like the fan of a peacock. About his feet a great army of scorpions and dogs, lions, elephants, and many other wild beasts. He stretches forth his arms to heaven and cries: In the crackling of the lightning, in the rolling of the thunder, in the clashing of the swords and the hurling of the arrows: by thy name exalted!

Streams of fire come out of the heavens, a pale brilliant blue, like plumes. And they gather themselves and settle upon his lips. His lips are redder than roses, and the blue plumes gather themselves into a blue rose, and from beneath the petals of the rose come brightly coloured humming-birds, and dew falls from the rose – honey-coloured dew. I stand in the shower of it.

And a voice proceeds from the rose: Come away! Our chariot is drawn by doves. Of mother-of-pearl and ivory is our chariot, and the reins thereof are the heart-strings of men. Every moment that we fly shall cover an aeon. And every place on which we rest shall be a young universe rejoicing in its strength; the meadows thereof shall be covered with flowers. There shall we rest but a night, and in the morning we shall flee away, comforted.

Now, to myself, I have imagined the chariot of which thee spake, and I look to see who was with me in the chariot. It was an Angel of golden skin, whose eyes were bluer than the sea, whose mouth was redder than the fire, whose breath was ambrosial air. Finer than a spider's web were her robes. And they were of the seven colours.[9]

Crowley's vision of NIA has several symbolic components which are linked through the system of magical correspondences to the Tree of Life cosmology. The hurling of arrows is linked magically to the Path of Sagittarius (Tau) on the Middle Pillar, a path often identified with the magical act of 'rising on the planes'. The fan of a peacock Crowley understood as a reference to Juno, and hummingbirds and doves were traditionally sacred to Venus and recorded in the tables of correspondences as such. Consequently, although the Aethyr refers to a warrior clad in armour, there are also decidely feminine components in his vision. It is characteristic that the warlike role of the chariot is transmuted into a chariot drawn by doves; the rose angel proposes to take the magician to a paradise world of flower meadows and is herself identified with the seven colours of the rainbow.

In a later part of his visionary account Crowley describes the ecstatic nature of his trance:

I see through those eyes, and the universe, like whirling sparks of gold, blown like a tempest. I seem to swell out again … My consciousness fills the whole Aethyr, I hear the cry of NIA ringing again and again from within me. It sounds like infinite music, and behind the sound is the meaning of the Aethyr.[10]

Then his vision twists around and takes a more hostile form. It now resembles the ecstasy/death/re-emergence theme of traditional shamanism and also the Siberian myths of the blacksmith at his forge:

> All this time the whirling sparks of gold go on, and they are like blue sky, with a lot of rather thin white clouds in it, outside. And now I see mountains round, far blue mountains, purple mountains. And in the midst is a little green dell of moss which is all sparkling with dew that drips from the rose. And I am lying on that moss with my face upwards, drinking, drinking, drinking, drinking of the dew.
>
> I cannot describe to you the joy and the exhaustion of everything that was, and the energy of everything that is, for it is only a corpse that is lying on the moss. *I am the soul of the Aethyr*.
>
> Now it reverberates like the swords of archangels, clashing upon the armour of the damned; and there seem to be the blacksmiths of heaven beating the steel of the worlds upon the anvils of hell, to make a roof to the Aethyr. [11]

## LIT (*AETHYR 5*)

There is a shining pylon, above which is set the sigil of the eye, within the shining triangle. Light streams through the pylon from before the face of Isis-Hathor, for she weareth the lunar crown of cows' horns, with the disk in the centre; at her breast she beareth the child Horus.

And there is a voice: thou knowest not how the Seven was united with the Four; much less then canst thou understand the marriage of the Eight and the Three. Yet there is a word wherein these are made one, and therein is contained the Mystery that thou seekest, concerning the rending asunder of the veil of my Mother.

Now there is an avenue of pylons [not one alone], steep after steep, carved from the solid rock of the mountain; and that rock is a substance harder than diamond, and brighter than light, and heavier than lead. In each pylon is seated a god.

There seems an endless series of these pylons. And all the gods of all the nations of the earth are shown, for there are many avenues, all leading to the top of the mountain.

Now I come to the top of the mountain, and the last pylon opens into a circular hall, with other pylons leading out of it, each of which is the last pylon of a great avenue; there seem to be nine such pylons. And in the centre is a shrine, a circular shrine, supported by marble figures of men and women, alternate white and black; they face upwards, and their buttocks are almost worn away by the kisses of those who have come to worship that supreme God, who is the single end to all those diverse religions. But the shrine itself is higher than a man may reach.

But the Angel that was with me lifted me, and I saw that the edge of the altar, as I must call it, was surrounded by holy men. Each has in his right hand a weapon – one a sword, one a spear, one a thunderbolt, and so on but each with his left hand gives the sign of silence. I wish to see what is within their ring. One of them bends forward so that I may whisper the pass-word. The Angel prompts me to whisper: 'There is no God.' So they let me pass, and though there was indeed nothing visible therein, yet there was a very strange atmosphere, which I could not understand.

Suspended in the air there is a silver star, and on the forehead of each of the guardians there is a silver star. It is a pentagram – because, says the Angel, three and five are eight; three and eight are eleven. [There is another numerical reason that I cannot hear.]

And as I entered their ring, they bade me stand in their circle, and a weapon was given unto me. And the password that I had given seems to have been whispered round from one to the other, for each one nods gravely as if in solemn acquiescence, until the last one whispers the same words in my ears. But they have a different sense. I had taken them to be a denial of the existence of God, but the man who says them to me evidently means nothing of the sort: What he does mean I cannot tell at all. He slightly emphazised the word 'there'.

And now all is suddenly blotted out, and instead appears the Angel of the Aethyr. He is all in black, burnished black scales, just edged with gold. He has vast wings, with terrible claws on the ends, and he has a fierce face, like a dragon's, and dreadful eyes that pierce one through and through. And he says: O thou that art so dull of understanding, when will thou begin to annihilate thyself in the mysteries of the Aethyrs? For all that thou thinkest is but thy thought; and as there is no god in the ultimate shrine, so there is no I in thine own Cosmos.

They that have said this are of them that understood. And all men have misinterpreted it, even as thou didst misinterpret it. He says some more: I cannot catch it properly, but it seems to be the effect that the true God is equally in all the shrines, and the true I in all the parts of the body and the soul. He speaks with such a terrible roaring that it is impossible to hear the words: one catches a phrase here and there, or a glimpse of the idea. With every word he belches forth smoke, so that the whole Aethyr becomes full of it.[12]

In his vision of LIT Crowley perceives the magical symbol of the eye of the triangle, which is invariably identified as the eye of Horus. The triangle also links the source of light to the first three sephiroth upon the Tree of Life which form the Triangle of the Supernals. LIT thus begins with a reference to high spiritual authority. It also contains familiar cosmological motifs: pylons which reach up to the heavens and a mountain which is at the centre of the world: '… all the gods of all the nations of the earth are shown, for there are many avenues, all leading to the top of the mountain.'[13]

As in many shamanic accounts the vision begins to acquire its revelatory nature at the top of the mountain. Initially the magician is told that there is no God but he later discovers that his own misconceptions have led him to a wrong conclusion. He discovers amidst a mighty roaring sound that God is present 'equally in all the shrines and the true I in all the parts of the body and the soul'. The magician thus finds the source of his connection with the cosmos. Later the supreme being reveals itself as 'the Great Dragon that eateth up the Universe'. In Hermetic magic the dragon with its tail in its mouth is a symbol of totality embracing the whole universe; in this context it also poses as a magical test: 'Unless he pass by me, can no man come unto the perfections.'[14]

# THE MAJOR ARCANA
# OF THE TAROT

While the Tattva and Enochian systems of trance magic bring about highly specific visionary states, a more complete transformational process is found when Major Arcana images from the Tarot are used in conjunction with the Tree of Life. Like the Tattvas and Enochian squares, Tarot images form the basis of an entry-stimulus to a visionary trance state, but because the archetypal mythology of the Tarot is much more developed, the cosmological parallels with the shamanic process become more apparent.

Tarot cards have been traditionally associated with gypsy fortune-telling and divination rather than magical visualization, and it was not until the nineteenth century that the French occultist Eliphas Lévi (1810-75) proposed combining the Major Arcana of the Tarot with the Kabbalistic symbol of the Tree of Life.

The 22 cards or Major Arcana of the Tarot – as distinct from the 56 standard cards which are divided into four suits – describe a number of archetypal images. These 'mythic' cards take the form of various male archetypes, including the Magus, the Emperor, the Charioteer and the High Priest, and female counterparts like the High Priestess, the Empress, Justice and the Moon. There are also cards which are symbolically 'neutral' – that is to say, neither male nor female – like Death and the Wheel of Fortune.

Employed magically, the Tarot cards of the Major Arcana

represent symbolic paths to spiritual transcendence, and since the time of Eliphas Lévi they have been positioned on the Kabbalistic Tree of Life to produce a composite framework of archetypal magical consciousness. However, while the Kabbalah itself is central to the Jewish spiritual tradition, the Tarot draws for its imagery on other spiritual traditions. In some Tarot packs, for example, there are Egyptian motifs – the Wheel of Fortune, for example, is sometimes shown with the jackal-headed god Hermanubis, and the High Priestess is invariably shown seated between Egyptian-style temple pillars. And figures like the Magus, while medieval in terms of their imagery, are essentially Gnostic in tone – a hint that the medieval Tarot may have been disguising mystical ideas which in the Middle Ages would have been considered heretical.

In most Tarot packs the Magician is shown directing spiritual energy from a higher source – the Infinite World of Light – down to the manifested world of form, represented in turn by the symbols of Earth, Water, Fire and Air.

Although there are various combinations in the occult literature the usual sequence of Tarot paths upon the Tree of Life is as follows:

| | |
|---:|:---|
| *The World* | Malkuth-Yesod |
| *Judgement* | Malkuth-Hod |
| *The Moon* | Malkuth-Netzach |
| *The Sun* | Yesod-Hod |
| *The Star* | Yesod-Netzach |
| *The Tower* | Hod-Netzach |
| *The Devil* | Hod-Tiphareth |
| *Death* | Netzach-Tiphareth |
| *Temperance* | Yesod-Tiphareth |
| *The Hermit* | Tiphareth-Chesed |
| *Justice* | Tiphareth-Geburah |
| *The Hanged Man* | Hod-Geburah |
| *The Wheel of Fortune* | Netzach-Chesed |
| *Strength* | Geburah-Chesed |
| *The Chariot* | Geburah-Binah |

| | |
|---:|:---|
| *The Lovers* | Tiphareth-Binah |
| *The Hierophant* | Chesed-Chokmah |
| *The Emperor* | Tiphareth-Chokmah |
| *The Empress* | Binah-Chokmah |
| *The High Priestess* | Tiphareth-Kether |
| *The Magus* | Binah-Kether |
| *The Fool* | Chokmah-Kether |

We can now consider each of these mythological cards of the Major Arcana in turn, beginning at the lowest level on the Tree of Life:

## The World
*The World* represents the descent into the underworld of the subconscious mind. In Greek mythology this theme is personified by the descent of Persephone into the land of the dead. However, symbolically, death is the other side of life and Persephone symbolizes the wheat grain which grows and dies, and undergoes a perpetual cycle of harvests. Persephone dies to live again: her existence is manifest both in the realm of the living and the dead. In *The World* she is androgynous, representing both male and female polarities despite her more obvious femininity.

Because Persephone rules the underworld as queen of the night and the dead, she is also seen as a reflection of the lunar sphere Yesod. Appropriately, *The World* links Malkuth to Yesod.

## Judgement
In the same way that Persephone represents both death and life in Greek mythology, *Judgement* is similarly associated with the theme of rebirth. Here we see figures rising from coffins with their hands in the air. They are gesturing with their arms to form the word L.V.X. – 'light' – as they rise in triumph from the grave of ignorance. One of the Correspondences upon this path is Hephaestos, the blacksmith of Greek mythology, and this figure also resembles the Siberian deity who forges a new identity for his shaman-candidates.

## The Moon

*The Moon* typically mirrors the symbolism of the lunar sphere Yesod, and a lunar crescent dominates the imagery of the card. Two dogs are shown barking at the sky, one of them domesticated and the other untamed. The dog is sacred to the lunar goddess Hecate, who is also associated with Persephone in her deathlike aspect. *The Moon* depicts the ebb and flow of the tides and is symbolic of spiritual evolution – a lobster is shown emerging from the sea to reinforce this effect.

## The Sun

*The Sun* reflects the light of Tiphareth which is positioned above it on the Tree of Life. Young naked twins – a boy and a girl – are shown dancing in a magical ring beneath the Sun. They represent both a type of innocence and also the synthesis of opposite polarities – a common theme in the Tarot. They are clearly ruled by the Sun, representing unity and vitality, and the path of enlightenment. However here they are separated from the cosmic mountain by a wall. In an occult sense, the children are still young and inexperienced in their mystical quest and barriers still exist denying access to the more sacred regions of the Tree of Life.

## The Star

*The Star* is associated with intuition, meditation and the hidden qualities of Nature, represented by Netzach. The beautiful naked White Isis – a lunar deity – kneels by a pool pouring water from flasks held in both hands. One of these flasks is made of gold (equating it with the Sun) and the other of silver (equating it with the Moon). Reaching up towards a golden star in the sky the goddess transmits its life energy down to the world below.

## The Tower

The symbolism of *The Tower* is instructive. As a path upon the Tree of Life, *The Tower* reaches right up to the highest sphere of Kether – that is to say it embraces the entire universe. A lightning flash strikes its upper turrets causing it to crumble, and figures are shown falling to their death. *The Tower* serves as a reminder that humility is required on the inner journey, and that the influx of divine energy from the higher realms of the Tree will produce a devastating effect unless our 'magical personality' is well balanced and has a solid foundation. *The Tower* is ruled by Mars, who ruthlessly destroys ignorance and vain conceptions.

## The Devil

Here we are shown a 'demonic' man and woman bound by chains to a pedestal upon which sits a gloating, torch-bearing Devil. Capricorn the Goat represents darkness and bestiality. Upon his brow rests an inverted pentagram indicating that his spiritual aspirations are directed more towards earth than towards the transcendental realms of higher consciousness. In this context *The Devil* reflects the plight of all unenlightened human beings, with their limited knowledge and understanding. Nevertheless, the light of Tiphareth lies beyond ...

## Death

Like *The Devil, Death* indicates humanity's shortcomings, and the limited nature of the ego-bound personality. But in the mystical traditions death is also the herald of new life, and beyond the scythe-wielding skeleton figure in the foreground we see new light appearing on the horizon. The scythe is associated with Kronos – the ancient Greek creator-god who transcended time – and on the Tree of Life the path of *Death* leads into Tiphareth, the sphere of spiritual awakening. So, despite its confronting imagery, the path through *Death* leads to rebirth.

## Temperance

This card represents the line of direct mystical ascent to a state of spiritual illumination. The archangel of Air, Raphael, stands astride a river of light, pouring the waters of Life from a Sun-vessel into a Moon-vessel. This constitutes a 'tempering', or union of opposites – a blending of solar and lunar energies. Raphael has one foot on earth and the other in water and he is also shown reconciling a white eagle (representing the Moon) and a red lion (representing the Sun). Above him arches a beautiful rainbow symbolizing God's covenant with humanity, and new light is dawning over a distant mountain peak.

### The Hermit

Having reached Tiphareth, the visionary magician now begins to move towards Kether at the mystical peak of the Tree of Life. The path between Tiphareth and Chesed is ruled by Mercury who in turn connects with Chokmah and Thoth – the 'Great Father' archetypes of the Kabbalah and the Egyptian mysteries. The Hermit wends his way up the magic mountain but his final goal is firmly in his mind, and the lamp he holds aloft illumines his pathway.

### Justice

In Eastern mysticism *Justice* would be considered a path of *karma* – a path where one experiences the consequences of one's own actions. *Justice* demands balance, adjustment and total impartiality. Ruled by Venus, this path leads to the sphere of her lover Mars, and is appropriately designated by the figure of Venus holding scales and the sword of justice. On this path the magician begins to discover his or her true, inner self by overcoming the illusory aspects of outer appearances which are in themselves barriers to true realization.

### The Hanged Man

This path, like that of *Justice*, leads to Geburah, the sphere of action. The Hanged Man swings by his foot, symbolizing sacrifice, but because of his position he also seems like a reflection in water, the element ascribed to the path. The head of the Hanged Man is all aglow – shining like a beacon – and we see that he is reflecting inspirational light through to lower levels of the Tree of Life. The waters themselves flow from Binah, the Great Mother, and the magician must now remain receptive to their healing energies.

## The Wheel of Fortune

Appropriately, this card symbolizes the forces of fate and destiny. In Kabbalistic magic, words composed of similar letters have related symbolic meanings and TARO or ROTA – the word inscribed upon the Wheel of Fortune – reads ATOR in reverse. This is a variant spelling of the White Goddess, Hathor, showing her influence on this path. The path itself leads to Chesed and understandably comes under the jurisdiction of Jupiter. Chesed lies in the region of pure archetypes – a realm of sacred being just below the Trinity on the Tree of Life.

## Strength

This card is positioned horizontally across the Tree of Life and occupies an equivalent position to *The Tower*, but higher up. Whereas *The Tower* separates the ego-based personality from the true spiritual self, *Strength* represents the gulf between individuality and universality. On this card we are shown a woman prising open the jaws of a lion – a clear indication of the triumph of spiritual intuition over brute strength. This symbolizes complete mastery over any vestiges of the 'animal soul' that remain in the magician's psyche.

## The Chariot

The chariot represents motion and this Tarot card provides a direct reference to the *Merkabah* (chariot) tradition in Kabbalistic mysticism which describes the visionary journey of the soul from one heavenly palace to another. Here the chariot carries the king to the furthest reaches of his realm, while on the opposite side of the Tree, in Chesed, the ruler of the universe views his kingdom from the stationary vantage point of his heavenly throne. On this path the king is a mediator, reminding us that we all need to become a receptor or vehicle for light. This is indicated by the central symbolism of the card, which shows the king bearing the sacred vessel of the Holy Grail.

## The Lovers

On this path The Twins (representing Gemini) stand naked in the innocence of Eden regained, the Holy Guardian Angel towering above them, bestowing grace. Greek mythology records a legend describing the bond between the half-brothers Castor and Polydeuces (Pollux) – one mortal and the other immortal. In an act of compassion, Zeus allowed both of them a common destiny, placing them in the sky as the constellation known as Gemini. The path of *The Lovers* flows upwards from Tiphareth (Harmony) and shows the happy and enduring union of opposites.

## The Hierophant

This path reminds us that the paternal, merciful qualities of the Great Father (Chokmah-Chesed) are enhanced by the love and grace of Venus, who rules this card. We find here an enduring bond of wisdom and mercy. The inspiration of the Spirit manifests in *The Hierophant* as an archetypal expression of enlightened intuition. Divine authority owes its inspirational origin to this realm of the Tree of Life.

## The Emperor

The Emperor faces towards Chokmah, the 'unmanifested' Great Father of the trinity, and draws upon his spiritual energy as a basis for his authority in governing the universe of Creation below. In the Emperor we find the qualities of divine mercy, for although he is capable of aggression in his Geburah aspect, he extends compassion to all his subjects. And the universe itself has come into being through his union with the Empress, or Great Mother.

## The Empress

On this path we enter the realm of pure illumination.The Empress is warm and beneficent. Laden with child, she is symbolically the Mother of All, since from her womb will flow all the potential images and forms capable of existence in the entire cosmos. Mythologically she is Hathor and Demeter, and she epitomizes Love and Nature on a universal scale. She sits in a field of wheat amidst luxuriant trees –

with the River of Life flowing forth from her domain. The Empress is the feminine embodiment of the sacred life-energy which emanates from the highest spheres of the Tree of Life.

## The High Priestess

This path, unlike *The Empress*, reaches to the very peak of Creation – the first sephirah: Kether, *The Crown*. And the High Priestess herself has an element of untaintedness about her – she is unsullied and virginal. She has the potential for motherhood but has not yet brought to fruition the possibility of giving birth – of bringing essence through into form. To this extent she is very much a goddess who belongs in the highest spheres of the Tree of Life. Those who follow her path undergo a dramatic transformation for they begin to rise above form itself, returning to a pure and undifferentiated state of being.

## The Magus

Linked mythologically to Mercury – the cosmic intelligence – the path of *The Magus* represents the masculine aspect of transcendental spirituality which has not yet found union with its feminine counter-part. This path reflects a type of masculine purity which equates with the virginity of the High Priestess. The Magus stands above Creation in an archetypal sense. He raises one of his hands to Kether so that he may draw its energy down, and transmit it to the lower reaches of the Tree of Life.

## The Fool

The Fool is a symbol for 'he who knows nothing', and this can be interpreted esoterically as well as in an everyday sense. On this path the magician draws near to the veil of non-existence – *No-Thing* – that which is unmanifest, or beyond the tangibility of Creation. This is a realm of true Mystery and of this dimension of reality nothing can meaningfully be said, or attributes ascribed. On the card itself we are shown The Fool about to plunge into the Abyss of formlessness – embracing the infinite and sacred transcendence of *Ain Soph Aur*, the Limitless Light.

# RISING IN THE PLANES

As we have seen, the 22 Tarot paths upon the Tree of Life provide an important framework for the contemporary trance magician. Like the shaman he has a clearly delineated cosmology and this serves to distinguish order from chaos. While the magician in trance or through meditation is exploring the Tarot paths there are additional factors which arise beyond visualizing the reality of the symbolic doorways.

Since occultists stress the will and regard trance as a domain where the willed imagination actually produces tangible visionary experiences, the technique of willing oneself to rise from one level to another is crucial. In *Flying Roll XI*, Frater Deo Duce Comite Ferro (MacGregor Mathers) notes that this effect can be produced by a willed aspiration to a higher symbolic level upon the Tree:

> Rising in the Planes is a spiritual process after spiritual conceptions and higher aims; by concentration and contemplation of the Divine, you formulate a Tree of Life passing from you to the spiritual realms above and beyond you. Picture to yourself that you stand in Malkuth – then by use of the Divine Names and aspirations you strive upward by the Path of Tau towards Yesod, neglecting the crossing rays which attract you as you pass up. Look upwards to the Divine Light shining down from Kether upon you. From Yesod leads up the Path of Temperance, Samekh, the arrow cleaving upward leads the way to Tiphareth, the Great Central Sun of Sacred Power. [15]

In this statement of practical advice from a leading occultist to his colleagues a clear transcendental direction is perceived, and the ecstasy of union with Tiphareth is brought about by visualizing oneself coursing like an arrow to a higher dimension. Mathers delineates the technique of passage from Malkuth through Yesod to Tiphareth, making it clearly into a Middle Pillar ascension upon the central axis of the Tree of Life. This technique provides one of the clearest parallels between shamanism and modern western magic.

However other factors are involved as well. The sacred names of power – the god-names associated with each Sephirah – provide protection and also reinforce the shamanic purpose. In this sense, willed concentration not only provides the means for altering one's state of consciousness to enter trance but continues to provide direction once the magician finds himself operating on that level. Mathers further notes that the magician can incorporate Hebrew letters of the alphabet (each of which was ascribed in the Golden Dawn to the Tarot Major Arcana) as a means of intensifying and authenticating trance visions:

> There are three special tendencies to error and illusion which assail the Adept in these studies. They are, Memory, Imagination and actual Sight. These elements of doubt are to be avoided, by the Vibration of Divine Names, and by the Letters and Titles of the 'Lords Who Wander' – the Planetary Forces, represented by the Seven double letters of the Hebrew alphabet.
>
> If the Memory entice thee astray, apply for help to Saturn whose Tarot Title is the 'Great One of the Night of Time'. Formulate the Hebrew letter Tau in Whiteness.
>
> If the Visions change or disappear, your memory has falsified your efforts. If Imagination cheat thee, use the Hebrew letter Kaph for the Forces of Jupiter, named 'Lord of the Forces of Life'. If the Deception be of Lying – intellectual untruth – appeal to the Force of Mercury by the Hebrew letter Beth. If the trouble be of Wavering of Mind, use the Hebrew letter Gimel for the Moon. If the enticement of pleasure be the error, then use the Hebrew letter Daleth as an aid.' [16]

A complete trance vision recorded in November 1892 by Soror Sapientia Sapienti Dona Data (Mrs F. Emery) and Soror Fidelis (Miss Elaine Simpson, later the mistress of Aleister Crowley) survives in *Flying Roll IV*. It is particularly interesting because it indicates the trance magician's direct sense of encounter with the deities upon the Tree of Life. A blend of Christian and Egyptian elements is apparent, the Grail Mother is seen as an aspect of Isis, and a ritual gesture appropriate to the Roman goddess Venus is also included, indicative of the eclectic blending of cosmologies found in modern magical practice:

The Tarot Trump, The Empress was taken; placed before the persons and contemplated upon, spiritualised, heightened in colouring, purified in design and idealised.

In vibratory manner pronounced Daleth. Then, in spirit, saw a greenish blue distant landscape, suggestive of medieval tapestry. Effort to ascend was then made; rising on the planes; seemed to pass up through clouds and then appeared a pale green landscape and in its midst a Gothic Temple of ghostly outlines marked with light. Approached it and found the temple gained in definiteness and was concrete, and seemed a solid structure. Giving the signs of the Netzach Grade [because of Venus] was able to enter; giving also Portal signs and 5° = 6° signs in thought form.[17] Opposite the entrance perceived a Cross with three bars and a dove upon it; and besides this, were steps leading downwards into the dark, by a dark passage. Here was met a beautiful green dragon, who moved aside, meaning no harm, and the spirit vision passed on. Turning a corner and still passing on in the dark emerged from darkness on to a marble terrace brilliantly white, and a garden beyond, with flowers, whose foliage was of delicate green kind and the leaves seemed to have a white velvety surface beneath. Here, there appeared a woman of heroic proportions, clothed in green with a jewelled girdle, a crown of stars on her head, in her hand a sceptre of gold, having at one apex a lustrously white closed lotus flower; in her left hand an orb bearing a cross.

She smiled proudly, and as the human spirit sought her name, replied:

'*I am the mighty Mother Isis; most powerful of all the world, I am she who fights not, but is always victorious, I am that Sleeping Beauty who men have sought, for all time; and the paths which lead to my castle are beset with dangers and illusions. Such as fail to find me sleep – or may ever rush after the Fata Morgana leading astray all who feel that illusory influence – I am lifted up on high, and do draw men unto me, I am the world's desire, but few there be who find me. When my secret is told, it is the secret of the Holy Grail.*'

Asking to learn it, [she] replied:

'*Come with me, but first clothe in white garments, put on your insignia, and with bared feet follow where I shall lead.*'

Arriving at length at a Marble Wall, pressed a secret spring, and entered a small compartment, where the spirit seemed to ascend through a dense vapour, and emerged upon a turret of a building. Perceived some object in the midst of the place, but was forbidden to look at it until permission was accorded. Stretched out the arms and bowed the head to the Sun which was rising a golden orb in the East. Then turning, knelt with the face towards the centre, and being permitted to raise the eyes beheld a cup with a heart and the sun shining upon these; there seemed a clear ruby coloured fluid in the cup. Then Lady Venus said:

'*This is love, I have plucked out my heart and have given it to the world; that is my strength. Love is the mother of the Man-God, giving the Quintessence of her life to save mankind from destruction, and to show forth the path to life eternal. Love is the mother of the Christ-Spirit, and this Christ is the highest love – Christ is the heart of love, the heart of the Great Mother Isis – the Isis of Nature. He is the expression of her power – she is the Holy Grail, and He is the life blood of spirit, that is found in this cup.*'

After this, being told that man's hope lay in following her example, we solemnly gave our hearts to the keeping of the Grail; then, instead of feeling death, as our human imagination led us to expect, we felt an influx of the highest courage and power, for our own hearts were to be henceforth in touch with hers – the strongest force in all the world.

So then we went away, feeling glad that we had learned that

*'He who gives away his life, will gain it.' For that love which is power, is given unto him – who hath given away his all for the good of others.'*[18]

### Notes

1   Quoted in Francis King, (ed.) *Astral Projection, Magic and Alchemy,* 1971, pp. 73-74

2   See Celia Green, *Out of the Body Experiences,* 1973, and Nevill Drury and Gregory Tillett, *Other Temples, Other Gods,* 1980, p.161

3   Francis King, op.cit., p.69

4   Quoted in Israel Regardie (ed.) *The Golden Dawn,* 1940, vol.4, p.43

5   Francis King, op cit., p.82

6   Yod is the sacred first letter of the Kabbalistic Name of God, JHVH

7   Francis King, op.cit., pp.82-84

8   See Isabel Regardie's introduction to Aleister Crowley's *The Vision and the Voice,* 1972

9   Aleister Crowley, *The Vision and the Voice,* 1972, pp.57-58

10  ibid., p.61

11  ibid., pp.61-62

12  ibid., pp.199-201

13  ibid., p.199

14  ibid., p.201

15  Francis King, op.cit., p.66

16  ibid., p.67

17  This is a reference to a ritual grade within the Golden Dawn. The grade of 5° = 6° equated with Tiphareth on the Tree of Life

18  Francis King, op.cit., pp.58-59

# CHAPTER 6

# OTHER VISIONARY APPROACHES TO MAGIC

Since the days of the Golden Dawn, several prominent occultists and metaphysicians have developed trance and 'active imagination' approaches to magic which in many ways resemble the techniques of traditional shamanism. Since magic stimulates imagery from the deep mythic resources of the subconscious mind, it is not surprising that the new approaches to trance consciousness have produced encounters with specific archetypes from the western pantheons: The Wise Man (Merlin), The Universal Woman (Aphrodite), Diana, Pan, Abraxas and so on. In each instance these contemporary 'inner space' magicians have developed ways of combining the will and the imagination in order to explore a wide range of 'alternative' realities. This chapter will explore the work of four prominent visionary metaphysicians – Austin Osman Spare, Edwin Steinbrecher, Dion Fortune and Dolores Ashcroft-Nowicki.

## AUSTIN OSMAN SPARE

### THE MAGIC OF ATAVISTIC RESURGENCE

While the Hermetic Order of the Golden Dawn was fragmenting amid schisms and dissent just prior to the onset of World War I, a remarkable visionary artist and magician named Austin Osman Spare was developing a unique system of practical magic through his exploration of ecstatic trance states. Spare was probably the first modern occultist to evolve a self-contained working hypothesis about the nature of psychic energy which could be applied without all the paraphernalia of traditional rituals and magical implements. His system of magical sigils showed how an effort of will, when focused on the subconscious mind, could unleash the most extra-ordinary psychic material.

One of five children, Spare was born in Snow Hill, London, on 30 December 1886, the son of a policeman. The family later moved to south London and Spare attended St Agnes' School in Kennington Park; he would live in this area of the city, in modest circumstances, for most of his life.

Spare showed artistic talent early in his life, and at the age of twelve began studying at Lambeth Evening Art School. In 1902, when he was sixteen, he won a scholarship enabling him to attend the Royal College of Art, South Kensington, and in 1905 examples of his work were exhibited at the Royal Academy. The President of the Academy, John Singer Sargent, proclaimed Spare to be a genius and he was soon commissioned to illustrate a handful of books, including Ethel Wheeler's *Behind the Veil* (1906) and a book of aphorisms titled *The Starlit Mire* (1911).

Spare's visionary art teems with magical imagery and when he began to self-publish his own illustrated magical books – works like *Earth: Inferno, The Focus of Life* and *The Book of Pleasure* – it became evident that his was an eccentric rather than a mainstream artistic talent. Indeed, there is little doubt that his unconventionality has pushed him to the sidelines of cultural history. He nevertheless remains a legendary figure in the twentieth century western esoteric tradition and is one of its truly original thinkers, his approach to trance states and his technique of 'atavistic resurgence' representing a unique contribution to the study of magical consciousness.

## Zos and Kia

Spare postulated the existence of a primal, cosmic life force which he termed *Kia,* and he believed that the spiritual and occult energies inherent in *Kia* could be channelled into the human organism, which he called *Zos.* As we will see, his technique of arousing these primal energies – an approach he termed 'atavistic resurgence' – involved focusing the will on magical sigils, or potent individualized symbols, which in effect represented instructions to the subconscious. When the mind was in a 'void' or open state – achieved, for example, through meditation, exhaustion or at the peak of sexual ecstasy – this was an ideal condition in which to direct magical sigils to the subconscious. Here they could 'grow' in the seedbed of the mind until they became 'ripe' and reached back down into the conscious mind. In such a way one could learn to manipulate one's own 'psychic reality'.

How did Austin Spare stumble upon his special approach to magical states of consciousness? Clearly it was no accident. His magic draws on a variety of inspirational sources, encompassing the mythic images of ancient Egypt, a fascination with the sexual energies of the subconscious mind, and his close personal relationship with an unusual psychic mentor whom he always referred to simply as Mrs Paterson.

Spare visited Egypt during World War I and was impressed by the magnetic presence of the classical gods depicted in monumental sculpture. He believed the ancient Egyptians understood very thoroughly the complex mythology of the subsconscious mind:

> They symbolized this knowledge in one great symbol, the Sphinx, which is pictorially man evolving from animal existence. Their numerous Gods, all partly Animal, Bird, Fish … prove the completeness of that knowledge … The cosmogony of their Gods is proof of their knowledge of the order of evolution, its complex processes from the one simple organism.[1]

For Spare, impressions from earlier human incarnations and potentially all mythic impulses could be reawakened from the subconscious mind. The gods themselves could be regarded as a form of internal impetus. 'All gods have lived (being ourselves) on earth,' he wrote, 'and when dead, their experience of Karma governs our actions in degree.'

However, while the classical gods of ancient Egypt made a marked impression on him, Spare learnt his actual technique of trance activation from an elderly woman called Mrs Paterson, who was a friend of his parents and used to tell his fortune when he was quite young. Mrs Paterson claimed a psychic link with the witches of the Salem cult and also appeared to have an extrasensory ability to project thought-forms. According to Spare, she was able to transform herself in his vision from being a 'wizened old crone' to appearing quite suddenly as a ravishing siren, 'creating a vision of profound sexual intensity and revelation that shook him to the very core'.[2]

The archetypal female image recurs in all phases of Spare's artistic work – he was a master at depicting the sensuous naked female form – and the Universal Woman would become a central image in his mythology of the subconscious. In his definitive magical credo, *The Book of Pleasure*, he writes:

> Nor is she to be limited as any particular 'goddess' such as Astarte, Isis, Cybele, Kali, Nuit, for to limit her is to turn away from the path and to idealize a concept which, as such, is false because incomplete, unreal because temporal.[3]

Spare employed a technique of ecstasy which frequently combined active imagination and will with the climax of sexual orgasm. Spare believed that his magical sigils – representing symbols of the personal will – could be directed to the subconscious mind during the peak of sexual ecstasy since, at this special moment, the personal ego and the universal Spirit, or *Kia*, were united in a state of blissful, transcendent openness. 'At this moment, which is the moment of generation of the Great Wish,' writes Spare, 'inspiration flows from the source of sex, from the primordial Goddess who exists at the heart of Matter ... inspiration is always at a *void* moment.'

Several of Spare's drawings depict the Divine Maiden leading the artist into the labyrinthine magical world. One of his most central works, *The Ascension of the Ego from Ecstasy to Ecstasy*, shows the Goddess welcoming Spare himself, who on this occasion appropriately has wings issuing forth from his head. Spare's 'ego', or persona, is shown merging with an earlier animal incarnation and two forms transcend each other in the form of a primal skull. Spare clearly believed that he could retrace his earlier incarnations to the universal 'Oneness of Creation', or *Kia*. According to Kenneth Grant, who knew the artist personally, Spare derived his formula of atavistic resurgence from Mrs Paterson:

> She would visualize certain animal forms and – the language of the subconsciousness being pictographic not verbal – each form represented a corresponding power in the hidden world of causes. It was necessary only to 'plant' an appropriate sigil in the proper manner for it to awaken its counterpart in the psyche. Resurging from the depths it then emerged, sometimes masked in the form to do the sorcerer's bidding.[4]

Undoubtedly, one of Spare's major objectives in using the trance state was to tap energies which he believed were the source of genius. According to Spare, 'ecstasy, inspiration, intuition and dream ... each state taps the latent memories and presents them in the imagery of their respective languages'. And genius itself was 'a directly resurgent atavism' experienced during the ecstasy of the Fire Snake – Spare's term for magical sexual arousal.

## SPARE'S MAGICAL COSMOLOGY

Spare's unique magical approach took several years to unfold, however, and while ancient Egyptian deities and other pagan entities abound in his drawings, his first book, *Earth: Inferno* – published as a limited edition in 1905 – seems to have been strongly influenced by the Kabbalah and other elements of the western mystical tradition. Here Spare tends towards dualism, regarding the phenomena of life as generally either positive or negative, spiritual or materialistic, real or delusory. His concept of *Kia* has a clear counterpart in the transcendent *Ain Soph Aur* of the Kabbalah, and there is a strong emphasis on the superficial and essentially false nature of appearances. 'Man', says Spare, 'should learn to shed his dependency on material security, which inevitably shrouds him in the falsehoods of conventionality. Instead he should search beneath his 'mask' to uncover the potentials of his subconscious.'

In *Earth: Inferno* Spare is intent on exploring the relationship between *Zos* and *Kia* – between individual awareness and the Universal Consciousness or Primal Energy. He concurs with the traditional mystical perspective that the Godhead lies within, and by now has begun to embrace the view that he should follow the beckoning of the Universal Mother of Nature – the 'Primitive Woman' – who can guide him pantheistically back to the Source of All Being. Spare has also taken a magical name to epitomise his mystical quest: *Zos vel Thanatos*.

In *Earth: Inferno* Spare makes it clear that the magical journey is one which is undertaken beyond 'the parapet of the subconscious' . Here Spare depicts the world of everyday awareness as a circular pathway along which visionless old men dodder hopelessly, looking to their candles for light while simultaneously remaining unaware of the 'Great Beyond'. Spare also shows us a depraved young man making lustful advances to the Universal Woman in his failure to see beyond her enticing outward appearance. This clearly involves an issue of insight: the Universal Woman is the wise and all-seeing Sophia of the Gnosis and is not to be mistaken for the Scarlet Woman of Babylon. Spare maintains that he himself did not commit this error: 'I strayed with her, into the path direct. Hail ! the Jewel in the Lotus !'

Nevertheless, at this stage Spare still finds himself caught between the inner and outer worlds: as he proclaims in his text, 'I myself am Heaven and Hell.' He has begun to encounter the dark night of the soul, and realizes that he will have to venture through the illusions of everyday life and the debris of the subconscious in order to experience the transcendence of *Kia*. Spare talks of this in a reflective way: 'The barrenness of this life but remains, yet in despair we begin to see true light. In weakness we can become strong. Revere the *Kia* and your mind will become tranquil.'

Spare already believed that every human being is innately divine, though most of them failed to perceive it. 'I have not yet seen a man who is not God already,' declares Spare provocatively. All man has to do is confront himself as he really is, and he will find God. This in turn involves the death of the ego, for it is the ego which isolates us from the realisation of the unity which sustains all aspects of Creation. For Spare, death could even be seen as a positive element because it destroyed the pretence of the personality. 'From behind', writes Spare, 'Destiny works with Death.' And death is a precursor of enlightenment. In *Earth: Inferno* Spare presents us with a vision which draws on both the Kabbalah and the Major Arcana of the Tarot:

> *On entering at the Gates of Life*
> *Lo, I behold Knowledge the Jester*
> *Capsizing the Feast of Illusion.*
> *The drawing aside false Truth*
> *He shewed us all –*
> *The World,*
> *The Flesh*
> *and*
> *The Being.*
> *This is the Alpha and Omega.*

On the Kabbalistic Tree of Life, Kether is the first emanation from the infinite formlessness of *Ain Soph Aur* – the first act of Creation 'out of nothing' – and this is the highest level of spiritual awareness any human being can theoretically attain. It is shown symbolically on the Tarot path which leads to Kether as the Jester, or the Fool – the person who knows No-thing. The Jester is therefore the wisest among all men for he has reached the highest possible state of consciousness. He has experienced *Kia*, or transcendent reality.

All of this involves a relatively orthodox western mysticism, but Spare was already developing his own individualized philosophy – a system of magical thought which he hoped would be free of dogma or 'belief'. As he saw it, Spare was now liberating his perception from the vices of the world – 'fear, faith … science and the like' – and was preparing to plunge into his own personal unknown: *his inner self.*

With this perspective in mind, he now produced a book which would be the *magnum opus* of his magical and artistic career. Entitled *The Book of Pleasure (Self Love): The Philosophy of Ecstasy*, it featured many of his finest drawings as well as describing the essence of his new magical approach. Released in 1913, *The Book of Pleasure* was privately published and included a number of important new concepts.[5]

It is true that prior to this time a number of occultists had been emphasizing the role of the 'will' in magical procedures. Golden Dawn member Florence Farr had outlined the need for intense mental concentration in her articles in the *Occult Review* (1908), and Aleister Crowley had emphazised the need for both a spiritual and magical focus in his central dictum 'Do what thou wilt shall be the whole of the Law'. Austin Spare was briefly a member of Crowley's order, the Argenteum Astrum,[6] and he adopted this view too, but only up to a point: he then moved in a different direction.

## SIGILS AND ECSTASY

In *The Book of Pleasure* Spare explored methods of concentrating the will. Since the degree of effectiveness of any action is related to a thorough understanding of the command behind the action, Spare developed a way of condensing his will so that it was more readily grasped *as a totality*. He did this by writing his 'will' (=desire) in sentence form and by combining the basic letters, without repetition, into a pattern shape, or 'sigil'. This could then be simplified and impressed upon the subconscious mind. Spare describes the process:

'Sigils are made by combining the letters of the alphabet simplified. Illustration: the word "Woman" in sigil form is:

     〜   or   〜   or   〜   etc. The Word

   tiger   〜   or   〜   Hat   〜   Come   〜

     Moon   〜   It   〜   or   〜   etc. etc.

The idea being to obtain a simple form which can be easily visualized at will ...'[7]

What was to be done with the sigil once it was arrived at? And what was the significance of the sigil itself? We must first of all consider some related ideas.

As has been noted earlier, Spare spoke of *Kia* as the Supreme Principle in the Universe: it was akin to a dynamic, expanding Vortex of Energy, ever in a state of becoming. Most human beings were unaware of its full potential simply because they did not let it manifest within themselves. ('Are we not ever standing on our own volcano?') Instead, most people would shut themselves off by means of the various 'insulating' devices employed by the ego. The only way in which the cosmic energy could manifest, or be aroused within, was by thoroughly opening oneself to it.

According to Austin Spare it was when the individual was in a state of mental 'vacuity' – or ultimate openness – that *Kia* became 'sensitive to the subtle suggestion of the sigil'. This state could be arrived at by emptying the mind of all its thought-forms in an effort to visualize non-manifestation – for example, by meditating on blackness or emptiness. This in turn usually involved inducing a state of meditative trance in which the individual became oblivious of his surroundings as he focused only on the Inner Void.

Because we all proceed from the Godhead originally, argued Spare, it should be possible to track back through the mind to the First Cause. Like many mystics, Spare believed in reincarnation and he therefore regarded the subconscious mind as the 'potential' source of all his own earlier physical embodiments or personalities, right back to the Beginning.[8] The psyche, as it were, consisted of a number of different layers – the resulting impressions of successive lives, most of which were subconscious. All of these were an aspect of the individual's own 'reality':

> Know the subconscious to be an epitome of all experience and wisdom, past incarnations as men, animals, birds, vegetable life etc.: everything that has, and ever will, exist. Each being a stratum in the order of evolution. Naturally then, the lower we probe into these strata, the earlier will be the forms of life we arrive at: the last is the Almighty Simplicity.

Spare's intention was to gain knowledge of his concealed mental states through 'regression' and eventually to lose his sense of self in an indescribably ecstatic union with *Kia* – whose energy he had now come to consider as basically sexual. The dark void of the mind, emptied of thought-forms through an act of concentration, could now be penetrated by the will by employing a sigil suitable for one's purpose. In theory, and according to one's ability, one could project the sigil to all possible recesses of the subconscious mind and in this way gain access to the entire sphere of the imagination. In reality this was much harder to achieve than the theory suggests. Obviously, it depended upon a number of crucial factors:

- an ability to derive a suitable sigil
- an ability to prevent random thought forms from unintentionally disturbing the 'black void' and thus rendering 'impure' the individual's attempt to become a pure vessel for the energies of *Kia*
- an ability to reach further into the subconscious by totally renouncing the wordly context of one's aspirations. Ultimately this task would involve rejecting one's sense of humanity and eventually destroying the ego altogether – a most unwordly intention!

Naturally the last condition was the hardest to achieve. Spare acknowledged that 'total vacuity' was difficult and unsafe for those 'governed by morality, complexes etc.' – that is to say, for all those governed by the 'superstitions' and intellectual conceptions that most human beings surround themselves with. Indeed, Spare maintained that one would have to cast aside all contrived or finite rationalizations. He therefore tried to think of various situations where a sense of the rational was minimal or absent, and he emphazised three such circumstances.

The first of these was the state of physical exhaustion. If one had a 'desire' or 'concentrated thought' in this situation, Spare argued, the mind would become 'worried, because of the non-fulfilment of such desire, and seek relief. By seizing this mind and living, the resultant vacuity would become sensitive to the subtle suggestion of the sigil.' In other words, by exhausting the body, one made it impossible for normal mental intentions or commands to be carried out physically. The mind would then be forced into manifesting the concepts embodied in the magical sigil. Sheer exhaustion can be brought about in a number of ways, and this includes the climax of sexual orgasm itself. The tantric yoga technique of using orgasm as the 'leaping off' point to visionary states of consciousness was well known in western esoteric circles at the time Spare was writing.

The second method lay in exploiting the mental state of extreme disappointment, experienced, for example, when one lost all faith in a close friend, or when a cherished ideal had been destroyed. Spare felt that this state, too, could provide its own sense of opportunity:

When fundamental disappointment is experienced the symbol enshrining a quota of belief is destroyed. In some cases the individual is unable to survive the disillusionment. But if at such times the moment is seized upon and consciously experienced for its own sake, the vacuum attracts into itself the entire content of belief inherent in the person at the time of disappointment.

Spare is saying, in effect, that when we thoroughly lose faith in a belief or ideal, that we are given the option of transcending it, and transcendence of belief can lead to a state of ecstasy as we are drawn into the vortex of *Kia*.

However, Spare seems to have often preferred a third approach for bypassing the ego, a method which could be used for generalized changes in the personality and also for specifics. This involved a state of self-induced trance in which the body became rigid, ceased to function, and underwent what Spare called 'the Death Posture'. He describes a preliminary exercise designed to bring this about:

> Gazing at your reflection (e.g. in a tall mirror) 'till it is blurred and you know not the gazer, close your eyes and visualize. The light (always an X in curious evolutions) that is seen should be held onto, never letting go, till the effort is forgotten; this gives a feeling of immensity (which sees a small form ∞ whose limit you cannot reach').

Spare considered that the Death Posture exercise should be practised daily for best effect. 'The Ego is swept up as a leaf in a fierce gale,' he wrote. 'In the fleetness of the indeterminable, that which is always about to happen, becomes its truth. Things that are self-evident are no longer obscure, as by his own will he pleases; know this as the negation of all faith by living it, the end of duality of consciousness.' Here Spare is alluding to the *Kia* dimension, which it beyond time and space but which nevertheless represents the central basis for all life and human potential. Spare believed that achieving the state of openness necessary for *Kia* to manifest would also enable him to direct his magical will into the cosmic memory. By doing this he could acquire a full and detailed knowledge of the earlier life forms which were both an aspect of oneself and of *Kia* as a whole. The Death Posture provided the possibility of a link; the magical sigil confirmed the possibility.

A sigil, as we have seen, is a visual condensation of the will. However, what we 'will' can often be based on ideas of grandeur and self-deception. Spare points out that even if we imagine ourselves to be great this is not necessarily so, and all the desiring in the world cannot alter the fact. Spare notes: 'Realisation is not by the mere utterance of words ... but by the living act. The will, the desire, the belief, lived as inseparable, become realisation.' Hoping for something won't help us achieve it: we must *live* it and *enact* it for it to become true. According to Spare:

> Belief to be true must be organic and subconscious. The idea to be great can only become organic (i.e. 'true') at the time of vacuity and by giving it form. When conscious of the sigil form (any time but the magical) it should be repressed, a deliberate striving to forget it; by this it is active and dominates at the subconscious period; its form nourishes and allows it to become attached to the subconscious and become organic; that accomplished is its reality and realisation. The individual becomes his concept of greatness.

In summary, beliefs need to be 'organic' not theoretical; organic realities originate with *Kia* and lie dormant in the subconscious; we can use a sigil to embody our desire, command or will, and this should relate to what we want to do or become; the sigil can 'grow' in the subconscious but will lose its effect if it is consciously remembered; and, finally, the sigil will eventually manifest as a 'true' aspect of the personality since it comes from within.

Spare also relates this process to the faculty of creativity: 'All geniuses have active subconsciousnesses and the less they are aware of the fact, the greater their accomplishments. The subconscious is exploited by desire reaching it.' This implies that geniuses are not born, and that they can be created – an idea he shared with Aleister Crowley.

Spare's system of implanting sigils was capable of different levels of application, and from an occult perspective it could be applied both to high and low magic. While Spare often used his sigils to embody transcendent commands his system could also be used for comparatively mundane purposes. Kenneth Grant tells of a situation where Spare needed to move a heavy load of timber without assistance. A sigil was required which involved great strength, so Spare constructed a suitable sentence: 'This is my wish, to obtain the strength of a tiger.' Sigilised, this sentence would be:

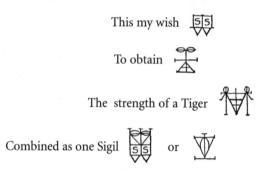

This my wish

To obtain

The strength of a Tiger

Combined as one Sigil　　or

Grant goes on to say: 'Spare closed his eyes for a while and visualized a picture which symbolized a wish for the strength of tigers [i.e the final sigil above]. Almost immediately he sensed an inner response. He then felt a tremendous upsurge of energy sweep through his body. For a moment he felt like a sapling bent by the onslaught of a mighty wind. With a great effort of will, he steadied himself and directed the force to its proper object. A great calm descended and he found himself able to carry the load easily.'[9]

Kenneth Grant makes it clear from his account that firstly dormant energy was awakened and then it was focused into a specialized activity. This was not always Spare's method, for in his more far-reaching atavistic resurgences he allowed the influx of *Kia* to obsess him. His mind would become flooded with preternatural influences and there was no semblance of control.

Spare, himself, considered this type of atavistic activity to be an act of bravery: 'Strike at the highest ... death is failure. Go where thou fearest not. How canst thou be great among men? *Cast thyself forth!* Retrogress to the point where knowledge ceases in that Law becomes its own spontaneity and freedom ... This is the new atavism I would teach: Demand of God equality – Usurp !'

Spare's method is thus clearly an act of stealing fire from heaven. His preferred method, the Death Posture, involved the 'death' of the ego through the negation of conscious thought – a positive, but 'unconscious' thrust towards transcendence.

What is unusual about Spare's cosmology and his occult trance techniques is that he believed in regression, rather than in the more conventional mystical concept of 'conscious evolution'. Indeed, he redefines his idea of magical evolution: The Law of Evolution is retrogression of function governing progression of attainment, i.e. the more wonderful our attainments are, *the lower in the scale of Life the function that governs them*. Man is *complex*, and to progress, must become simplified. This means that because more and more manifestations of *Kia* are appearing in the world all the time through reincarnation, as the Source of Creation expands 'outwards', the true magical direction is 'inwards' or more specifically 'backwards' to the First Cause.

Austin Spare's approach to magical perception is virtually unique within the western esoteric tradition. As with Aleister Crowley, he has retained an enthusiastic following to the present day. However in Spare's case, aspects of this renewed interest appear to be of a lower calibre than one might have hoped for. In the United States a group of so-called 'Chaos magicians' now claim to be utilizing Spare's sigil methods and an influential work titled *Practical Sigil Magic* by Frater U..D.., first published in 1990, purports to extend the practical applications of Spare's trance formulations. However, these practitioners appear to have fallen far short of Spare's magical vision and have seized hold only of its pragmatic 'low magic' applications. While Frater U..D.. writes that 'sigil magic is primarily success magic', Spare is embracing much wider realms than magical self-gratification: his is a unique response to the cosmos. It remains to be seen whether the resurgent interest in Austin Spare will be deflected by a trivialization of his unique contribution to the exploration of visionary magic.

# EDWIN STEINBRECHER

## THE GUIDE MEDITATION

A highly effective way of contacting the 'inner gods' has been developed in recent years by American metaphysician Edwin Steinbrecher of the D.O.M.E. Foundation in Los Angeles, an organization whose initials derive from the latin expression *Dei Omnes Munda Edunt*: 'All the Gods/Goddesses bring forth the Worlds'. Steinbrecher's approach draws strength from Dr Carl Jung's belief, put forward in *Mysterium Coniunctionis*, that internal mental images can be animated by concentrating attention upon them. The Guide Meditation incorporates Tarot symbols – which 'correspond to reality creating images within all of us' – and astrology which 'provides a map of the inner and outer worlds'. However, the essence of the D.O.M.E. Foundation system involves inner contact with a 'Guide' similar to the magical ally called by a shaman.

In 1969 Steinbrecher undertook Jungian analysis in Los Angeles which included using active imagination techniques and 'reworking and finishing' incomplete dreams. He had been reading *The Secret of the Golden Flower* and decided that the 'secret' was to force mental energy back along the same channels through which they had originally manifested. Accordingly he began to use his skills in active imagination to conjure into his consciousness specific images:

> I attempted to do this by inventing a staircase in my imagination that would take me within to those archetypal images I was seeking. And it worked! I reached a 'room' at the bottom of my stairway, thought of the High Priestess, and she was *there*, a living presence in that inner world, different from the picture on the Tarot card, but without a doubt the High Priestess as a reality in me.[10]

Following this initial attempt, Steinbrecher began to summon other archetypes from the Tarot mythology but had a frightening experience with the fifteenth trump, *The Devil*, who blocked his pathway and was menacing for some time until overcome by a sustained act of will. After this unfortunate encounter Steinbrecher resolved not to venture on the inner journey without an appropriate guide.

The D.O.M.E. Meditation technique utilizes a relaxed body posture with the back straight and both feet flat on the floor. The hands rest on the thighs, the palms face upwards and the eyes are closed. The meditator imagines himself entering a cave and tries through an act of will to enhance the sense of its being moist or dry, dark or light. Steinbrecher insists that the meditator should retain the sense of being consciously within the body rather than watching an external body image, and in this respect the D.O.M.E. method resembles identically the shamanic and magical concepts of transferring perceptual consciousness to an inner-plane event. Like the shaman, Steinbrecher has found it valuable to call for an animal ally who will in turn lead the meditator to the appropriate Guide. On various occasions such animals as deer, lions, dogs and cats have appeared and have led the way to the Guide who, in Steinbrecher's experience, has initially always taken a male form.

Steinbrecher warns against false guides but believes they can be distinguished by asking the figure to point 'to where the Sun is, in the sky of the inner world'. A false guide, he notes, 'will generally balk, change the subject, try to divert your attention in some way, hedge or will simply vanish'.[11]

Like Austin Spare, Steinbrecher regards the Guides as entities who lived on earth in a former time but who have now entered a psychic plane and have become 'humanity's lost teachers'. While Spare was inclined to run counter to the evolutionary process in tracking the origin of consciousness backwards through time to its abstract source, the D.O.M.E. method advocates focusing on and summoning the transcendent inner sun, which is the 'archetype of the self' – 'the inner life-centre'. The basic intent is to 'place spiritual authority back within the individual ... its true and holy place'.[12]

Specifically, Steinbrecher regards the Guide Meditation as a series of controlled encounters with the archetypal gods and, like the shaman, the occultist must retain control of all aspects of the situation. Steinbrecher notes that the Guides do not necessarily volunteer information and must be specifically asked for it; accordingly, all archetypal beings should be made to answer if their responses are elusive.

Following the Tarot archetypes in sequence, Steinbrecher makes the important observation that the inner god-images are able to bestow magical powers of gifts, very much in the same way that a shaman may treasure a power-object like a quartz crystal, or a sacred song given during initiation. The Major Arcana of the Tarot, in this sense, provides 'at least 22 symbolic gifts or powers in object form scattered throughout your body. A crystal may be in the centre of your forehead, an apple in the heart, a stick of green wood in the right hand, pearls around the neck.' These are gifts to be used in the outer, physical world:

> If the Tarot Empress has given you a copper rod which she explained would do healing, think of a sick plant in your environment and ask your Guide to bring it to where you and the Tarot Empress are – in the inner realm. Ask her to show you how to heal the plant with the rod and follow her instructions … these tools are for use in our everyday lives, not just on the inner planes.[13]

In the Guide Meditation system, astrology is combined with the Tarot in order to identify dominating and conflicting archetypes within the self, so that the encounter process becomes a form of therapy. For example, Aries equates with the Emperor and Mercury with the Magician, Venus with the Empress, Gemini with the Lovers and Aquarius with the Star. According to Steinbrecher, we are able to analyze the horoscope in order to identify the 'high energy' areas via squares, oppositions and opposing zodiacal fields; 'unions', or harmonizing forces, via the conjunctions, sextiles parallels and quincunxes, and basic archetypes via the Sun sign and ruler of the Ascendant. The horoscope is thus a chart and symbolic guide to the individual cosmos of each meditator.

In the final analysis, the Guide Meditation strives for the same kind of inner rebirth harmonizing found in both initiatory shamanism and Kabbalistic magic. The aim is self-integration, individuation, and a broader spiritual perspective. As Steinbrecher writes: 'Outer world perceptions become acute, and the world literally becomes *new*. The creative energy wells up from within and a knowledge of a *oneness* with all becomes a fact of being.'[14]

# DION FORTUNE

## THE FRATERNITY OF THE INNER LIGHT

Dion Fortune was born Violet Mary Firth on 6 December 1890 at Bryn-y-Bia, in Llandudno, Wales. By the time she had reached her teenage years Violet Firth had already turned to Christian Science – it is likely that her parents were also devotees although this has not been established – and she seems to have had an early inclination towards psychism and metaphysics.

Although details of her early professional life are scanty it is known that she worked as a therapist in a medico-psychological clinic in east London and later studied psychoanalysis in classes held at the University of London by a Professor Flugel – who was also a member of the Society for Psychical Research. Strongly influenced by the theories of Freud, Adler and Jung, Firth became a lay psychoanalyst in 1918. In Jung's thought especially, she found correlations between the 'archetypes of the collective unconscious' and a realm of enquiry which would increasingly fascinate her – the exploration of sacred mythological images invoked by occultists during their rituals and visionary encounters.

According to Dion Fortune's biographer, Alan Richardson, her first contact with occult perspectives seems to have come through her association with an Irish Freemason, Dr Theodore Moriarty. Firth probably met Moriarty at the clinic where she worked; he in turn was involved in giving lectures on occult theories in a private house in the village of Eversley in north Hampshire. Dr Moriarty seems to have been a very fascinating individual. His interests were both Theosophical and metaphysical, encompassing such subject matter as the study of psychology and religion, the so-called 'root races' of lost Atlantis, mystical and Gnostic Christianity, reincarnation, and the occult relationship between mind, matter and spirit. He was also interested in the psychic origins of disease, the karmic aspects of pathology, and the influence of black magic on mental health.

It is not clear whether Dr Moriarty had any personal connection with the Golden Dawn magicians – many of whom were also Freemasons. However Violet Firth had a close friend, Maiya Curtis-Webb, whom she had known from childhood and who was also an occult devotee, and through her she was introduced to the Golden Dawn Temple of the Alpha and Omega in 1919. Based in London, this temple was a southern offshoot of the Scottish section of the Golden Dawn headed by J. W. Brodie-Innes. Maiya Curtis-Webb became her teacher at the Alpha and Omega temple, and Firth found the magical ceremonies powerful and evocative. However there was also a certain gloom about this particular group: 'The glory had departed ... for most of its original members were dead or withdrawn; it had suffered severely during the war, and was manned mainly by widows and grey-bearded ancients.'[15] Taking her leave a year later, Violet Firth now became a member of a London temple headed by Mrs Moina Mathers, who was continuing the esoteric work of her husband following his untimely death from influenza in the epidemic of 1918.

In the Golden Dawn, Violet Firth took the magical name *Deo Non Fortuna* – 'by God and not by luck' – which also happened to be the Latin motto inscribed upon the Firth family crest. She now became known in esoteric circles as Dion Fortune – a contraction of her magical name – and in 1922 formed her own meditative group. It was originally known as The Christian Mystic Lodge of the Theosophical Society and would later become The Fraternity of the Inner Light.

This connection with the Theosophical Society is not as surprising as it may seem, because there was a substantial overlap in membership between the Golden Dawn and the esoteric branch of the Theosophical Society in London at this time, and Dion Fortune herself felt a strong psychic and spiritual connection with the Theosophists. In her mind the two organizations did not need to compete with each other, but were complementary. The Christian reference in the name of her mystical group is harder to account for. It can in part be explained by the fact that Dion Fortune's teacher, Dr Moriarty, seems to have been a Gnostic Christian who believed strongly that the Christian gospels were esoteric allegories. In her book *Applied Magic*, Dion Fortune also reveals that, like Dr Moriarty, she too held an esoteric view of Jesus Christ, describing him as 'a high priest after the Order of Melchizedek', and comparing his spiritual role with that of other 'saviours' like Orpheus and Mithra. Dion Fortune even found her own version of the Golden Dawn Secret Chiefs in a cosmic being called Manu Melchizedek, 'Lord of the Flame and also of Mind', who would become her guiding force on the inner planes.[16]

But there would also be a specific, and ongoing, connection with the Golden Dawn. According to Dion Fortune's account in *The Occult Review*, The Fraternity of the Inner Light was established by her 'in agreement with Mrs Mathers, to be an Outer Court to the Golden Dawn system …'[17]

Dion Fortune seems to have got along reasonably well with Moina Mathers until 1924 when a dispute arose over the publication of Fortune's book *The Esoteric Philosophy of Love and Marriage* – a book which put forward the view that a sexual relationship between two people could be considered as an energy exchange on many levels of being, not just the physical level. While today this seems reasonably innocuous, and perhaps even obvious, Moina Mathers charged Dion Fortune with 'betraying the inner teaching of the Order'. Fortune protested that she had not actually received the relevant degree from Mrs Mathers' temple and she was then 'pardoned'. Nevertheless, the dispute with Moina Mathers continued. Soon afterwards, Fortune writes, 'she suspended me for some months for writing *Sane Occultism*, and finally turned me out because certain symbols had not appeared in my aura – a perfectly unanswerable charge'.[18] Dion Fortune eventually severed her connection with Moina Mathers after claiming she had attacked her magically on the inner planes.

Despite falling out with Moina Mathers, Dion Fortune continued to explore the ceremonial and visualization techniques she had learned in the Golden Dawn temples and she set up a temple of her own in Bayswater. Her temple was loosely affiliated with the Stella Matutina which had been formed by Dr R. W. Felkin and other Golden Dawn members following the earlier rift with MacGregor Mathers. Dion Fortune finally moved beyond the Golden Dawn altogether, establishing her own magical society, The Fraternity of the Inner Light, in 1927.

Dion Fortune's unique contribution to visionary magic really begins with her work in The Fraternity of the Inner Light. Here she increasingly engaged herself in the mythological dimensions of magic – venturing into what she now came to regard as the collective pagan soul of humanity, and tapping into the very heart of the Ancient Mysteries. Reversing the male-dominated, solar-oriented tradition which MacGregor Mathers had established in the Golden Dawn, Dion Fortune now committed herself completely to the magical potency of the archetypal feminine, and began exploring goddess images in the major ancient pantheons. Her two novels *The Sea Priestess* and *Moon Magic* contain allusions to what appears to be a Rite of Isis:

> Those who adore the Isis of Nature adore her as Hathor with the horns upon her brow, but those who adore the celestial Isis know her as Levanah, the Moon. She is also the great Deep whence life arose. She is all ancient and forgotten things wherein our roots are cast. Upon earth she is ever-fecund: in heaven she is ever-virgin. She is the mistress of the tides that flow and ebb and flow, and never cease …
>
> In the heavens our Lady Isis is the Moon, and the moon-powers are hers. She is also priestess of the silver star that rises from the twilight sea. Hers are the magnetic moon-tides ruling the hearts of men …

In the inner she is all-potent. She is the queen of the kingdoms of sleep. All the visible workings are hers and she rules all things ere they come to birth. Even as through Osiris her mate the earth grows green, so the mind of man conceives through her power ...

But there was a different emphasis here as well, for Dion Fortune had begun to explore the symbolic and sexual polarities in magic, including those of the Black Isis. Isis is best known as the great goddess of magic in ancient Egyptian mythology, as the wife of the sun-god Osiris and the mother of Horus. It was Isis who succeeded in piecing together the fragments of Osiris's body after he had been murdered by Set, and it was she who also tricked Ra into revealing his secret magical name. However Dion Fortune was interested in a different aspect of Isis – a dimension associated with what occult writer Kenneth Grant has called the 'primordial essence of Woman (*sakti*) in her dynamic aspect'. While Isis was a lunar goddess and the Moon is traditionally considered passive – a receptacle or reflector of light – the Black Isis was said to destroy all that was 'inessential and obstructive to the soul's development'. This in turn led to an exploration of the magic of sexuality. According to Kenneth Grant, the basis of Fortune's work at this time involved 'the bringing into manifestation of this *sakti* by the magically controlled interplay of sexual polarity embodied in the priest (the consecrated male) and the specially chosen female. Together they enacted the immemorial Rite'... and this formed a vortex on the inner planes 'down which the tremendous energies of Black Isis rush(ed) into manifestation'.[19]

If Grant is correct, and he met her in the 1940s around the same time that he knew Aleister Crowley, this was clearly a type of visionary magic which ventured into new realms, encompassing the use of transcendent sexual energies and the fusion, in ritual, of male and female polarities. It seems to have involved some form of western magical tantra, and was a clear departure from the Golden Dawn, which tended to downplay the sexual dimensions of magic.

However, while one can only speculate on the sexual aspects of the most secret Inner Light rituals, it is also clear that Dion Fortune's main emphasis was not so much on physical magical activities as on astral encounters with the mythic archetypes of the mind. The Fraternity of the Inner Light continued the experimental work with magical visualization that had first been undertaken in the Golden Dawn during the 1890s, and the Inner Light magicians now developed a practical approach to magical 'pathworkings' as a direct means of exploring the subconscious mind. An important essay titled *The Old Religion*, written by an anonymous senior member of Dion Fortune's group,[20] confirms that the Inner Light members believed that astral ventures of this kind could arouse 'ancient cult memories' from previous incarnations. Dion Fortune believed that the key to understanding human life and achievement lay in understanding the nature of reincarnation,[21] and the archetype of the Great Mother, in particular, could be thought of as a symbolic embodiment of the World Memory – a concept which has a parallel in the Theosophical concept of the Akashic Records. Through the universal potential of the Great Mother one could access details of one's earlier lives on earth, and in this way could divine one's sacred purpose ... According to the author of *The Old Religion*:

> Most of the members of these groups have, in the past, served at the altars of Pagan Religions and have met, face to face, the Shining Ones of the forests and the mountains, of the lakes and seas ... In the course of these experiments it was discovered that if anyone of the members of a group had in the past a strong contact with a particular cult at a certain period, that individual could communicate these memories to others, and could link them with cult memories that still lie within the Earth memories of Isis as the Lady of Nature.[22]

In many mythic traditions the magical journey to the ancient gods and goddesses begins on a path which leads through a gateway to the underworld. We have already mentioned that the Golden Dawn magicians conceived of Malkuth, the tenth emanation upon the Tree of Life, as the doorway to the subconscious mind – and this was like entering the underworld of the human psyche. Utilizing classical Roman mythology, members of the Inner Light drew on the imagery of the Cumaean Gates which, according to legend, were located near Naples and were guarded by the Sibyl attending the Temple of Apollo. It was through these gates that Aeneas was said to have passed, after deciphering the labyrinth symbol inscribed upon them. Aeneas sought safe passage in the mythic world by first obtaining the golden bough, which would be given as a gift to Persephone. He also encountered evil spirits, supernatural monsters and former colleagues, numbered among the dead. Then, having been reunited with his father Anchises, he perceived the 'great vision' – a panorama of past and future Roman history – and was granted access to mysterious secrets of the universe.

The Inner Light members had a special interest in visionary journeys of this sort and incorporated them into their guided imagery meditations, although under Dion Fortune's leadership they tended to focus primarily on the feminine aspects of the underworld encounter. Reflecting Dion Fortune's early interest in the psychological concepts of Carl Jung, there is more than a hint here of Jung's concept of the animus and anima:

> … it is the woman that holds the keys of the inner planes for a man. If you want to pass the Cumaean Gates you must become as a little child and a woman must lead you … It was Deiphobe, daughter of Glaucus, priestess of Phoebus, and of the Goddess Three-wayed who, for King Aeneas, opened the keyless door and drew the veil that hides life from death and death from life.[23]

The Inner Light guided meditations helped heighten personal awareness of specific mythic imagery and facilitated a switch of consciousness away from one's waking perception to the symbolic inner locale concerned. The author of *The Old Religion* describes a series of inner journeys – 'The By-Road to the Cave in the Mountain', 'At the Ford of the Moon', 'The High Place of the Moon', and 'The Hosting of the Sidhe' – the culminating experience being a merging of one's awareness with the ethereal Isis in her 'green' aspect as Queen of Nature.

The following account is given from the viewpoint of a male occultist who is initiated by the feminine archetype:

As he watched, the green of the beech-leaves and the faint silver colour of the bole seemed to merge in a form that was not the tree, and yet it was the tree. He was no longer seeing the tree with his eyes – he was feeling it. He was once again in his inner, subtler, moon-body, and with it he saw and felt the moon-body of the tree. Then appeared the tree spirit, the deva, the shining one who lives through the trunk and branches and leaves of the beech tree as a man lives through his torso, limbs and hair. That beech was very friendly and moon-body to moon-body they met, and as his moon-body merged into that of the lady of the beech tree, the sensation of the nature of the seasons of the caress of the sunlight, of the stimulation of the bright increase of the waxing moon, and of the sleep-time that comes with the decrease of the waning moon, were his.

'You can merge thus into all life', he was told; and then he saw, as the fairy sees, the flowers, the waterfalls, the rivers, and the brightly coloured holy mountain of Derrybawn, which means the home of the Shining Ones. He merged himself into the roaring life that was at the summit of that great and sacred mountain – and in so doing he took the initiation of the lady of Nature – the Green Isis – in her temple on the heather-clad hill-top that is above the deep ravine.[24]

Dion Fortune died in 1946 but her unique approach to magical consciousness did not come to an end with her death. The work of The Fraternity of the Inner Light would be further developed by a contemporary magical order known as the Servants of the Light (SOL), a group whose headquarters are currently located in St Helier on the island of Jersey.

# DOLORES ASHCROFT-NOWICKI

## SERVANTS OF THE LIGHT

One of Dion Fortune's close associates in The Fraternity of the Inner Light was the well-known occultist W. E. Butler. Like Dion Fortune, Butler had assimilated a vast knowledge of the Kabbalah, western mythology and esoteric symbolism into a practical system of magic and after her death he established the Servants of the Light to continue this work. In his later years, Butler passed the leadership of the SOL on to the present Director of the Order, Dolores Ashcroft-Nowicki, whose many publications include a collection of visionary magic pathworkings titled *Highways of the Mind*.

Like Dion Fortune, Dolores Ashcroft-Nowicki is of Welsh ancestry and was born into a family with an extensive esoteric lineage. Her great-grandmother was a full-blooded gypsy and her grandmother practised gypsy magic. Both of her parents were third degree initiates at a time when magic and Wicca were far less accessible than they are now. Dolores herself was tutored in the Inner Light by C. C. Chichester and W. E. Butler and is the author of over a dozen books, including recent publications like *The Tree of Ecstasy*, *Daughters of Eve* and *Building a Temple*. However it is her earlier work which is of special interest here, because it deals substantially with magical pathworkings.

The initial exercise described in *Highways of the Mind* – a meditative journey embracing the four elements – resembles the psychotherapeutic techniques of active imagination. The following is an extract for the element Air:

> Look up at the sky; above you are the clouds and the warm sun. Deep inside you there is a pull upwards. Yield to it, and let the power of the sun draw you up to the clouds. Let

yourself be made part of the clouds. There the winds dry you and make you part of the kingdom of the Air. Beside you are a throng of fellow sylphs; together you race across the ocean you have just left towards a range of high mountains capped with snow. Up, up and over them you go, revelling in the snow flurries that blow constantly from their summits. Rush down into the valleys, sweeping through the forests and making the branches sing in thin, high voices ... Ride on the backs of birds nestled among the wing feathers, looking down on the earth below. [25]

Dolores Ashcroft-Nowicki refers to two different types of path-workings, the first which proceeds between fixed and known points and which involves familiar symbols (this is the 'active' method) and the second which uses a familiar symbol of entry such as a Tarot card or Tattva but which allows unfamiliar images to present themselves (the 'passive' method). The first approach is advocated as a safer method for occultists relatively unfamiliar with magical journey techniques since the second approach allows for unknown and potentially frightening symbols from the subconscious to present themselves.

Nevertheless, there comes a time when any aspiring magician must venture into new realms of the mythic universe and trust his sense of personal integrity and concentrated will. Such experiences are sometimes referred to by occultists as semi-structured or unstructured pathworkings and within the SOL system they are regarded as appropriate only for advanced practitioners. Examples of such workings which derive from the SOL tradition will be discussed in part three of this book.

In the final pathworking of her 'Highways' series, a visualization which belongs to the 'active' rather than to the 'passive' category, Dolores Ashcroft-Nowicki builds the imagery of an appealing woodlands scene which heightens the personal sense of well-being and peace with Nature. Nestling in a clearing is a small stone chapel where a sacred transformation will occur:

*When you feel ready, close your eyes and build in the mind's eye a door in the wall facing you. It is made of heavy dark oak with iron hinges and a massive lock. Study it carefully noting the iron handle. Now, move from your chair and walk towards the door. Put out your hand and turn the key, feeling the effort needed for it is large and ancient and a little rusty. Now take hold of the handle, turn it and open the door.*

*Before going through, study the scene before you. It is a wood in early springtime, a beaten track obviously much used leads from the door into the heart of the wood. The air is warm and soft as if after a shower, the scent of damp earth and moss all around you. Step through the door and walk a few paces forward then turn and look behind you. The door is half open, the room beyond is dim and hazy. Above the door is carved your name in letters of gold. You are clad in a long cloak of grey wool with a hood that is thrown back and fastened at the throat with circular clasp which, when closed brings together an equal armed cross engraved within it.*

*Take the path and walk through the wood, try and record the scents and sounds around you. Birds singing very clearly as they do after rain, the feel of wet branches and leaves as they brush against your face and hair. The softness of damp earth beneath your feet. The whole wood is carpeted with wild flowers, see if you can name them. On the branches there are tight green buds just beginning to form.*

*As you walk another sound comes to the ear, the chime of bells. Follow it and the track leads you to a large clearing in which stands a small chapel of grey stone. The bells fall silent and you wait. To the door of the chapel comes a friar clad in a white robe. The face is neither young nor old, austere yet with untold compassion and understanding in the eyes. He opens the door wide and gestures to you to come into the chapel.*

*Inside all is light and the full glory of the stained glass is visible. It is sparsely furnished, no pews, just a high-backed chair facing the Altar with a small wooden bench in front of it. On the*

*Altar all is ready and waiting. Take your place in the chair and make your own prayer. On the Altar there is a silver chalice, small and plain and in a covered dish the Holy Water. The Eastern Window is in shades of Rose and Gold with touches of Blue and Green. The Central theme is a child holding a dove in His hands. The priest comes from behind you carrying what seems to be another chalice, but covered with white silk. This he places with great care on the Altar, the cover is constantly stirring as if in a gentle breeze, the scent of roses fills the chapel and though noone else is present there is an unheard song of praise that fills the inner ear.*

*Kneel now at the bench and prepare yourself to become a receiver. Empty yourself as completely as you can, leaving the mind, not blank but 'ready'. The priest comes to you with the communion which you take. He then departs from the chapel taking the small chalice and the plate with him.*

*Take your seat again and fix your eyes on the covered object on the Altar. Now, in this state, already on a higher level than the physical, go into a meditation thus passing into the next level. Let the covered chalice be your doorway. It becomes larger until it fills your vision, its shape shining through the cloth. Let 'It' fill your mind, which you have emptied ready for whatever may come. Try and grasp what is being impressed on your higher state of consciousness.*

*Gradually the Grail returns to its former size and the chapel becomes visible around you once more. Hold on to whatever it is that has been passed to you. Make your thanks and go to the door, pause there and look back. All the light within the chapel is coming from the covered Grail and a low musical humming sound fills the air.*

*Outside all is quiet and peaceful, just a lovely wood full of flowers. Retrace your steps until you come to the door, go through it closing and locking it behind you. Sit down in the chair. Feel the physical body close around you and when you are ready open your eyes. Record your 'Grail message' at once before you forget.*

*This may take time and tire you a bit for you are passing through
the astral to the mental plane using one as a stepping stone to the
other, but a short rest should be enough to restore you.*[26]

Because the SOL provides magical training through a system of
correspondence courses it has been able to extend its international
influence much further than the Golden Dawn was able to in its
day. The Golden Dawn had temples only in Britain and France, with
affiliated Orders in the United States, whereas the SOL currently has
lodges in Australia, Canada, Mexico, the Netherlands, Sweden,
Britain and the United States and around 2,600 students scattered
across 23 countries. Dolores Ashcroft-Nowicki periodically visits
her SOL members in these different countries and is able to manage
the growth of the SOL and its core magical procedures by utilizing
the resources of the Internet and by frequently updating her website. The SOL remains one of the most prominent contemporary
organisations dedicated to the exploration of visionary magic in the
world today.

### Notes

1   Austin Osman Spare, *The Book of Pleasure,* privately published, London 1913,
    pp.52-53. Reissued in facsimile edition by 93 Publishing, Montreal 1975
2   Gavin W. Semple, *Zos Kia,* 1995, p.7
3   Quoted in K. Grant, *Images and Oracle of Austin Osman Spare,* 1975, p.73
4   ibid., p.33
5   This book had been preceded by *A Book of Satyrs* (c.1911) which contained
    'satires' on the Church, politics, officialdom and other 'follies'. It is not a
    major work.
6   Spare became a member of the Argenteum Astrum in 1910 after contributing
    some drawings to Crowley's occult journal *The Equinox.* However Spare later
    distanced himself from Crowley altogether.
7   See *The Book of Pleasure,* op.cit., p.50
8   Spare believed that the self lived 'in millions of forms', and that it was obliged
    to experience 'every conceivable thing' – all the infinite possibilities inherent in
    the manifested universe. Any incomplete existence or situation required a
    reincarnation to finalize it or make it whole.

9   Kenneth Grant, 'Austin Osman Spare', *Man, Myth and Magic*, vol.1, London 1970

10  E. Steinbrecher, *The Guide Meditation*, 1975, p.30

11  ibid., p.48

12  ibid., p.69

13  ibid., pp.54-55

14  ibid., p.58

15  Quoted in Alan Richardson, *Priestess*, 1987, p.112

16  A Gnostic sect, the Melchizedekians, maintained that there was a spiritual power greater than Jesus Christ. This was Melchizedek, 'the light gatherer', who is said to have performed a comparable role in the heavens to that of Jesus on Earth.

17  See Alan Richardson, *Priestess*, op.cit., p.117

18  Quoted in R. A. Gilbert, *Revelations of the Golden Dawn*, 1997, p.124

19  Kenneth Grant, *The Magical Revival*, 1972, p.177

20  See chapter by 'FPD', 'The Old Religion', in Basil Wilby (ed.), *The New Dimensions Red Book*, 1965

21  Dion Fortune, *Applied Magic*, 1962, p.4

22  FPD, 'The Old Religion', op.cit., p.147

23  ibid., p.49

24  ibid., p.78

25  D. Ashcroft-Nowicki, *Highways of the Mind* in 'Round Merlin's Table', no.50, pp.14-15

26  *Round Merlin's Table*, no.53, pp.5-6

Part Three

# VISION-QUEST

CHAPTER 7

# PATHWAYS OF
# THE MIND

This section of the book now becomes more personal, and describes my own exploration of the relationship between shamanism and visionary magic. Although this personal enquiry began over thirty years ago, this subject continues to fascinate me even now. I continue to hold workshops utilizing shamanic drumming and magical visualization and I never cease to be amazed at how readily magical imagery can be aroused into everyday conscious awareness – even among people who have not ventured into these psychic and spiritual realms before.

Nevertheless, when I first began to explore the various approaches to magical consciousness in the late 1960s I was surprised to discover that there had been very little overlap between occultists and those who were part of the Human Potential Movement, as it was then known. The latter was, and is, a diverse group of people, mostly made up of psychologists but also including anthropologists, physicists, theologians, musicians, pharmacologists and philosophers, who are interested in the furthest reaches of human consciousness. Although one could justifiably assume that psychology *ought* to be all about the study of consciousness, this had not been the case since the time of William James. Since his day, psychology had gone off on a behaviourist tack and had veered away from the study of what actually makes us conscious. Perhaps human consciousness studying *itself* could never be regarded as sufficiently scientific or impartial.

The home of the Human Potential Movement in these early years was the Esalen Institute located in very picturesque countryside in the Big Sur, south of Monterey in the USA. The workshops conducted there on 'spiritual psychology' were far-ranging, and included a wide variety of topics including bodywork therapies, polarity balancing, Tai Chi, Zen, creative sexuality, dance, hypnosis, shamanism, Taoism and special lectures on the Gnostics and Findhorn for example. For many years through the late 1970s and into the 1980s the scholar-in-residence at Esalen was Czechoslavakian psychiatrist Dr Stanislav Grof. Dr Grof had also been President of the International Association of Transpersonal Psychology, a movement which grew out of humanistic psychology and which encouraged research into visionary consciousness, peak-experiences and mysticism, in addition to all forms of well-being and holistic health. Transpersonal psychology had developed from its humanistic roots as a result of the very considerable efforts of Anthony Sutich and Abraham Maslow in the late 1960s and its growth as a school of psychology has paralleled the emergence of the personal growth movement ever since. In Maslow's view, psychology had allowed itself to become much too dominated by the study of pathology and neurosis and was not sufficiently involved with those states of supreme well-being that we all strive after. Maslow had also gone on record stating that religious values and mystical experience were a vital part of the human make-up, and deserved serious scientific and experiential study.

Since it was clear to me that magic also had the aim of putting human beings in touch with their sacred origins, I wondered why there had been so little interchange between students of the Western Mystery Tradition and their 'higher consciousness' brothers and sisters in California? The one exception in the literature at that time was an essay on western magic by William Gray in Charles Tart's anthology *Transpersonal Psychologies*, but apart from that there had obviously been very scant sharing of information. I still don't know the reason why.

One of the areas where there was potentially a certain amount in common was so-called 'active imagination' work. The occultists in the Golden Dawn had made extensive inner journeys of the mind by focusing on Tarot cards and the Hindu Tattva symbols of the four elements and had thereby learned to trigger controlled self-hypnosis states at will. Although Ralph Metzner had published a book called *Maps of Consciousness* which included descriptive chapters on the Tarot and alchemy, the only 'experiential' book I could find to throw light on these inner processes of visualization was *Mind Games*, a book of guided imagery exercises. Its authors were Robert Masters and Jean Houston, Directors of the Foundation for Mind Research in Pomona, New York.

*Mind Games* – which has since become something of a classic and has now been reissued – presents a series of graded exercises in which members of a small group are guided by a leader into sensory areas of the imagination. Typically the early games begin with a relaxation exercise and lead progressively into areas which involve focusing, for example, on the body-image or on the sensory qualities of music. The games then progress to more complex visualizations where the participants imagine complete scenes – often of a mythic or fantasy nature – and learn to transfer consciousness to them, so that in an experiential sense they become real. Members of the group gradually learn to move in and out of the trance state at will, and to have encounters with sacred beings and the 'Group Spirit'. The final sections of the book lead the participants through deep self-examination and towards the exploration of spiritual values, culminating in the experience of the quest for the Holy Grail and symbolic death and rebirth.

# A MEETING WITH
# ROBERT MASTERS

I could see the occult applications of these mind game techniques
and resolved to make contact with the authors. Finally I managed to
combine a professional publishing visit to New York with a journey
to their home, located just outside the rural town of Suffern. Jean
Houston was on a lecture tour at the time but she later told me that
her husband Robert Masters was much more inclined towards
mysticism and the occult than she was. And there was evidence of this
in the environment they had created within their home. Located in
lush, wooded countryside, the house was richly decorated with
paintings, ornaments and wall hangings that made it into a
mythological event in its own right: a fur mandala from Greece hung
on one wall, several Huichol peyote paintings on another. In Masters'
study there were two authentic sculptures of the Egyptian lion-
hearted goddess Sekhmet, one of which had an extraordinary psychic
presence and seemed to follow you around the room with its eyes. I
wasn't alone in this impression. Apparently anthropologist Margaret
Mead had had the same feeling when she saw the sculpture, and had
been very disturbed by it.

When I met with him, I found that Robert Masters had moved on
from the *Mind Games* work and was now much more involved with
the symbolism of Sekhmet and in linking mind research with the
ancient Egyptian mysteries. He gave me a copy of his article *The Way
of the Five Bodies*, which is an extraordinary statement of magical
purpose specifically grounded within the framework of Egyptian
mythology. For Masters the only true spiritual transformations
involve the two most subtle bodies of man, known by the Egyptians
as *Khu* – the magical body – and *Sahu* the spiritual body. (The other
three bodies are *Aufu*, the physical body, *Ka*, the double, and *Haidit*
the so-called 'shadow'.) When the three main bodies are fully
operative the magician interacts with the gods and goddesses of the
highest planes of being and becomes a participant in 'the war within
the heavens'. Life is then lived on a profound, cosmic level, far

transcending ordinary reality. For Masters, the polar opposites are symbolized on the one hand by Sekhmet and her associated deities representing the forces of Light and Cosmos, and on the other by the dark god Set and his cohorts of Evil and Chaos. The most profound magical work results in sacred knowledge and self-realisation being conveyed to the occultist in a visionary state, directly by the god – in Masters' case, through Sekhmet.

This was impressive material, and far more grounded in occult mythology than I had expected from reading Mind Games, which is not aligned to a particular metaphysical system. In Masters' view a type of spiritual energy arousal was produced by his personal communication with Sekhmet, which paralleled the Yogic *Kundalini*. Although we did not discuss intimate details of the actual process for arousing this energy, the symbolism of Sekhmet (or Sekhet as she is sometimes known) is instructive. The husband of Ptah in the cosmology of Memphis, Sekhmet was regarded as guardian of the sun god and was also the Eve of Ra, whose energy she radiated forth. Kenneth Grant, an occultist working in the Tantric tradition, describes Sekhmet as 'the lion-headed goddess of the South; the type of solar-phallic or sexual heat ... considered by the ancients as the divine inspirer or breather, the spirit of creation. Sekhet gave her name to the Indian concept of Sakti or Shakti, the creative power of Shiva ...'[1] So Sekhmet/Sekhet had many of the qualities which are universally symbolized as typifying the magical quest: a force or spirit underlying creativity and a unique blending of polarities – a feminine bodily form, coupled with the lion's head and the 'fire of life' traditionally associated with male deities. Androgynous gods, those which display the fusion of male and female in one form, have mythologically been regarded as the highest gods of all. The process of spiritual transformation in the Kabbalah similarly leads the magician beyond male and female polarities to the 'high neutrality' of *Kether*, the Crown – the peak of the Tree of Life and doorway to the 'infinite light' of *Ain Soph Aur*.

At the time of my meeting with Robert Masters, it is fair to say that I was not yet ready to embrace such a highly specific magical system as that presented by the Sekhmet cosmology. Although my more recent work with shamanism has now led me towards similar conclusions regarding the aims of magic – which in the final analysis involves powerful interactions with the sacred archetypal gods of the subconscious – I was still at that time interested in specific active imagination techniques like those presented in *Mind Games*. One of my aims was to construct a complete system of visualization pathways based on the Kabbalah and the Tarot – the magical systems most familiar to me.

There was also another topic on which I sought Robert Masters' opinion: the controlled use of psychedelics. I was interested in his views about sacred plants and their derivatives because of their role in shamanism, and I was also aware that he and Jean Houston had spent fifteen years researching non-addictive psychedelics and had compiled one of the classical texts on LSD, *The Varieties of Psychedelic Experience*. They had also written the superbly visual, but long out-of-print *Psychedelic Art*, which I had finally managed to track down in a second-hand bookstore in Berkeley. I was particularly keen to have Masters' views on certain specific drug-states because I knew that Aleister Crowley had experimented with a variety of hallucinogens and had endeavoured to incorporate the resulting altered states of consciousness into his magical rituals. I was also aware that there was still considerable interest in psychedelics at Esalen, despite the legal constraints. Stanislav Grof had researched the psychotherapeutic applications of LSD for over twenty years and when I first visited Esalen in 1979 I discovered that several members of staff were very intrigued by the potential applications of ketamine hydrochloride, a dissociative anaesthetic that caused out-of-the-body experiences. John Lilly had also begun using ketamine extensively, and had written about it enthusiastically in his book *The Scientist*.

Robert Masters obviously still valued the insights that psyche-delics could provide but cautioned me against the use of ketamine although he had not tried it himself. I told him about an article I had read by Grof's protégé Rick Tarnas, who believed that ketamine had an extremely safe medical record and was virtually guaranteed to produce mystical states of consciousness. It seemed too good to be true. Masters was not convinced, and felt that the drug could possibly anaesthetize the breathing apparatus unless used with extreme care.

So I put aside the question of the magical use of psychedelics. When I returned to my home in Sydney I found that nobody I knew had any knowledge of ketamine at all, let alone whether it had magical applications or not. In the meantime I decided to stick to mind games and to construct a series of visualizations that could be used to tap archetypal and mythological areas of consciousness. My starting point was the Major Arcana of the Tarot.

# FIRST ENCOUNTERS
# WITH THE TAROT

Intrigued by the visual beauty of the Tarot, I had already begun researching the symbolism of the cards in the early 1970s. A spate of decks had flooded the market in response to the demands of the counterculture, but the best-known Tarot pack was still the comparatively dull Rider Pack designed by A. E. Waite and Pamela Colman Smith. By contrast, the visionary pack of Aleister Crowley and Frieda Harris came as a revelation, although it was clear that Crowley had incorporated some of his own mythological ideas into the card sequence. For example, he had replaced *Strength* with *Lust* in deference to the Whore of Babylon, and replaced *The Emperor* with *The Star* – both personal aberrations.

I knew that Tarot cards were linked in the popular mind to gypsy fortune telling but learned that they had been present in Italy a century before the gypsies arrived there – so the origin of the Tarot remained a genuine mystery. Some people claimed that the Tarot originated in ancient Egypt, among them the French theologian Antoine Court de Gébelin, author of one of the earliest books on the subject, *Le Monde Primitif.* De Gébelin had encouraged these fanciful theories by claiming that the Tarot was part of an initiatory procedure in the Great Pyramid. However the medieval nature of the cards – which included all the symbols of chivalry and armoured knights – clearly discounted this theory. De Gébelin's view was typical of the romantic obsession with lost cultures. Many people interested in occult origins have looked back to a golden age which possessed a secret esoteric wisdom and have located the source of this wisdom in various countries, including ancient Egypt and the legendary 'lost continents' of Atlantis and Lemuria.

But even if de Gébelin's theories concerning the historical origins of the Tarot seemed dubious, his concept of the initiatory application of the Tarot struck a powerful chord with me. There did seem to be a pattern of spiritual growth in the cards, especially in the 22 mythological trumps of the Major Arcana.

I found as I read further that the French occultist Eliphas Lévi had been responsible for combining the Major Arcana and the Kabbalistic Tree of Life and that for the first time this presented the Tarot cards as potential pathways into the areas of the mind concerned with mystic consciousness. This eccentric blend of esoteric symbols, subsequently decried by orthodox Kabbalistic scholars like Gershom Scholem, was taken up as a working system by the occultists in the Order of the Golden Dawn, and has since become central to western magic.

Having already worked with visualizations based on the Middle Pillar of the Kabbalistic Tree of Life, I felt that Tarot pathways upon the Tree were a good place to start. So I began to explore the symbolism of the Major Arcana starting with the entry card of *The World* and culminating with the paradoxical symbol of *The Fool*. By 1974, when I assembled my notes for an article titled *The Inner Mythology*, my sequence on the Tarot looked something like this:

**The World**
This card represents the descent into the underworld of the sub-conscious. The dancer is reminiscent of Persephone, symbolizing the perpetual cycle of the harvest, and therefore life and death. She is also androgynous – her genitals are hidden – and she represents both male and female, despite her apparent feminity.

## Judgement

The figures rise from death towards the new life and light of the magical quest. They are shown gesturing with their arms to form the word L.V.X. ... A new personality, a magical identity, has to be formed. Hephaestos, the blacksmith is ascribed to this path ... he is like the great shaman who forges a new identity for his magical candidates in trance.

## The Moon

This card is also evolutionary: the lobster emerges from the waters; the wild dog becomes tame and less aggressive. The tides of life are cyclic.

## The Sun

The young naked twins dancing show a sense of innocence, and the synthesis of sexual opposites. The magic mountain is still far off in the distance.

## The Star

The White Goddess kneels beside a pool of water, the river of consciousness towards which the magician slowly makes his way. The card symbolizes intuition and fertility, and the cup is reminiscent of the Holy Grail ...

## The Tower

The Tower of Babel – an arrogant attempt by man to scale the heights of heaven. *The Tower* is also the body, and a thunderbolt of divine energy – the lightning flash – would be devastating and harmful to the occultist who was not inwardly prepared. A hint here of the Kundalini power?

## The Devil

Man and woman bound in chains, still trapped by their lower, bestial and materialistic nature. A card which reminds us all of our limited frameworks and the need for transformation.

## Death

The skeleton slayer strides across the horizon. Death and carnage are everywhere, but death leads to new life. The river of consciousness flows into the sun in the distance ... and actually leads to Tiphareth, at the centre of the Tree of Life.

## Temperance

A wonderful card. The union of opposites, male and female, and the four elements all blended together. All the aspects of the lower subconscious find unity on this path. Tiphareth, the level of God-in-Man, is within reach.

## The Hermit

The Hermit is like the Ancient of Days, rising above the cycles of Time and wending his way up the magic mountain, following the lantern of his own inner light. For the first time on the journey, the inner qualities take priority over outer ones. His outer persona is limited, for he is hidden in his cloak.

## Justice

A path demanding balance, adjustment and total impartiality. The love of Venus combined with the stern justice of Mars. Here the mystic encounters his accumulated wrongdoing – his karma, if you like. Only truth can be admitted in the Hall of Justice. Reminiscent of the goddess Maat in ancient Egyptian religion.

## The Hanged Man

At first glance a man upside down, perhaps even a parody of Christ. On a deeper level, a reflection of a greater mystery beyond. In Crowley's pack, his head is a beacon, showing that he transmits light from a more profound source.

## The Wheel of Fortune

The Tarot's 'mandala' – a symbol of universal cycles of fate and destiny. An essentially 'neutral' card; the magician must learn to transcend opposites as the wheel turns from feminine to masculine and back again.

## Strength
The intuitive woman overcoming the brute strength of the lower animal nature. Complete mastery over the earlier stages of evolution; opening the mouth, or pathway, to a more universal consciousness.

## The Charioteer
The reflector of truth, the eye of the heavens – a very mobile form of the guardian god. A form of Mars but ruled by the love and spirit of the Great Mother.

## The Lovers
Another card bringing the polarities of male and female together. The twins of *The Sun* in a more spiritually evolved state of being. A wonderful path flowing out of the harmony of Tiphareth. Innocence regained.

## The Hierophant
A reminder that the priest is one who channels divine inspiration to the gathered congregation. A blend of wisdom and mercy.

## The Emperor
Another form of the Great Father, more stationary than the dynamic Charioteer, and seated on a throne hewn out of rock, overlooking the manifest world below. The Tarot's version of Zeus ...

## The Empress
The Great Mother, ever supportive and beneficent. The Mother of all ideas and concepts, which flow from her infinite womb into the finite world of forms. The partner in Life of the Great Father. Surrounded by a field of wheat, she is also the mother of Persephone, whom we met on the first path.

## The High Priestess
The Great Goddess but in a colder, more aloof aspect. She is virginal, and does not yet know man. Mythologically, her virginity is a symbol of purity.

## The Magus
The virginal Male God, again pure and unsullied. He reaches upwards to the supreme mysteries of infinite awareness but has not yet combined with the Great Goddess to produce the manifested universe. Linked to Thoth, the word and rhythm sustaining the Universe.

## The Fool
The supreme paradox: he-who-knows-nothing. He who therefore knows 'that which is beyond everything' – the unmanifested world of pure spirit. The Fool stands on the peak of the magic mountain; spirit and infinity are all around him. The Fool embraces that-which-is-not.

There seemed no doubt to me that the Tarot contained all the ingredients of a total initiatory system. The lowest card on the Tree, *The World*, led directly into the subconscious mind, and resembled the classical tales of descent into the underworld. Then the cards began to form clusters around the lunar and solar archetypes. *The Star*, *The Moon* and *The Sun* were good examples of these, but it was interesting that on the pathway of *The Sun* the children were presented as still very young, and not yet spiritually mature.

Around the centre of the Tree were Tarot paths which forced a person through a process of rigorous self-assessment and an honest encounter with all the follies of the ego – *The Devil*, *The Tower* and *Justice*, while in the form of *Death* it was clear that all of these illusions and vanities had to be destroyed prior to the experience of spiritual rebirth. *Temperance*, with its fusion of the four alchemical elements, was a superb example of harmony, as was *The Wheel of Fortune* located nearby.

The paths leading upwards from Tiphareth at the centre of the Tree were also symbolically appropriate: *The Lovers,* showing the gradual blending of sexual opposites (a theme also found in yoga) and *The Hermit,* in which the magician's personality was clearly less important than the spiritual quest itself. *The Hanged Man,* which in fact portrayed the reflection of spiritual light from above, similarly pointed the way to more sacred domains of consciousness.

The remainder of the cards were primarily reflections of the great Male and Female archetypes, either in their dynamic forms *(The Charioteer, Strength)* or more static and regal counterparts *(The Emperor, The Hierophant, The Empress).* Virginity was also presented as a mythic form of purity, symbolic of very sacred pathways of spiritual consciousness, and here *The Magus* and *The High Priestess* were particularly appropriate. And the final pathway, paradoxically titled *The Fool,* was one of the most interesting of all. Here the individual was seen yielding totally to the cosmic spirit, surrendering all personal possessions and stepping from the cliff-edge of finite existence into the ocean of infinite light.

I was convinced that the Tarot needed to be presented as a meditative journey of the spirit. Most books on the Tarot were either heavily laden with obscure symbolism or else focused on the fortune telling aspects which, from my point of view, had become quite a minor consideration. The actual processes of spiritual growth portrayed in the Major Arcana seemed comparatively straight-forward but, as always in the occult traditions, the central themes had become clouded by metaphysical details – a problem that one also finds with the Kabbalah. The answer seemed to lie in adapting the Major Arcana into a system of meditations and visualizations comparable to the guided imagery of Masters' and Houston's *Mind Games.* I undertook the project with great enthusiasm.

# TAROT MEDITATIONS

The first Tarot meditations that I produced in this style were simple in the extreme. Here are some examples:

## THE WORLD

*Tides of energy are all around us, for we are in the presence of the sacred maiden of the earth. Her pure face is filled with sunlight which nourishes the leaves and flowers in the deep, abundant valley, and her flowing hair is the colour of golden wheat.*

*In her eyes are the reflections of the moon, for she will lead us into the twilight world beneath the earth and beyond the sky, where her dark sister rules the land of shadows.*

*But while she is with us now, Persephone is like a beacon. In her movements are rays of enrichment and warmth, and her radiant hair glistens like the newly risen sun across the fields.*

*She is the first path.*

*She is the entry to the world beyond time.*

*She is the Maiden of the World.*

## THE STAR

*In the night sky a golden star glows with crystal light. The maiden of the stream guards the life essence which she captures from the sun with her flask. Shimmering light flows through her body like a translucent vessel as she pours the waters of life into a pool below, and suddenly the earth all around her springs to life with new possibilities. She tells us that we too can transmit the light, heralding new hope and new abundance.*

*She is the fifth path.*

*She is the mediator between the golden star and earth.*

*She is the Star Maiden of the Life Stream.*

## TEMPERANCE

*Before us stands the angel of day and night, guardian of the sun and moon, and master of the four elements which unite the whole universe in the magic cauldron. Here in the womb of the world, man can be born again from the ashes, and arise phoenix-like in quest of the inner sun.*

*We enter the flux, allowing ourselves to be refashioned after the manner of the gods, encompassing the cycles of life, death and rebirth, and journeying by night and day along the universal road.*

*Temperance shows us the elixir of new life, the magical Philosopher's Stone.*

*Temperance is the ninth path.*

*Guardian of new life and ruler of the four elements of the Universe.*

## THE EMPEROR

*Amidst the textured rocks of the timeless mountains sits the throned ruler of the Universe. He is awesome and all-knowing, yet also merciful and just. His crown blazes with pure light and his vestments are fashioned from the fabric of the Universe. He presides over life in all its forms; his domain is illumined by fire, kindled by the Sun of Sacred Knowledge.*

*The Emperor sits vigilantly, ever patient upon his throne, surveying the world of man. From his vantage point he looks out, ever watchful for imbalance. He shows us the flux of life and death which sustains the Universe in an ageless cycle.*

*He is the eighteenth path.*

*He is the Monarch of the Universe.*

*The timeless and ever present Ancient of Days.*

I still felt, though, that the aspect that I most wanted to include, that of the magical journey itself, was missing. Finally I undertook the lengthy task of presenting the complete Major Arcana as a continuous sequence. I was also interested in combining the magical visualizations with electronic music, and found such records as Fripp and Eno's *Evening Star*, Tangerine Dream's *Rubycon* and *Zeit*, Edgar Froese's *Epsilon in Malaysian Pale* and several albums by Klaus Schulze, including *Mirage* and *Moondawn*, to be especially useful. The haunting vocal effects on the film soundtrack of *2001*, 'Requiem' and 'Lux Aeterna', also had an appropriate magical quality.

In practical terms, however, I soon discovered that a journey through the 22 pathways of the Tarot was far too demanding for most people, including occultists experienced in visualization and relaxation techniques. I therefore decided to condense the journey into the essential initiatory pathway that had formed the magical focus of the Golden Dawn – the Middle Pillar ascent to Tiphareth at the centre of the Tree of Life. I have found this guided visualization to be excellent in group work, following a basic relaxation exercise, and I use a tape which combines 'Crystal Lake' from Klaus Schulze's *Mirage* and 'Maroubra Bay' from Edgar Froese's *Epsilon in Malaysian Pale* to establish the mystical setting. The following is the complete text of the magical visualization, which is read to the group while the music plays:

*We find ourselves in a field of grass, with the wind blowing gently and birds whistling in the distance. We are at peace with the environment and feel the sun warming our skin. Nature's rhythms and energies flow through us.*

*As we walk through the field we see looming before us a rocky cliff-face, hard and worn with time. The granite textures seem ageless, and there are rifts and channels, like wrinkles upon the face of an old man. Suddenly these fissures in the rock deepen and an opening appears in the cliff, becoming a doorway. We pass into the rock, through the space that leads down between the worlds into the land beyond time itself.*

*Before we entered the rock it was warm and bright. Now we are entering a world that is dark, damp and cool. And yet, despite the fact that we are in an unfamiliar domain, the earth welcomes us. All around us, forces and powers are at work,* sustaining living things growing in the soil, and in the rock streams, and in the sun-filled air above.

As we continue, we detect an ethereal glow at the end of the path. A misty green-brown light plays on the walls of the cave, and we see for the first time, as our vision grows clearer, that in the flecks of light-energy a figure is dancing. She is naked, and youthful in appearance and yet, as we watch, her body takes different forms. As if in a mirror, we see in her the fields of ripened wheat, and a golden light shines from her face. Then she darkens, hardening into rock. Waters now seem to flow over her form, dissolving its hardness, and she resembles the currents and eddies of a country stream carrying the grains of sand in their flow.

A soft breeze rustles through her golden hair. As she dances she calls to each one of us in her own way, saying that she is both death and life and that she can teach us, through her movements, the motions of the world itself – with its cycles and seasons, its patterns and rhythms. Streams of energy flow from one hand to another and everything about her being is related to motion. There is no constancy, no sense of being able to stand back and watch. We embrace her in the life force, and dance with her.

Now a circle of misty light comes up around us and we feel we are dancing in the dawn of the first days of the world. And yet we know that our journey has just begun. We have made our first venture into the underworld of myth and legend, and we must continue.

We call now for an ally, one who can help us attain new heights of mystical vision. A deep blue haze has formed around us but within it, having answered our call, is Sagittarius the centaur. He is a magnificent figure, with the robust muscles of a warrior and the bodily form of a stallion. He is bearded and has friendly eyes that twinkle as we behold him. Meanwhile we notice above him a magnificent rainbow that has manifested in the heavens.

In his right hand Sagittarius holds a magnificent golden bow and as we contemplate it he explains that it has magical qualities. For he can fire arrows into the sky which shower golden light, and which open for us a pathway to a higher place in the cosmic sky.

We watch a golden flare ... a magnificent array of sparkling lights which marks a new pathway for us. We are drawn by its power, drawn by its magnetism, and we are rising in the air, rising, floating, floating, floating.

As we float in the sky we are overwhelmed by the beauty of the luminescent particles of the arrow flare and these droplets now flow together in a path which has become a river. We gather momentum in the current which seems to be drawing us towards the sun. We experience an exalted sense of freedom, of liberation, as we float in the ocean of the sky ...

Now, as we contemplate the nature of the tide that is carrying us along, we see that it has brought us into a strange domain. Looking to either side, we see as we look closely that one side of the stream has become dark while the other retains the luminosity of the new day and the two aspects seem to mingle in the stream of light that bears us along. We know now that we are pursuing a path of delicate and profound balance. Still the fibres of energy draw us along and we become increasingly one with the stream.

Now we see that this sacred domain also has a guardian and he has an imposing form. We are given his name: Raphael ... He is an enormous winged figure with trailing orange and blue drapes and he stands majestically before us. In his right hand he holds a water vessel and in his left a glowing torch.

At first we cannot clearly see his face, for it is sheathed in light. But our attention is drawn to his chest and the decorative embroidery upon his cloak. We see here, in essence, the fabric of the whole universe ... a bright vibrant sun shines from his breastplate and circling around it we observe the motion of all the planets and constellations. Raphael says to us: 'You see that the sun and his companion stars in the dark night of the heavens are brothers and sisters.'

*Then the golden luminosity in his chest fuses with the glow around his head and his whole form is ablaze with light. Gradually we are able to adjust our vision and we see that he has one foot in the stream and one upon dry land. And he is the overlord of two creatures as well.*

*One of these is a ruddy lion which lies angrily scowling near his foot. The other is a silver eagle on his left, whose wings whip ferociously in the air in an act of defiance. But we do not fear them because we are in the presence of the Lord Guardian.*

*He tells us now that he will show us how to control their tenacious qualities. Uplifting his water vessel from the stream, he pours its silvery glistening waters upon the head of the lion. The crystal fluids seem to pour right through him, and he is instantly transformed and subservient to his master. Then the Lord Guardian lowers his torch above the head of the eagle, which seems then to be of glass, reflecting the glowing embers of the torch. A spark of flame falls down into the eagle's heart and fills its entire translucent body with an orange-red glow. And the eagle ceases any longer to menace his master.*

*Again the Lord Guardian addresses us, reminding us that we are transforming our very being. His voice speaks to us in its own special way and, as we listen, it becomes like music, a mantra, a visionary rhythm which has special significance for each of us. We listen, listen, listen.*

*He beckons us now to enter his domain and we follow the stream of life towards a mountain cleft between two command-ing peaks. We see pinky golden rays of the rising sun lighting the mountain. We see the sun eroding the shadows on the mountain slopes, and it is rising slowly, slowly, higher and higher, and we are riding in the stream, feeling the healing rays of light get warmer and warmer upon us. We are merging with its beauty. We feel a deep, deep peace, a deep, deep peace, and we rejoice in its sacred, cleansing light.*

Guided magical visualizations, or pathworkings, like the one described above, are not in themselves a new approach, although most magical groups have neglected these 'occult mind games' in favour of ceremonial and ritual activities. Nevertheless, as mentioned earlier, when Dion Fortune was a member of the Stella Matutina group she developed the pathworking technique to tap archetypal images and 'ancient cult memories', and guided imagery work subsequently became an important part of the activities of the Servants of the Light.

In 1979 I had the good fortune to meet three practising members of SOL who had been experimenting with new pathworking techniques. We found that we had a great deal in common and soon began undertaking 'magical journeys' together. Cheryl, Moses and Cathy had begun to break down the linear structure of guided pathworkings and were writing new 'entry' material themselves that focused on specific magical symbols or mystical deities without constricting or enclosing the journey. Such visualizations led only to a certain point, but no further. After that you were on your own. This modification of technique allowed for a great deal more spontaneity and, in a sense, was more challenging. Now, instead of being summoned under tight controls, the gods were being invited to speak on their own terms!

The technique itself was completely simple. One person would read the 'entry' details for the visualization aloud while the others relaxed and flowed meditatively with the imagery. After each journey was completed – a process often taking around a quarter of an hour – the contents of the visionary sequence were immediately written down. We would wait until everyone was 'back' and had recorded an account of the journey before discussing what had happened.

One day Moses proposed a meeting with Merlin and the Jaguar. I didn't even know that Merlin *had* a jaguar but I was willing to give it a try! Perhaps Moses was deliberately throwing aside orthodox mythology to allow the imagination more free rein. As we gathered in Cathy's small inner-city flat I wondered what was in store. Moses has a deep and haunting voice and the charm of a great storyteller.

As we lay on the floor, completely relaxed and breathing slow, deep breaths, he began to read to us:

*Imagine a wall in front of you, with a doorway. You stand in front of the doorway and try to see what is on the other side. All you can see is a black mist filling the doorway. You step through the mist and find yourself on the edge of a clearing. In the centre of the clearing is a statue of a jaguar made of green jade. Of this stone tiger, this beast 'made of living water turned to stone', it is said that if you sit on its back it may come to life and take you wherever it may take you.*

*Beside the statue of the jaguar stands a man, an old man with long white hair and beard. He wears a long, white robe. He is Merlin, the Lord of the Jaguar.*

*Step into the clearing and begin your journey...*

My experience was quite intense and much more dramatic than I expected. Here is my account:

*It is easy visualizing Merlin although he seems also like an ancient Greek sage – the archetypal wise man. The statue of the jaguar is considerably larger than Merlin, and the giant cat is poised as if ready to strike. Looking up towards the heavens, it sits upright on its rear legs.*

*As I draw near, I allow the jaguar to jump and devour me, as it strikes for my heart. I am surprised that I do not die but instead find that I have conquered the jaguar, who has now become my ally. He is immediately more subdued, and I am able to ride on his back.*

*We soar into the heavens and it is very dark. At times I seem to see another jaguar alongside us, but it is really Leo the Lion striding through the constellations in the night sky. I feel some degree of dissociation as the darkness intensifies. The jaguar is taking me down, not upwards as I wished! It is another trial of strength. It is now time for me to become Merlin myself. The*

*change takes place … I feel I am Merlin. I am in control and the*
*trial is over. Still in a state of slight dissociation, I awaken and*
*gradually recover full consciousness of my surroundings.*

This journey gave me two valuable insights. The first was that I should never underestimate the power of the internal mythic images as they become increasingly real within the field of consciousness. The second was not to panic at moments of overwhelming crisis. On many occasions since this journey I have been devoured by my magical ally, but death seems to be no barrier at all in the imagination – the magician invariably finds that he can keep bouncing back! I have learnt also that no image should ever be allowed to dominate the consciousness so strongly as to cause a retreat; this indicates a lack of control. Far better to go with the flow of images, even if they seem to contradict logic completely … And of course, in magical reality there is no logic at all. Everything is possible. One soon learns to take a stand with both feet planted firmly in the clouds.

Cathy also had an interesting and evocative journey with the jaguar:

*The jaguar comes alive and Merlin and I mount on its back.*
*Merlin seems to merge with the body of the jaguar but still*
*retains his shape also. We leap into the sky in one enormous*
*bound, over the top of the trees ringing the glade. We fly over*
*mountains and valleys, trees and plains. Higher and higher we*
*fly until we are above the clouds, flying on into the sunset itself*
*– and to the land behind the sun.*

*We finally come down through the clouds and land in a*
*green field where some people are sitting in a circle. There are*
*fires blazing and a bard is playing a harp. Merlin dismounts*
*with me and the jaguar is frozen back into immobility. Merlin*
*turns to me and says 'These are my people'. As we walk among*
*them they make a kind of obeisance to him, by touching their*
*hands to their faces.*

*We sit in the main circle and a bard sings a song of a drowned city. This city, or town, was by the coast and people made a rich living from the sea and the surrounding land, which was very fertile. In the beginning they gave thanks to their Gods, bringing gifts in appreciation. But as time passed they forgot from whom their wealth came, and they grew greedier. Finally they became so corrupt that the Gods rose in anger and caused the water to rise, drowning their city and submerging all the land around them ...*

*The whole scene and story seems incredibly familiar to me, and I feel a real kinship with these people, and a great sense of belonging. When the bard has finished his song I ask Merlin if I may speak with him, and Merlin agrees. I feel very close to the bard, who is young and golden, but his eyes contain at the same time an expression of great age and sadness. He hands me his harp and I play it. I sing the song of my own journey – my searching and yearning – and the people listen, finally it is time to go. But I feel as though at last I have come home, and have found the place of my own roots, my beginning.*

*We mount the jaguar and Merlin holds me as we fly. He tells me I am one of his people. As we land he kisses me on my forehead, and this activates a silver star of energy. I am bathed in an intense white light and Merlin tells me to return whenever I wish.*

It was obvious that the new, less structured pathworkings were capable of unleashing a very rich source of imagery. Cathy's tale, quite aside from the parallel with the Atlantis legend, had revealed her own psychic origins. She had found her place in the mythic cosmos and, in a very profound and personal way, had discovered magical allies previously unknown to her. All of us were deeply moved as Cathy related her story, and I was intrigued by the potential of these less formal magical pathworkings.

On another occasion we undertook a journey somewhat comparable to the mind games except that we ascended rather than descended into the unconscious. And rather than be guided all the way, this time the entry visualization offered us a threefold choice. Cheryl read her entry to us:

*You are standing at the foot of a spiral staircase of very simple design. You commence the climb. Up and around it leads you, until at last you emerge in the centre of a very strange chamber. It is triangular, and in each of its three walls is set a white door. Approaching one of the doors you see an inscription which says: 'There is sweet music here.'*

*Moving further around you read the inscription on the next door: 'There is a play within.'*

*And the last door says: 'Buried treasure.'*

*Return now to the centre of the hall and choose which door, if any, you wish to pass through. Enter that door to find what is waiting, knowing that you may return whenever you wish.*

On this occasion I chose the doorway leading to buried treasure, I suppose because it sounded the most spectacular. However it soon became apparent to me that the treasure was not personal wealth but a metaphor for self-realisation and gifts of a visionary kind:

*I am assailed by a group of motley, bizarre creatures who hurl missiles at me and who roll their bodies into wheels, obstructing my pathway. I persevere, and come to the domain of a winged griffin who sits in a cave filled with golden light. His body glistens with radiance and at first it seems that a treasure hoard lies all around this awesome creature. The griffin tells me that the treasure itself is of a paradoxical nature. If I overcome the griffin and gather the treasure into my possession, claiming it as my own, I am bound to lose it. The treasure is only meaningful, he tells me, if I fail to be dazzled by it, and if I recognize that it has always belonged to me – in fact, to everybody. The griffin says he serves as a reminder to people approaching the hoard of treasure as a goal, that the journey itself is an illusion. I am impressed by this advice and wake up empty-handed. I have not attempted to assail the griffin for his treasure.*

Needless to say, I found this Zen-like journey extremely meaningful.

In the West, our cultural upbringing attunes us to strive for goals and to acquire wealth in order to improve the quality of our lives. Sometimes we forget what we possess already.

Now it was my turn to prepare entry visualizations for the group. The first of these was an entry to The Empress, the archetypal Great Mother of the Universe, and a central figure from the Major Arcana of the Tarot. This time, as I read the visualization to the others I found I was also able to continue with the journey myself, something I hadn't thought possible:

*We enter a cave door and descend by a flight of ancient stone steps to the palace of the Empress. At the bottom of the steps we come to a magnificent door encrusted with silver discs and beautiful sea-blue gemstones. The door swings in and we enter the antechamber. The floor is pearly and translucent and the walls of the chamber shimmer like starlit mirrors.*

*A young maiden presents herself as mistress of the star-chamber and we tell her that we would like to meet the Empress. The maiden says that she may allow us to enter one of three doorways and that she will give us a gift to enable us to be effective in the Goddess's domain. The gifts are: a scythe with which to harvest wheat; a silver goblet from which to drink; and a luminous crystal to guide us beneath a lake.*

*We see symbols of these on the doorways before us and take our gifts and enter. We are told that when we meet the Goddess we should account for ourselves, telling her in what manner we have travelled in her domain and what we have learnt. And now we step forward …*

The imagery took effect immediately:

*In the antechamber the gift that I chose from the maiden was the goblet from which to drink. Almost immediately I was aware that I was in a different domain. I was travelling on a precipitous mountain track which climbed perilously above me on a very vertical incline. I had a guide – a youth with a beautifully proportioned body and superb golden hair, who carried a fiery torch. The glow lit the landscape and it was craggy with green-blue colouring and potentially very hard to climb. I seemed to follow the light rather than watch where my feet were.*

*Then I was aware of a coiled dragon above me, curved around the central peak of the mountain. A warrior came forward and slew the dragon and then his own head was cut off. I didn't see how this occurred but a sense of self-sacrifice was implied. I passed by, and came towards the great Empress seated on her throne. She had long, flowing golden hair but I found it difficult to focus on her face as if her eyes were in many places at once.*

*She held out another flask for me to drink – instead, I was not aware of actually having taken the goblet from the maiden in the first place and maybe the sacred drink was the goal, not a gift given initially. I drank, and as the fluid poured into me I felt I was expanding and could almost float away. It was a very liberating, expansive feeling and it seemed that something precious had been given to me.*

I found this a very satisfying journey and it was the beginning of a number of encounters with sacred beings where some sort of gift would be bestowed. Usually, I found out, the actual properties of the gift would be intangible, even if the object was familiar. The giving of a gift seemed to symbolize a degree of interaction in itself much more significant than the gift itself. Later, in the shamanic work, I would discover that many of the gifts were power objects, energy sources planted directly within my body by the sacred beings themselves.

On Cheryl's journey to the Empress, she was asked to give a gift to the Goddess, not the other way around! Her journey began by combining two of her magical options, rather than focusing on just one:

*Through the doorway is a field of wheat which I work, with others, to harvest. When it is complete we return to their village for a celebration, during which a youth tells me I might reach the*

*Empress through the caves in the Misty Mountains.*

*I journey towards the mountains and on my way I am approached by an old man with a dog at his heels. He offers his services as a guide but I refuse. He then gives me a gift saying 'This is your pearl,' and leaves me.*

*The caves are made of limestone, full of strange and beautiful formations. The luminous crystal I have been given as a gift by the maiden of the antechamber lights the caves beautifully. Rivulets run everywhere but I have no real difficulty in passing through. I leave the crystal to shine in the caves.*

*Finally I pass through a door to the Empress. Her hair is of gold and silver, elaborately arranged in the form of a rising sun. She asks for a gift and I reply that I have not brought one. She says she would like the pearl. I am loath to part with it, but I give it to her and she places it on the floor. Softly touching it, she makes it grow until it becomes a huge, translucent dome.*

*A doorway appears and I step inside. The pearl chamber is silent and peaceful and yet I tingle with a kind of vibration. In the centre is a column of water which, because the liquid is not flowing, seems to be suspended in time. I stand in this column as if to blend with it, and here the voyage ends.*

The next journey I prepared was a brave one indeed to the domain of the Gnostic deity Abraxas. I was very pleased with the entry material after I had written it, both with regard to the symbolism, and also because in the form of the waterfall I had found a dynamic visual image for propelling the meditator into a new dimension:

*We look into the sky and are overwhelmed by the radiant beauty of the sun which radiates light that falls to earth in the form of fiery droplets. The droplets begin to shower in a golden haze. Days pass, then months, and by the time a year has passed the luminescent shower has become a wide river.*

*We journey down the river in a strange, archaic vessel that seems oriental – perhaps Persian or Indian – and which is*

*painted so that one side is black and the other white. We gather
momentum on the golden stream and are suddenly aware that
we are approaching a waterfall and that the boat is quite
incapable of avoiding floating over the edge. We do so, and the
feeling is one of liberation and freedom.*

*We float in the ocean of the sky and are once again aware of
a golden haze. As we draw nearer to the source of this light we
perceive a strange and awesome deity whose name we are told is
Abraxas.*

*Abraxas has a human body, the head of a hawk and legs of
serpents. In his left hand he holds a dagger and in the right an
ancient shield. Abraxas says that he can offer to lead us into the
land of night or the land of day and that whatever our choice he
will protect us with his weapons. He takes us to his temple, a
superb and majestic structure which stands on the peak of a high
mountain. There are two gateways in the temple from which we
may choose to commence our journey of the magical spheres. One
will lead us to the night and the other to the kingdom of the new
day, but we will not know which until we enter … for indeed
Abraxas is an unpredictable and awesome god. However, we must
be courageous in his presence for he is protecting us. We make our
choice of doorway and enter …*

Once again I found I was able to participate in the visionary process
released by the visualization:

*I enter the right door of the temple of Abraxas. It has high arches
inside and a seemingly infinite heavenly vault. There are people
here, holding their hands heavenwards, and I am aware of a
fluttering motion. At first I think it is a palpitating heart, then a
sacrifice, but now I see a white dove flying aloft. I feel extremely
peaceful and inwardly reassured.*

*Now I dwell on the form of Abraxas. He is very much a
composite, his hawk-like head suggesting he is a god of flight and
ecstasy while his body belongs to man's domain. His serpent legs*

*reach down below the earth. Now Abraxas changes form and I am shown a night-owl with angry yellow eyes in the place of Abraxas's hawk head. He pecks at my heart, but I allow him to – for I know that I cannot be harmed. Abraxas is showing me his night-side, but I do not feel any sense of panic. I am given to understand that these are the two facets of a great high-god who lives in the clouds in the ceiling of the celestial chamber. I am told that Abraxas holds the key for passing beyond this domain, but I remain within it and feel a protective sense of peace.*

I was very nervous before this pathworking. I knew from Jung's account of this deity, and also from the Gnostic literature, that Abraxas was difficult to fathom and certainly impossible to predict! On many inner-plane occasions since, I have been attacked and even devoured by magical creatures but have always found it best to yield rather than panic. It would of course be quite normal to fear actual death and to sense the imminent destruction of the ego, but inevitably one comes through these experiences with a feeling of renewal or integration.

Meanwhile, Moses' encounter with Abraxas proved to be much more testing than mine, and he engaged himself in a struggle with the god, although it was not without its humorous moments. Unlike the experiences of Cathy, Cheryl and myself, Moses' often had a strong conversational content:

*I enter through the right door. There are stepping stones which are like pillar tops in the water. The pillars become taller and taller, reaching into deep space. The last one I have to leap across. Abraxas speaks: 'Now you must fight me.'*

*He suddenly has wings and swoops into the air and down towards me. I grab his snake legs and he zooms up into the air with me. It is as if he has bird claws clutching my scalp, as I clutch his feet. It is like being on a circus trapeze. Then far below I notice a silver dome on the ground. He brings me down. 'Call me when you want to go back.' He swoops up into the air again. I sit on the silver dome and then a giant white worm comes and circles around me. Abraxas comes zooming down. I catch his snake legs and he rises up with me. Again, it is like being at a circus. I am twirling round and round, holding onto his right serpent-leg.*

'Now let go – if you dare.'

*(I let go and I can fly. It is a beautiful, slow-motion sequence.)*

'Now you must fight me.'

*(I have a sword in my right hand and a shield to the left. Abraxas changes his knife into his right hand and his shield to the left to oblige me. We perform a mock battle – clashing weapons and shields as we fly into space. Now I drop my shield and I am falling down, down, down … but there is a net stretching across space which propels me back again …)*

'It is time to go back.'

*(I grab the snake legs and we come shooting out through the temple doorway and land.)*

'Abraxas,' I ask, 'What was the meaning of what I saw and did?'

'The images are mine, the meanings must be yours,' he tells me.

'What was the experience?'

'A testing.'

'A testing of whom?'

'Of you, and also of me.'

'Who was the tested and who the testing one?'

'You were the tester. I was the tested one. The snake did not bite you …' [A reference to my holding his snake legs?]

'What was the silver dome?'

'A tortoise.'

'What was the worm?'

'I know not.'

'What was the net?'

'The rising of the sun.'

*Abraxas continues:* 'Go back my child, with my blessing. Go back my child with fear. Go back my child with loving.'

We were finding the pathworkings extremely interesting and evocative. Each evening as we gathered for a new journey we had the sense of a magical adventure before us. We were enjoying the ventures into the symbolic, mythic areas of our imagination because they were exciting and full of personal meaning – although we were not always able to pin down analytically just what that meaning was. One of the feelings which we all experienced at various times was the sense of participating in a personal fairy tale, of being able to transform from one shape or location to another, all in the blink of an eyelid!

I did not realize at the time that the pathworkings were leading me towards shamanism. I possibly should have been aware of this direction because the journeys were really a form of light trance produced by a combination of will power, visualization and relaxation, and the shamanic journey of the spirit – familiar to me from anthropological reports – had many features in common. The first shamanic content finally presented itself during a pathworking based on the symbol of the Tao, in which my journey was seemingly quite unrelated to the entry symbol. Once again, Moses read to us with his warm expressive voice:

*Imagine yourself in a dim temple of oriental design. In the centre of the temple sits an ancient monk whose eyes are sightless, and yet he smiles. Across the blind monk's knees lies a long-handled object, and behind him is a huge gong. Depicted on the gong are two fish, one of black, the other of white. And you recognize the disc of Tao, which is the gong. And you realize that the object across the old man's knees may be used to strike the gong. If you choose to remain and act, it may be that you will hear the striking of the gong of Tao, and learn something of its voice. Do then, as you will ...*

My journey was a curious one:

*I do not strike the gong but notice instead that the yin yang circle of the fishes becomes a doorway to a tunnel which leads down through waves to a place in the underworld. I am told that I am journeying to the domain of the sea-goddess Sedna (an Eskimo deity familiar to me from anthropological accounts of shamanic practices) and that my task will be a difficult one.*

*Sedna seems to be guarded by fierce tigers (I certainly wasn't expecting those!) and I can see their teeth snarling with rage. Later I notice that the waves of the stormy sea raging around Sedna's domain are not waves at all, but wolves who protect her from the unwary. And yet I am still confident that I will snatch a glimpse of her.*

*As it turns out, it is only a momentary flash, but I see her twice. On the first occasion I see her in the distance, standing in front of her throne. She has wild hair which lashes back from her forehead and a robe falls loosely around her form, exposing one of her breasts. Her manner is very hostile but after I have been able to prove that I am immune to the sea-wolves a new sense of calm comes over me. A serene wash of blue sweeps into my vision. I summon the water pentagram to view and vibrate the water mantra 'Shaddai' (a technique learnt from western magic) but the goddess does not come. I call her by her name, Sedna the Sea Goddess, and I seem to float into an underwater cave. I catch glimpses of old men asleep, but then find myself at the foot of her throne. I look up and she towers above me. Whether I sit at the base of a huge column or whether her form is huge I cannot tell, but I desperately want to see her face. This is not granted to me.*

*I ask her to pour her waters into my body and I feel that to a degree, but not totally, this request is granted. She tells me that I should come to see her again. Then I catch a glimpse of her face, mirrored in the waves, but like a glassy haze it disappears. I know I will have to go back to see her.*

It was surprising enough finding myself on a symbolic pathway to Sedna's domain, and the imagery of the sea of wolves was extraordinary, but the next journey gave me my first inkling of my magical allies. Moses had been interested in psychodrama and symbolic role play for some time, and one night – at his suggestion – we decided to try something different.

Moses had cleared the main room in the small, semi-detached house so that it was almost totally devoid of furniture. The room was perfectly square except for the area built up around what had been an open fireplace, and which now constituted a fifth wall across one of the corners. It was here we decided that the ritual shaman would sit on a small chair, presiding over the sacred space and either drumming or shaking the gourd rattles we had brought for the purpose. Moses proposed that he would take the shaman role while I would summon an animal spirit and begin to dance its characteristics in spontaneous ritual form, within the cleared space.

Moses suggested that, as the impressions began to come through strongly, I should retire to the corridor and prepare a mask from paper, wool and crayons that had been put aside. Moses, as presiding shaman, would then summon me to come forth from the corridor and return to the main room, wearing the mask and dancing in league with the magical ally as the drumbeat intensified.

The room was now darkened, and illuminated only by a solitary candle. Moses took his position on the chair and after a while began to beat a mantric rhythm on the large flat drum. I called forth several times seeking an animal spirit and then began to loosen my body in spontaneous dance gestures as Moses increased the beat of the drum. The image of a large hawk flashed into my vision several times. I went out to the corridor, made myself a rudimentary hawk-head mask with paper and crayons, donned it and began to dance hesitantly into the main room. The effect was eerie. I had made eyeholes in the mask but my vision was extremely restricted. In the darkness I could make out the figure of Moses seated in the distance. He looked stern and remote, his dark curly black hair and beard lost in the shadows flickering around the candle.

I began to dance the hawk in front of him, my arms moving freely in an undulating fashion suggestive of flight. The energies of the hawk now seemed to rise up within me and, beckoning to my shaman guide, I asked him to dance with me. Our wings rose and fell in slow, rhythmic fashion as we whirled around the room and I began to lose all awareness of the space we were occupying. Instead, I found we were soaring to the peak of a sacred mountain.

It was an exhilarating flight. The earth was now far below us, lost in the distance, as I became – for a timeless moment – the large and awesome hawk that had presented itself as my magical ally. Exhausted from the dance, I sank down on the floor and returned to the more familiar location of the small room in Moses' house in Trafalgar Street. For a while I was unsure what had occurred. My body had felt alive with a new energy, yet now I was physically tired and strained by the experience. I wondered what sort of magical reality Moses and I had tapped into, and where my hawk image had come from. As it turned out, it was not long before I was provided with some of the answers.

CHAPTER 8

# THE SHAMAN'S DOORWAY

Moses and I had heard that the International Transpersonal Association would hold a major conference in Australia in 1980. Several
leading members of the Human Potential Movement associated with
the Esalen Institute, including Stanislav Grof, James Fadiman, and
Ralph Metzner, were to give papers. We made enquiries through the
Australian organizers at the Blackwood Centre in Victoria, and to
our surprise and delight both Moses and I were asked to give papers
and workshops as part of the conference proceedings. Moses was to
deliver a workshop based on 'Death and the Soul', including story-
telling, mythodrama and the ritual use of masks and fantasy, and I
agreed to present the Major Arcana of the Tarot as an initiatory
sequence using the superb slides prepared by the Servants of the
Light. I also suggested a guided imagery session which would take
participants up the Middle Pillar of the Tree of Life to the accompaniment of appropriate electronic music. Unfortunately Moses
became sick prior to the conference and could not attend, but I was
able to present the core of the material that I had found to be most
valuable in tapping the essence of the magical tradition.

These sessions went well. However the conference had a strange
consequence for me as a result of an unexpected contact. Anthropologist Michael Harner was attending the conference to give lectures

and workshops on the shamanic journey. Dr Harner was well known to me through his excellent scholarly works on shamanism and had been the reader for my Masters thesis. He had been a visiting professor at Columbia, Yale and Berkeley and, understandably, I had an image of him as a solid and thoroughly respectable academic. I hardly expected him to be a shaman as well! However Harner arrived at the conference carrying a shaman's drum, gourd rattles, and a set of feathers and bones used by the Salish Indians for a mind-control game. As a result of his extensive field research in the Upper Amazon, Mexico and western North America, he had learnt shamanic techniques from the Indians and was now adapting their approach for a Western audience, showing how we too could tap the inner magical universe.

Harner's lectures and workshops were superb. He was a large friendly man with a dense black beard and mischievous dark eyes, who would chuckle when presenting the paradoxes of the shaman's universe. He told us about power animals and magical forces in Nature without at all attempting to present a logical rationale. He explained how, for the Jivaro Indians, a man can only reach maturity if protected by special power allies that accompany that person and provide vitality and purpose. He showed us how to meditate on the mantric, repetitive rhythm of a beating drum and ride it into the inner world, journeying in the mind's eye down the root system of the cosmic tree or up smoke tunnels into the sky. He also asked us not to judge these events when they occurred to us but to dwell with them on their own terms. We were, he said, entering a shamanic mode of trance consciousness where *anything* could happen – and invariably would! If we found ourselves engaged in strange, surreal events, or encountered mythic animals in unfamiliar locales, we should not recoil from such situations but should participate in the process of discovering a new visionary universe within ourselves.

Harner's workshop technique was remarkably simple. After blessing the group with his rattles, Harner would start pounding his large flat drum and encourage us to dance free-form around the room with our eyes half-closed, attuning ourselves to any expression that would flow through. We were endeavouring to contact our magical allies in a manner rather similar to the one Moses and I had stumbled on by ourselves.

After quite a short while, many people adopted animal postures and forms, and began to express these spontaneously in very individual ways. Some people became bears and lumbered slowly around the room. Others became snakes or lizards. There were several wild cats, the occasional elephant and a variety of birds. Once again my eagle-hawk presented itself to me as I winged around through the group.

Harner then asked us to lie down on the floor and close our eyes. He would begin drumming in a monotonous rhythm, to allow us to ride down into the shamanic underworld. He had explained to us that this was not an 'evil' domain but simply the magical 'reverse' of our familiar, day-to-day world, a place where a different kind of reality prevailed. The technique was to imagine yourself entering the trunk of a large tree through a door at its base. Perhaps there were steps inside but soon one would see the roots leading down at an angle of around 45°. Following a root-tunnel you then wound down, down, down – all the time propelled and supported by the constancy of the drumming.

Finally you would see a speck of light at the end of the tunnel. Gradually drawing towards it you had to pass through into the light and look around at the new surroundings. Various animals would pass by, but we were asked to look for one that presented itself to us four times. That animal was possibly our own magical ally. Perhaps we would engage in conversation, be shown new vistas and landscapes in Nature, fly in the air, or be given gifts or special knowledge. Harner emphasized that any of these things could happen but it was up to us to accept the visionary experience on its own level. If elephants finished up moving through the air, so be it. There was no question of the experience being put down as 'just imagination'. Imagination, in Harner's view, was a different type of reality, not an illusory world to be rationalized away or belittled.

Since my first guided imagery journeys I have always kept records of my experiences, and invariably I have written them down immediately afterwards so that all the details remained in a clear sequence. The following is my diary record of my first shamanic journey at the Transpersonal Conference:

> *I summon the image of the huge angophora tree that grows in the garden next door to ours at home, and pass through a doorway at its base. Using the rhythm of Michael's drumming I ride along the root system of the tree, down into the earth. The tunnel is large enough to flow down with ease, and I go through various twists and bends as I follow the root system.*
>
> *We have been taught to flow towards the light, and yet it seems to be a considerable length of time before the flickering light of day trickles in through the end of the tunnel.*
>
> *I find myself in a lush, primeval glade with huge, soaring trees reaching for the sky amid trailing vines and creepers. The undergrowth is quite dense and the trunks of the trees rise majestically to an enormous height. I am immediately aware, through an array of images, that my power animal is a hawk – confirming the earlier experiment with Moses in Sydney. I look for the home of the hawk and am immediately transported to a nest at the top of the tree. I see the hawk very clearly and seem to merge with it for a while. Its wingspan is impressive and I hear its cry.*
>
> *I am pleased that this creature seems to be my ally in the underworld. Coming back, I re-enter the tunnel and rise to the surface ...*

Encouraged by both the directness and essential simplicity of the shamanic technique, I decided to participate in a day-long workshop that Michael Harner was holding in Melbourne after the conference. We were asked to minimise our food intake and I managed to restrict my diet to an apple and a small piece of cheese for the whole day – a considerable effort!

As we gathered in the large hall, Harner took us through the same techniques that he had explained earlier. In addition we paired off within the group so we could practise contacting power animals on behalf of others – bringing the magical allies up the tunnel in order to transfer them to our partners. The theory behind this was the Indian concept that disease was linked to soul-loss. One of us would pretend to be 'dis-spirited' while the other would take the role of shaman and seek a power animal as a source of new vitality for that person. After an animal offered itself in the shamanic world we would scurry mentally back up the tunnel with the animal held close in our arms. We would then 'breathe' it into the chest and head of our partner, imagining that at that time its essence was transferring to the sick person.

We also did a great deal of dancing, and soon our power allies began to present themselves much more spontaneously in our movements and gestures. I am sure that much of this activity provided an appropriate environment and atmosphere for our magical journeys. We seemed to be entering a quite new dimension which soon became as familiar and real as the outside world. My first journey took me through both night and day, and my link with the hawk was now much more specific:

*I travel down the tunnel beneath the angophora and this time take less time to reach the light at the end of the tunnel. However, there is a problem: the tunnel has opened onto a cliff-face with a precipitous drop to the sea. I have to summon my power animal to me ... The hawk appears in the distance, flying with its wings gracefully extended. It has powerful dark black and yellow eyes and a mix of black and brown feathers. As it approaches the cave entrance it turns around, allowing me to mount up on its back. We ease away, flying over the sea.*

*It is daylight at this stage. We come along the cliff-edge and I see a domed building overlooking the sea. Then there is a very clear scene of a building like a restaurant – with white stucco walls – fronting onto the sea. A large number of tourists are clustering around.*

*Leaving them, we now fly into the sky and night falls. I seem to merge once again with the hawk as we fly over a hamlet with a number of high-gabled houses huddled together. The darkness shrouds them but their ancient medieval roofs peer through.*

*Now it is daytime again and I land amidst a crowd at a fairground. The people seem pleased to see the hawk land, and they welcome us. Then we rise up again, and darkness returns. We fly over the sea, moonlight glinting over the waves. Rocky crags reach up out of the sea, but I feel secure. I can see the original rock face in the distance. I enter, and return up the root system to the tree in my garden.*

The feeling of entering into a new experiential domain was very impressive. It really did seem at the time that I was flying, and I could see the waves of the sea crashing against the rocks beneath me. These journeys seem distinctly different from dreams; the imagery is much clearer and at times it seems like watching a film – except that one is actually participating in it!

The climax to the workshop, for me, came in the evening. Harner told us that he had been experimenting with journeys up into the sky, as well as down into the underworld. He asked us to imagine entering a smoke tunnel either by wafting upwards on smoke from a campfire or by entering a fireplace and soaring towards the sky up a chimney. As we entered the smoke tunnel, he explained, we would see it unfolding before us, taking us higher and higher into the sky. At some time or other, Harner said, a water bird would present itself as an ally, to lift us still higher into the sky-world. Why this should be a water bird was not explained. He was also keen to see whether any of us would see any 'geometric structures', although he didn't wish to elaborate on this in case his comments had the effect of programming us into a specific visionary experience. As it turned out, several people in the group had visions of geometric, 'celestial' architecture.

The room was quite dark as Harner began to beat on his drum. I found it easy to visualize the fireplace in the front room of our house:

*I enter the fireplace and quickly shoot up the chimney into a lightish grey whirling cloud tunnel. Soon I am aware of my guardian – a pelican with a pink beak. Mounting the pelican's back I ride higher with it into the smoke tunnel. In the distance I see a golden mountain rising in the mist ...*

*As we draw closer I see that, built on the top of the mountain, is a magnificent palace made of golden crystal, radiating lime-yellow light. I am told that this is the palace of the phoenix, and I then see that golden bird surmounting the edifice. It seems to be connected with my own power-hawk.*

*I feel awed and amazed by the beauty of this place, but the regal bird bids me welcome. Then the hawk comes forward and places a piece of golden crystal in my chest. I hold my breath deeply as I receive it, for it is a special gift.*

*The drum is still sounding but soon Michael asks us to return. However I am still high in the sky and find it very difficult to re-enter the smoke tunnel. When I finally do begin to return, the heavens remain golden, and as I travel down into the tunnel I look up to see saint-like figures around the rim of the tunnel, bidding me farewell.*

This journey was a very awesome one for me. After returning to an awareness of the workshop location and the people around me, I found it very difficult to articulate my thoughts. I seemed lost for words but anxious, nevertheless, to communicate some of the importance that the journey had had for me. I felt I had been in a very sacred space. The direct interaction with the hawk that had planted a crystal in my chest was totally unexpected, although I remembered reading about events like that in Aboriginal mythology.

There was a minor embarrassment as well. Some of the people attending Harner's workshop had also been to the Transpersonal Conference and had participated in my guided imagery session using Tarot imagery and electronic music. Many of them had told me afterwards that they had got a lot out of it. Now, by contrast, I found myself in a state of mind where I had experienced a quite different type of magical reality that seemed to go beyond anything I had achieved in western magic. There was a total directness and natural authenticity in the shamanic journey. Harner's notion that shamanism pre-dated the split of Eastern and Western religious consciousness also gave it a primeval quality which added to its appeal. Suddenly shamanism seemed much more valid and real, and in our group discussion – when I finally did manage to assemble some thoughts – I made this point to the other people present. Events since then have shown me that this idea of a split between magic and shamanism is quite illusory and one can tap a universal mythology through both methods. In fact, as I was to discover, at times the two traditions fuse together. Nevertheless, at the time, I was convinced that I had found something else. I returned home delighted with having made so many good contacts at the Transpersonal Conference, a definite convert to shamanism.

# HAWK AND CROCODILE

Several of my close friends were interested in visionary magic. As an experienced SOL member Cheryl had found our magical path-workings extremely evocative and she wanted to try the shamanic technique. A friend from the conference, Sue, and another friend named Ly, who had spent many years with Nature worship, Wicca and western magic, were also keen to explore the new approach. After the conference we began to hold regular shaman gatherings at each other's homes. One of us would drum while the others would journey on the vision-quest. The following are entries from my magical records of that period:

**January 28**
> *I find it easy enough to get into the tunnel and rise upwards. I am soon aware of a bird coming to get me. It is delicate, yet broad in wingspan, and has a long curved beak. I think it is a heron but am told it is a curlew.*

*We fly upwards and come again to the domain of golden crystal although it is not as well defined as before. But my power bird – magnificent ally! – is there, and faces me directly. This time instead of receiving a gift from him, I have to reach for it. My hand passes into his neck and from it I take a green gem; bottle green rather than emerald in hue.*

*Now the bird shows me his transformations. He passes through a number of forms, the most notable being a pigeon. Perhaps he is telling me that he can be docile and peaceful as well as hostile.*

## March 2

*I travel with the drumbeat through the smoke tunnel and this time the pelican is there to assist. However the atmosphere is very turgid and it is difficult to ascend with any speed. It feels more like a DC-3 than Concorde!*

*As I rise in the air my first impression is of a huge giant digging the soil with a spade. He hurls his implement in the air and I follow it: it has become a totem-pole surmounted with the image of my hawk. The pole now rises, rocket-like, into the air and becomes a torch … we are reaching more elevated ground.*

*I have come to a marbled courtyard and look towards a stylish palace that combines both futuristic and art deco architecture – as if belonging both to the past and an era yet to come. I enter the hall and it is very dark inside. Through the shadows I see an Ibis-headed god, seated on a throne. It is a form of Thoth, presumably, but this is not clear to me.*

*There is an Egyptian bas-relief on the wall behind the god. Two hands are visible in profile, holding a flask. The hands now become three-dimensional and, lifting out from the wall, pour water onto my head which passes down into my body. I feel I am turning into glass or crystal.*

*The drumming has ceased but I still feel quite rigid. It is some time before I am 'back'.*

## July 13

*I visualize a large door at the base of my angophora. The door is regal and stately, and I prepare to enter. However, almost imme-diately I find forces blocking my entry. A procession of hostile*

*Egyptian forms, including a 'dark' version of Horus, impedes my path, and a black swan tries to peck me.*

*I persevere, and enter the tunnel which by now is full of people. The hustle and bustle is unpleasant and, again, I have the feeling that something or someone is barring my way. I continue to fight my way along – quite an unexpected experience – and eventually discover that this tunnel is quite straight, not twisting like a root system, and I can see quite clearly where I am going.*

*The people have formed a stream on either side of me and are now travelling in the same direction as me, not against me. Rather than emerge from the tunnel into the light I notice that the left-hand side of the tunnel has become translucent and the line of people begins to curve outwards. Gradually the figures form a circle which encloses what I take to be a sacred area. Within the circle there is a stylized island surrounded by water. A large tree is growing on the island and I begin to climb it, anticipating an encounter with my hawk. But it is not to be ...*

*I become increasingly aware that I am in the presence of a crocodile entity. At first I see him from the side and wonder whether he is a new ally. Gradually I become more and more aware of his snout and his interlocking teeth. I see his eyes quite clearly. Now he turns full on, and begins to eat me. I yield to him and there is no pain. There is a vague, slightly disquietening feeling that some of my limbs have been separated off, but this is apparently no obstacle, for I continue on my way. Higher up the tree I come at last to the domain of my hawk. But he is not fully visible, and a quite extraordinary sight presents itself. The 'room' I am in has a layer of dense grey cloud near its 'ceiling' and the legs of the hawk are visible protruding through it. But I am not granted a complete vision of my power animal. Perhaps the hawk is punishing me for not coming to see him more often!*

Certain themes seemed to be emerging on these journeys. The power-hawk was beginning to show itself to me in different forms and the familiar shamanic images of the power-crystal, the water bird allies, the cosmic tree, and even its symbolic representative, the totem pole, continued to appear. However, certain other aspects were puzzling. I seemed to have another power animal in the form of a crocodile. There was certainly no obvious rationale for this since I have never lived in a tropical region and crocodiles have only been of passing interest. Nevertheless, the crocodile has since appeared to me on several occasions.

More surprising than any of these aspects, though, was the emergence of strong Egyptian imagery on the journeys. My expectation had been that shamanism would strike to the 'earliest' and 'deepest' core of mythic imagery, and that somehow my experiences would now be more primeval. This was not the case at all. Since my earliest ventures in shamanism, Horus, Ra, Isis, Thoth and other images from classical Egyptian mythology have continually arisen during the visionary journeys and of course they dominate the symbolism of the Western Mystery Tradition and the magic of the Golden Dawn.

One particular journey from this period brought home to me what now seems obvious, namely that shamanism does not confine itself to native Indian symbolism but can tap a vast resource of mythic imagery in the subconscious mind. I was with Cheryl, Moses and Ly in the Trafalgar Street flat where Moses and I had first experimented with shamanic dance and ritual masks. The evening began in the usual way, and on this occasion Moses was drumming. From the start the journey had a very specific direction:

*It is the day before full moon ... My initial desire is to undertake a journey of ascent, but it seems that tonight I have no choice but to go down! My eagle-hawk is there and immediately offers to carry me down the tunnel on his back.*

*We come out over fierce, lashing waves and the scenery is dark and forbidding. For a while I am unsure where we are, but the hawk lifts me into the sky. The sun begins to appear from behind the dusky clouds and we fly towards it. The light is more radiant now and we are flying very high. I seem to go through a 90° shift as I ascend and feel almost two-dimensional. I now have to lift myself out of that vertical plane and face a gathering of people who are bathed in light.*

*I am with a gathering of spiritual devotees who are dressed in robes. An orange-golden light pervades the scene. At first I stand on the periphery. A man rides his horse into a large fire which is glowing in the centre of the group. He is unaffected by it. Now I see a figure with four arms, moving in mudras, revealing spiritual motion. He has a distinctly Buddha-like appearance.*

*It is my turn. I have a 'baptism of fire' but am unscathed by the flames although they lap all around me. Looking down I see I am sitting on a silvery pentagram which seems to have a magnetic-field effect – shielding me from the destructive power of the flames which billow all around in waves.*

*Now a new figure begins to dominate my vision. It is a deity with a hawk's head and a human body and seems to be related to my power animal. He is about to speak to me as Moses ceases drumming and I have to return ...*

For some time Moses had been interested in a technique he calls 'image taking'. If a paradoxical image presents itself during a guided imagery journey, the idea is for the practitioner to 're-conjure' it into consciousness, and almost become possessed by it, while other members of the group ask questions about its origin and purpose. Puzzled by the nature of the hawk-entity that had appeared at the end of my journey, I resolved to call it forth. I sat on the small chair that we had agreed should be the 'shaman's seat' and began to focus all my attention on actually *becoming* the mysterious bird-god. Moses and Ly began to ask me questions:

*I tell them I am a bird-man. Moses asks me who I am.*

*I answer: 'I am Abraxas.'*

(This was truly extraordinary, because I had never made a conscious connection between the hawk-headed Abraxas and my magical hawk ally, although it seems obvious enough now.)

*I am an eagle with soaring, expansive wings who flies at the top of the vault of the universe, confined only by the curve of the sky. It is a great pressure for me to combine with a human form. I feel at times that the lower part of my body is constricted as if by a straitjacket, a difference of densities between the cosmic sky and my ventures on the earth plane.*

(Now a moment which Moses later told me was sad and poignant ...)
*I tell them I am losing my wings and becoming more human. My body seems to constrict all over and I become sweaty and clammy ...*
Gradually I awake.

It was this journey, more than any other, that demonstrated that in reality a variety of magical techniques can lead towards the same regions of inner space. In essence, shamanic meditation and ritual drumming are guided imagery techniques which make full use of sensory deprivation. When external visual stimuli are cut off, it is quite normal for internal imagery to manifest in a compensatory manner, and if the venture inwards is specific enough – focused, for example, on the cosmic tree or magical flight – a universal layer of mythic imagery can be tapped.

What was happening now was that the range of symbols that I found personally meaningful was resurfacing in a new way, rather like new casks for old wine ... The Gnostic content of the image-taking was also quite apparent. In the early centuries of Christianity many of the Gnostic sects had been accused of denying the body, and regarding it as evil. It seems to me that perhaps what was meant by this Gnostic teaching was precisely a question of 'densities'. In the Gnostic conception there were sacred realms of being and profane areas too, and a continuum existed between them. The Gnostics characterized the mystic quest as a venture towards the spirit and, symbolically, the gross vehicle of the body – with all its sensory restrictions – was comparatively less important. Our image-taking experiment seemed to show that pure spirit found it difficult to coexist with the much 'denser' material of human existence.

Shamanism was certainly providing a challenge, and posed as many questions as it gave answers. In several respects, the journeys were also proving to be quite unpredictable. With hindsight I am sure that this was a good thing. We are all inclined to like our religious beliefs to be neatly packaged and enclosed – there is a type of security in being able to hold on to a body of religious concepts that for us represents 'ultimate certainty'. Shamanism did not provide that type of security. I was finding that it did not lead specifically *anywhere*; that sacred images from a wide range of cultures could appear at any time. Much of what I experienced was proving to be personally meaningful but there was something about each journey that kept one ever-watchful at the same time. I was constantly reminded of the Yaqui shaman don Juan's conversation with Carlos Castaneda: 'For me the world is weird because it is stupendous, awesome, mysterious, unfathomable ... you must learn to make every act count, since you are going to be here for only a short while; in fact, too short for witnessing all the marvels of it.' [1]

**Note**

1    Carlos Casteneda, *Journey to Ixtlan*, New York 1972

CHAPTER 9

# ALLIES OF POWER

During the next six months I noticed that certain patterns would recur during the shaman sessions. Often, in my mind's eye, I would find myself thrust into exotic cultures, for example among African natives or Red Indians or initiatory bands of Aborigines. The shaman's drum, by association, was leading me into areas where the mythologies had been rich and diverse, a clear contrast to the barrenness of mythic thought in our computer-dominated Western society.

Another quite distinct theme involved my being attacked or devoured, either by adversaries or by my power animals themselves. My crocodile, for example, usually showed his affection for me by eating me, but I would always find that inside his belly I felt protected and well armoured and not at all fragmented. It was as if something in me had to be broken down before a more integrated magical persona could be established. As a result of this perhaps, I felt increasingly that I was going through a 'rebirth' process.

Three of my journeys involved quite vicious attacks that symbolically involved my 'death' but which, in a positive way, culminated with impressive visions of the power-hawk and a feeling of my own 're-emergence'.

*The drumming is very effective tonight. I enter the tunnel immediately and am aware of thronging people. They are*

*negroid ... I am in Africa (Dahomey?). There are circular huts
with thatched roofs and the ground is very dusty. Huge palm
trees catch my attention, and one in particular seems to reach up
into the sky. I climb it instinctively, feeling that my power animal
must be up there.*

*Soon a hawk appears, turns around and lets me mount on
her back. We fly, but I am too frightened to look down, and I
wonder where we are going. We have arrived – at the domain of
a Giant Hawk, who towers far above me. I stand at its feet like a
grovelling earthworm.*

*Now I become aware of huge sculptures, some of them are
Egyptian and portraying hawk-like images. Others are less
distinct. They encircle me, in a manner similar to the monoliths
at Stonehenge. A young assistant dressed in Egyptian-style
clothing comes upon me with a cudgel and begins to beat me. I
become pulp-like but feel no pain.*

*Now, as I lie upon the ground on my back, a female hawk flies
down and rests gently on my genital area. There is no eroticism,
but it seems to be some kind of sexual encounter. I feel I am being
reborn as a young hawk. Energy courses into my arms and I feel
them turning into wings. I rise, hawk-like, from my body.*

*The drumming ceases, and I return through the tunnel. I am
pleased by tonight's adventure. It is good to re-establish a firm
bond with the hawk.*

*My entry tonight is through a fireplace which includes as part of
its design a decorative metal rim. I travel through a succession of
arches filled with golden light but eventually come to a more
hostile location where I am hemmed in by warriors. Once again
the figures are African. They raise their spears menacingly in the
air above me, as if I am some sort of sacrificial animal (a pig of
some sort ...?) I let them spear me, but there is no feeling of pain.*

*My vision now switches to a Red Indian locale and I see a
medicine-man performing a bird dance. Feathers adorn his hair
and arms. Meanwhile I am told that I am a hawk and I should
rise up from the carcass of the slain animal (the pig). I am
instructed that in tribute I should bare my chest-wound to the
sun, and allow its healing rays to fall upon the gash.*

*As the rays of sunlight warm my skin, a hand comes into view in the right side of my vision. It comes closer, and inserts a crystal into my body. I look down and see the crystal within, as if my body were hollow …*

*Now I rise up into the air and come to a mountainous domain where there are huge eagles and other birds of prey, much, much bigger than I. I see their heads clearly silhouetted against the bright blue sky and they are awesome to behold… Are they comrades of Abraxas?*

*The drumming begins and I have no trouble entering the tunnel. I come out in a grove of trees which fills the sky with branches and foliage, allowing only occasional glimpses of blue sky.*

*I come to a tree with a very straight trunk, and begin to climb upwards. The tree resembles an elongated silver birch. After climbing for a short time I come to a 'jungle'. (It doesn't occur to me at the time how preposterous this is!) Where I notice a dark-skinned crocodile frothing around in some marshy reeds. It seems smaller than other power-crocodiles I have encountered but it soon makes its presence felt by beginning to devour me, feet first. I allow him to do this, feeling no pain, and when I am inside his belly I feel protected and strong, as if encased in firm leather armour. I have to continue up the tree, however, so I cut myself out of his belly with a dagger, and begin once again to climb vertically.*

*I become aware of a pair of amber-orange eyes, and then the beak and visage of my bird of prey. It begins to peck at my throat, gradually dismembering me until I become a ball, and then an egg. The bird then sits over me, and I have the feeling that I have to fight to be 'hatched'. At times I seem to be under the nest as well as under the bird… almost as if I have to battle my way up on to its level. I gradually emerge from the egg and notice as I peer over the rim of the nest that other bird-men warriors are up there too – and they are dancing.*

*I become bird-like, and float off into the sky. I am not able to see clearly below, however, and my last impressions before the drumming ceases, are of the wind and a hazy blue light.*

*It is good to reaffirm my links with my power animals. When they eat me, I know they like me!*

Two subsequent sessions revealed interesting aspects of the symbol of the totem pole which is, of course, a form of the mythological 'world axis' that unites the different worlds or planes of the shaman's journey:

*At first I am not sure where I am, but gradually I become aware of a luxuriant orchard filled with citrus trees. A crystalline river flows through the orchard and its surface has a remarkable mirror-like sheen. I am somewhat surprised, but not unduly alarmed, when a crocodile comes towards me, showing itself four times to me. I have met it before, on other occasions.*

*The crocodile opens its jaws wide and I sit inside its mouth and cruise down the placid river as if in a small boat. There are figures dancing on the bank and they become increasingly dominant in my field of vision. The figures are leaping and dancing with amazingly slow, graceful motions, as if they are not subject to gravity. They then form into a column, standing upon each other's shoulders, and form a human totem pole. I rise up the pole, high into the misty blue sky, and for a time the journey seems endless.*

*Now a large Red Indian stands before me and I look very clearly into his eyes. He sings a chant, which becomes abstract and rhythmic: 'ne, ne, ne ... ' It is the first time I recall hearing sound from within the visionary sequence itself, during a shamanic exercise.*

*It is raining on the roof of the house where we are and this seems to influence the nature of the inner journey. The scene becomes dark and menacing, and rain begins to fall heavily within my vision also. Through steely-grey pellets of rain I discern the supremely 'central' and pivotal image of a great eagle-hawk and I look deeply into his right eye, which shines with a green-yellow glow. His feathers glisten dark brown, and his presence – as always – is quite awesome. I float back down, entering a Red Indian wigwam from the top. It feels protective, almost womb-like. Then as the rapid drumming commences, I return to the room where the journey began.*

*I do the drumming myself this evening but I find, to my surprise, that I can still enter the shamanic world; my drumming does not interfere.*

*I am with a band of Aborigines. I see them very clearly. Their dark skins glisten as they sit around the campfire and there are white daubs of paint on their foreheads and cheeks.*

*The figures are in a circle but soon they transform into a human chain, like a centipede, and in turn become a crocodile which chases its own tail (like the alchemical dragon). The form of the crocodile, reinforced by the drumbeat, creates a circular entry-point and I travel through the tunnel that has been created, into a region of watery depths. The waters part around me as I travel, and I feel rather like the Biblical Moses, parting the waves as I move along.*

*Now it has become dark and I am surrounded by a group of native shamans. This time they are not Aborigines, but Red Indians. As I watch, the chief of the band, who is resplendent in a feathered headdress, stands up and his head – minus his body – seems to ascend a totem pole. I rise up with him, and meet various rather solemn Indians whom I take to be ancestor spirits although I am not given their names. I anticipate meeting my hawk, but it is not to be. At the top of the pole is my crocodile's mouth. I am swallowed whole and come back down inside the totem pole!*

*I am back in a domain of watery textures and diffuse light. My last impression is of a light-bearing messenger riding towards me on a horse. There is no specific communication but he does not seem hostile. The quality of the light is very unusual and a sort of yellow incandescence rises from the ground.*

*Now I stop the drumming and return through a pool of water to the room where we had begun. I am impressed that the magical journey can also operate while one is drumming oneself. The activity becomes automatic after a while and does not intrude.*

A little while later I noticed that the imagery from the Western Occult Tradition was entering the shaman visions more distinctly. This tendency has since continued, perhaps not surprisingly.

An example of this 'parallel symbolism' occurred when the symbol of the Holy Grail appeared on one of the journeys. However shamanism and western magic and mysticism all involve personal transformation as part of the quest, and the Holy Grail is one such metaphor for the spiritual journey. The symbol of the cup – which at different times is the womb of the Great Mother or the cup of the spirit of life – is present in both orthodox Christian mysticism and the occult mythology of the Tarot. I also began to find that in a shamanic context it had the same type of meaning:

*We have a guest drummer tonight. Carmen has begun to drum after putting us all through an excellent progressive relaxation. Rose essence wafts through the air from an incense stick.*

*My initial intention is to travel downwards through the root system of the tree I have visualized. However the entire journey proves to be a rising through various planes within the hollow trunk of the tree. Initially I am in a ground-level chamber similar to our room in the house.*

*Immediately my mind is dominated by the image of Red Indians dancing in a circle, their feather headdresses uplifted in the breeze. I rise, bird-like, above them, and find myself approa-ching a ceiling of cloud. Having passed through it, I begin to dance like a bird myself, and gradually realize that I am in a large teepee. I look up and see what seems to be a disc of light, visible through the apex. I travel up towards it, and now encounter one of my two power animals: the crocodile.*

*I am rapidly engulfed by a chaotic slurring of crocodile images but they transform into a mandala of crocodiles, all with their snouts facing the centre. Out of this focal area arises a large, Grail-like cup filled with silver light. It rises slowly into the air and I follow it. I find myself summoning my hawk ally. I can only see the hawk dimly at first. Then I have the feeling of reaching a mountain peak and flying through the air gracefully at an enormous height. I am only vaguely aware of the valleys and rivers far below me but I return to the peak and am aware that the hawk has human characteristics – primeval and unfamiliar.*

*The hawk becomes even more human and a golden light emerges from his chest. I have a strong impression of an Egyptian figure, perhaps a priest, waiting nearby. The light now solidifies into the form of a golden goblet, and as I watch the hawk dissolves into it gradually. The Egyptian priest, solemn and dignified, remains in the background as the hawk's head disappears.*

*It is an impressive and mysterious sight. I have the sensation
of being bathed in golden light myself – somehow it has poured
down on top of me – and then the drumming summons me back.
I find it difficult to return. It has been a most enjoyable and
literally 'elevating' experience.*

Unfortunately, the pattern of regular shaman meetings became
disrupted at this stage. Ly was finding strong parallels between
shamanism and Wicca, and was being urged by members of her
coven to spend more time with them. Moses, meanwhile, returned
to his earlier role as a solitary magician in the urban wilderness.

For a while, to my regret, shamanism was relegated to a minor
role in my activities. It was difficult working alone because, even
though one could drum for oneself, it required a lot more concentration and was best shared by the group. However the shaman
sessions were able to begin again the following year – primarily as a
result of a chance encounter with two like-minded occultists whom
I had not met before.

## TOWARDS ABRAXAS

Several years earlier, while researching a book on different occult
groups, I had met a devotee of goddess worship named Marguerite
Moor. Marguerite had established a unique magical group called the
Order of Isis-Ishtar in a north shore suburb of Sydney and it attracted
many different types of people: marketing managers, accountants,
students, waitresses, labourers and radical feminists – all of them
interested in learning more about the feminine side of their inner
nature. Marguerite combined mythology, Tarot, astrology and ritual
in her Order and had nine grades encompassing many different forms
of the Universal Goddess. These included Geshtinanna, the Mesopo-
tamian goddess of wine and grapes; Cybele, the Titan earth goddess;
Astarte and Isis, the Phoenician and Egyptian goddesses of fertility,
and Venus/Aphrodite, the classical goddess of beauty and love.

One afternoon, at Marguerite's request, I held a shaman gathering
in her temple for members of her Order. After I had explained the

techniques, they began to dance around a candle in the centre of the temple floor, while I drummed from the periphery. Many of them had immediate impressions as they began to dance their power animals. One woman had an eagle, others had wild cats and one man had the front half of an elephant (two legs only!) The second dance proved more effective. This time the elephant manifested in its complete form, one girl discovered she had a Bengal Tiger for an ally, and there were two snakes – a boa constrictor and a cobra – both of them incarnating in very petite females. One man discovered that he had a snail as his power animal, something I hadn't encountered before. He rejected it outright as a magical ally and insisted that it depart from his vision, but it declined, and he had to accept it. Among other power animals that appeared were a black panther and a wolf.

It was a successful first venture into shamanic practice for the group, who were already well trained in visualization. Marguerite told me that she would invite me to a 'ritual feast', to be held soon, to meet the participants in a more casual environment. Marguerite was holding these meetings to encourage members of her Order to meet occultists working in other traditions, and she was keen to diffuse the sense of secrecy that was present in most occult groups.

Robert and Ian – the two young occultists who would be my partners in shamanic visualization later on – were discussing Aleister Crowley's magical system with Marguerite's Order members when I first met them. Interested in Crowley's sacramental approach to magic, and his diverse body of writings, Robert and Ian were involved in establishing a Kabbalistic research centre and also – as I later discovered – had the largest filing system on international meta-physical and occult groups that I had ever seen. We soon discovered a mutual interest in trance magic, and agreed to meet again as soon as possible – in order to exchange techniques and information.

Although their flat was comparatively small, Robert and Ian had put one room aside for ritual workings. There was a metal-frame pyramid on the floor, one or two crystal pendants appropriate for ceremonial (but also strikingly similar to shamanic power objects) and several mattresses and cushions to lie on while embarking on the mind-journeys. There was also a hi-fi stereo system to allow us to play electronic music as an accompaniment. I had recently obtained a cassette of Michael Harner's shaman drumming from a mail order company in Big Sur, and was anxious to try it as an alternative to actual drumming. The tape proved to be very effective indeed and had the advantage of running for 25 minutes on each side – at two different drum beats, fast and slow. I had found in our earlier shaman sessions that few of us could sustain a regular drum-beat for more than fifteen minutes and of course this was a restriction on the length of the journeys.

Our first meeting together produced excellent results. We positioned ourselves in turn beneath the metal-frame pyramid, which even seemed symbolically appropriate – a technological equivalent of the Red Indian teepee and the tomb of the Pharoahs ... Using the cassette tape of the drumming in the intimacy of a small, darkened room proved to be quite as effective as the actual drum. We each took turns and recorded a written account of the journeys afterwards. I was pleased that, despite a gap of several months, my magical allies had not deserted me:

*I feel a strong sensation of bright, geometric lights and pulsing energy and lie back on the mattress beneath the metal frame. I summon the cosmic tree and begin immediately to become my hawk. I am very aware of my heavy wings, propelling me through the air. The drumming is on 'slow beat' rather than on rapid. I fly over numerous snow-clad mountains, above pine forests, and into a grey misty twilight. At times I seem to be perched on top of a high mountain peak surveying the night-sky. The drum does not particularly propel me tonight, and at times it contains, rather than releases me... almost like driving nails into a coffin. This has an interesting shamanic effect, because of the task of constructing a new spirit body! A river of silver crystal begins to pour over me, making me a new body. I become very aware of the drumming and it is as if nails are being hammered into my body, not to harm me but to reconstruct my form. I breathe deeply, and new vigour and life comes into my new body ...*

*Now I can fly again, and through the forest I come to a huge mansion-like dwelling, half concealed by snow. The mansion itself is mountain-like, and drawn through one of the illumined windows, I come towards a silvery light source and look upwards.*

*A sacred being is seated on a throne. At first I wonder if it is a lunar form of Thoth – the deity looks Egyptian and is seated rather stolidly on a throne in the manner of the large Egyptian sculptures. The head at first glance looks Ibis-like, but as I draw closer I see that it is more the form of a crocodile. I observe it first in profile but its snout becomes more prominent and I know now that I will have to submit myself to it, as I have done with my power animal before. Its teeth are sharp filaments, more delicate than the teeth of a real crocodile, but I manage not to be frightened. As the snout comes towards me I see that the god is offering me a single lustrous pearl. Taking the gift, I lie in its mouth and its snout closes, holding me. I do not panic, but feel new assurance and confidence.*

*The drumming continues and again I am travelling over snow and dark forest. I sense that I am drawing near to the domain of a snow queen and look for her form in the light before me. Her eyes and hair are jagged with icicles and frost and there is a steely-grey light radiating from her body. She tells me her name is Sedna, and I have seen her before beneath the waves of an angry sea. Now she takes on aspects which remind me of the Tarot card Justice. She holds a steel sword above me which at first seems very threatening – almost like the sword of Damocles. But this then becomes the central axis for a pair of scales and I see that she is judging me. I sway back and forth beneath her and then I feel I am becoming a young child, rocking in her arms. The sense of peace and comfort is wonderful and reassuring.*

*The drumming ceases and I return.*

This journey had certain qualities which distinguished it from those which had preceded it. For the first time a quite particular archetype from the Tarot – the goddess of the Justice trump – had appeared in a shamanic context. I was also responding to the drumming in new ways, and learning that the drumbeat could be either a propelling or an inhibiting force, each of them appropriate in different symbolic situations.

On several occasions I have found my body being restructured in a mythic sense, and often the rhythmic drumbeats have seemed to be the hammerings of a deity at work. The formation of a magical body was one of the sequences on the next visionary journey:

*I ascend in a column of smoke which billows upwards from a campfire. Looking down I can see that I am rising quite high in the sky. Once again I have become immersed in a stream of liquid crystals which shine and twinkle with silver light. I am shown how the gods – it seems to be Thor specifically – fashion shamans from the quartz rock.*

*I can see a man's chest, and then other parts of his torso, being sculpted from the crystalline rockface on the side of a cliff. A person emerges from the rock. Now I realize it is me! But as I stand free of the rock I feel much shorter than I really am and realize that I am without a head! Paradoxically, this isn't at all alarming. I am now given a crystalline head to complete my body structure, and this is fitted to me almost like a medieval helmet.*

*I come now to a Red Indian teepee (the dramatic change of cultures seems quite natural at the time) where a figure is dancing. Bird feathers adorn his arms and body. There is a sense of the Indian being me as well. I am caught up in the dance, which is clearly totemic. My body changes its proportions and I begin to acquire an animal form. I have a long, muscular abdomen and short, lizard-like legs. Then, as I contemplate my form, I realize that I am dancing my crocodile!*

*It is a strange sensation: primeval and atavistic, with all the impressions of a lower animal intelligence but also a strong and vital force in Nature. The teepee has become a crystalline pyramid and, as I look upwards, I notice chunks of crystal falling upon the pyramid like heavy rain. A totem pole forms within the teepee, and I rise up. As I do so, I ask to see my other power animal.*

*I summon strong images of the hawk, and then see it seated on the top of the pyramid, which by now has become a mountain. The hawk has its back to me, and I prepare to mount it. Instead*

*I become the hawk, and as I merge with its body I am surprised by the sheer weight of the creature's wings as I endeavour to fly slowly through the air.*

*I now ask for a gift from my hawk, and we seem to separate. I am presented with what looks initially like small mussels. I then see that inside one of the shells, which must be oysters after all, is a bright, luminescent white pearl. The symbolism of the shell is impressed upon me ... the hard protective surface of the shell housing the precious gift within.*

*The drum has stopped and with some reluctance I return to the room.*

The renewed discipline of meeting regularly for shamanic journeys was obviously a positive factor. We were all finding the experiences to be rich in mythic imagery. For my part, the initiatory rebirth themes, the allusions to the Tarot archetypes, and the sense of par-ticipating in a new type of magical reality, continued at subsequent meetings:

### December 9

*At first I feel surrounded by evil, predatory forces. A large crab-like monster fills the sky as I endeavour to rise up in the smoke of the campfire. I see an Indian chief conjuring over the flames but he looks ominous. He is wearing a horned feather headdress and stares out at me with dark, pitted eyes. I feel drawn into the fire, but yield to it rather than become frightened... knowing that I should not panic. For a while I seem to float above myself ... a sense of dissociation.*

*The sky has now become a dull brown colour but eventually opens up, as a tunnel of silver light forms in the dark murkiness above me. I call to my hawk to free me and find myself able to stretch vertically. However, the drumming seems to be nailing my feet to the ground, and I am unable to pass through the tunnel.*

*The scenery now changes so that I come to resemble a Jack and the Beanstalk figure. I have become a huge giant traversing the heavens. Now there is another switch, and I have become microscopically small, standing beside the ankle of a huge giant who towers above me. The symbolism of the giant now disappears as I myself become the World Tree, heavily ornamented with diverse and very intricate 'universal' motifs. As I contemplate the complex beauty and grandeur of the Tree my perspective changes so that I perceive the huge axial trunk stretching upwards from my chest into the heavens, while roots come out of my back, reaching down into the earth. I am literally 'middle earth', extending horizontally in all directions: a most bizarre sensation!*

*I have become like liquid soil. Someone is stirring me, and I realize I am in a bubbling cauldron. The Tarot image of Temperance comes to mind immediately. My texture has become viscous. I am clinging to the stirring stick like a cocoon to a branch. My body meanwhile is changing shape. My crocodile is there to eat me also (as he always does!) and my form begins to break down into diffuse elements.*

*Now there is a distinct change. I experience a soaring effect as I become a knight in dark armour riding a white, winged horse. I am seeking the Holy Grail. I rise up the side of a mountain and can see a cross superimposed on top of it. The mountain – Calvary – is illuminated, and Christ-like, I find myself being crucified. There is a definite sense of detachment to this experience – no impression of passionate involvement.*

*I call for my power hawk but feel he has forsaken me. No vision of the Grail presents itself either. Meanwhile the drumming has ended but I know that I have not resolved my situation.*

I ask Robert and Ian to let me continue by turning the drum cassette over to the other side.

*(Slow drumbeat cassette)*

*I have come to another mountain. There is a heavy blizzard and deep snowdrifts hug the rocks. I see a dark, silhouetted figure ahead of me. He is hidden in a cloak and his face is not visible, but he has a lamp to guide him up the treacherous mountain path; I recognise him as the Tarot figure of the Hermit.*

*I merge with his form and feel I am being taken to meet 'The Goddess'. However, I do not see her fully: her downward stretching hand reaches towards me but her face is not visible.*

*Now my attention focuses on the drumbeat and my vision is*

*dominated by the texture of wood. I am shown 'The Drum' (an archetypal shaman's drum) and merge with its shape. It encompasses me like a womb.*

*My body, once again, seems to dissolve. It is totally liquid, without form. The rapid fourfold drum signal summons me back. Still I feel that the journey is unresolved, but has been preparatory for something else ... perhaps initiatory.*

*Something deep is stirring in me. I am re-forming. My essence is being channelled towards a new expression.*

## December 17

*My first visual impression is of a giant eagle, perched majestically on the top of a mountain, sedately surveying the world below. He seems lofty, distant, immovable. I am given his name: Abraxas.*

*Now I see a number of people bowing reverently to the earth. There are several intense points of light shining on the ground. They are luminescent pearls that give off radiation like laser beams and their colour changes from green through to purple. The people are awestruck by these marvellous power objects.*

*An imposing figure now stands before me. He reminds me of the Hierophant from Aleister Crowley's pack except that a large, all-seeing eye emanates from his chest, replacing the pentagram.*

*I am led into a large initiatory hall, the vaulted ceiling of which rises high into the sky. Huge Egyptian gods in close formation tower above me. It is as if I am an ant surveying a huge mural that has come alive. I recognise Thoth and Isis, and an alligator-headed god whom I later learn is Sebek-Ra, a form of the dark god Set. The ceiling of the temple now seems to dissolve into blue sky as the sun rises in the distance. We are all bathed in warm sunlight but the sun itself is not visible.*

## January 21

*As the drumming begins I rise up in the curls of smoke, I open my wings as I take the form of the hawk. Before me, in my focused vision, I can see a crystalline shape forming: it becomes a geometric, stylized mountain. I fly towards it in the greyish night sky.*

*I am shown a beautiful naked woman who seems to be enclosed in an alchemical type of flask – she is moving around inside it. At the same time, I am strongly aware of the beating drum, which seems to be the very pulse of life itself. I can feel its vibrancy in my body like an enhanced heartbeat and for a brief moment I become the drum.*

*What has been the crystal mountain now becomes the central pillar of the Tree of Life, except that it is formed of entwined human components – muscle, sections of the abdomen, the breast and so on. As I rise up it becomes a tunnel and I have the impression that it is the birth canal and I am becoming foetus-like. I am going to give birth to myself! My foetal body includes my power animals: I have images of the hawk and the crocodile, and also an elephant ... which is new to me. All of these are somehow combined.*

*For a while I seem to be plunging into an evil morass; a slimy devil with tentacles lurks around trying to engulf me, but I laugh at him and he dissolves. The scene lightens immediately...there seems to be an aspect of confronting one's karma here ...*

*As the drumming continues I feel the undulatory movements of a woman giving birth, although there is no sensation of pain (perhaps because, as a man, this is outside my range of experience). At times, as if from the viewpoint of the mother, I look down at my enlarged abdomen as if expecting the child to be born.*

*The sun is rising through the clouds, bringing the journey to a climax, but somehow I withdraw from going through the birth experience. At the end, the journey is unresolved, but nevertheless has strong initiatory implications. I am beginning to realize that the shamanic journey combines not only magical will, but also the capacity to surrender to a higher process. I suspect I am holding back on this ... Nevertheless, I feel very peaceful and relaxed after the journey.*

The shamanic vision-quest had now reached an interesting point. The Gnostic deity Abraxas had become clearly identified with my hawk ally in my own personal mythology. I was also finding quite remarkable fusions between the Tarot imagery, which had been part of my world for so long, and the rich and universal symbolism of shamanic rebirth. And, increasingly, the inner journey of the spirit was becoming an encounter with the abstract and infinite qualities of the Cosmos:

## January 28

*I raise my arms upwards as the drumming begins, and feel myself lifting away. I am becoming the eagle-hawk; my wings are extended and I am flying. Now I find I am becoming an egg. A shell encloses me and I feel I must break through.*

*Tonight I feel very fluid, as if I am surrounded by vibrant waves of energy. It is very astral and more abstract than usual. I have the strong feeling of the shaman's role to break through different planes of being.*

*I rise up out of the egg, a young eagle emerging into flight for the first time. I am very aware now of a dark god standing before me and feel it is a test of strength. The god is a dark form of Horus, and his black hawk eyes look at me piercingly. This negative god now becomes Baphomet, sinister and evil, but I am not frightened of him. Gradually his form dissolves and a silver pentagram replaces him.*

*I am now transforming myself by amalgamating the four elements. From being fluid, light and airy, I become dense and rock-like. I feel there is a shell or enclosing surface to break through into a different reality.*

*My clarity of vision improves and I am drawing very close to my two power animals. I see the head of my giant hawk extremely close: the texture of the feathers on the head in minute detail, the eye in profile. I merge with the hawk, but find as I do so that it now becomes a crocodile as well. My body becomes strong and armoured, and I can feel the tail moving. I am dense and heavily structured.*

*The drumming becomes more noticeable and somehow I am aware that I must be born in a new form which encompasses my power animals. I see a foetus swimming in blue fluid, and it feels as if I am in an oceanic womb. Then I become increasingly smaller and the sense of space dominates.*

*My field of vision becomes an exquisite and intense blue. There are thousands of people here, worshipping a force in the heavens. The sky tints with gold and it is very awesome, at times reminiscent of the Tarot card* Judgement *except that a drum rather than a trumpet heralds the presence of a great god.*

*I look upwards and the azure blue sky seems to take a vault-like shape, like the ceiling of a great cathedral. I am in the domain of Abraxas but he is mysterious and elusive.*

*I call his name and I see a huge hawk, but one thing is puzzling: he has no face. He seems to flow into infinity ... He is the 'bornless one'.*

*Once again I have a feeling of the enormity of space, and the strong impression that the magical journey itself, rather than any specific goal, is the important thing.*

*It is very Zen-like. Abraxas is the hawkless-hawk, the God-who-is-not. A form of space.*

It still seems very remarkable to me that archetypes from an essentially forgotten religion like Gnosticism can reappear in one's consciousness. Whether my concept of Abraxas is comparable to Jung's, or even to that of the third century Gnostic mystics, is hard to judge. Nevertheless, from the very beginnings of my journey through magic and occultism, the symbolism of Abraxas has always had a special appeal for me. More than any other deity I have been aware of, Abraxas represents the polar opposites of consciousness and therefore seems to me to be a much more complete deity than one who is specifically good or evil. If I have learned anything from magic, it is that the path ideally leads to a state of inner balance, and that means integrating both the positive and negative forces of the psyche.

In the final analysis, shamanism and visionary magic both lead to a similar place. It has been called the 'separate reality', the 'crack between the worlds', the sacred ground where self-initiation occurs. What is most remarkable of all, is that the old inspirational gods are still accessible. They are still there to help us on our journey.

This book really has no ending, for the shamanic quest itself is an ongoing process. I am convinced that the shaman's journey, in a very real and personal way, is a pathway to sacred space. In many so-called 'primitive' societies such a concept would be familiar enough, for here the myths and deities associated with creation, fertility, and the cycle of life, birth and death, are a function of everyday life.

In our increasingly clinical, and many would say alienating, modern urban society, access to the sacred and awesome areas of being is harder to come by. Some have found mystical experience or self-realisation through the auspices of a church, others through meditation or related approaches to heightened states of personal awareness. It seems to me that one should refrain from passing judgement on whether one spiritual path is superior to, or more appropriate than, another. In the final analysis we are all seeking a personal mythology, a framework of meaning which encompasses not only the complex realities of modern life but also the essentially mysterious and intangible realms of our inner being.

The path to the sacred introduces us to profound areas of true and lasting meaning. We begin to understand our place within the cyclical and universal processes of Nature and – perhaps for the first time – we are able to participate in the mythologies that enriched our western culture centuries before we were born. Shamanism and visionary magic are both expressions of the timeless adventure of the human spirit and, for me, their fascination is enduring. One can hardly say more than that.

# APPENDIX

## MUSIC FOR MAGICAL VISUALIZATION

During the mid 1980s, as ambient electronic music became more widely available, I began to research different types of music suitable for magical visualization and meditation. I was attracted to this genre of music because it was minimal and non-intrusive.

In my book *Music for Inner Space*, I presented the idea of identifying different selections of ambient music with the five elements, Earth, Water, Fire, Air and Spirit, since we often recognize these particular characteristics in different styles of music. I also thought this would be a useful correlation because the five elements are central to several mystical systems – including yoga, alchemy and the Western Magical Tradition. These elements, in sequence from lowest to highest are:

Earth    (level of everyday consciousness/feminine polarity)
Water    (correlates with the Moon/feminine polarity)
Fire    (correlates with the Sun/masculine polarity)
Air    (correlates with the Sky/masculine polarity)
Spirit    (transcendent awareness)

I thought it might be helpful to choose specific sequences of recorded ambient music – Earth music; Water music; Fire music, and so on – and then produce a series of composite tape recordings for personal use as musical backgrounds, especially when working with Tarot pathworkings or visualizations based on specific elements (e.g. the Tattvas, referred to in chapter five).

## THE QUALITIES OF MUSIC

Music is useful as a supplement to meditation and creative visualization because of its capacity to stimulate feelings and associations. Some types of music have a calming, relaxing quality, while other forms of music are intense and dramatic, and help sharpen the intellect or stimulate specific, well-formed images in the mind's eye. Some types of music instil a sense of harmony and balance, while other discordant forms might leave us restless, on edge, or lacking resolution. Some forms of music may seem to us to be trivial or whimsical, while other musical compositions have an impact that is profound or inspiring.

When choosing selections of music for visualization or meditation it is important that the music should be tested by the individual meditator to ensure that it evokes specific associations, so that – like an affirmation – it helps reinforce a particular focus or orientation. If the music and the visualization are competing against each other, on the other hand, the value of the music is obviously diminished …

In practical terms, selections of music chosen for the element Spirit are usually suitable as generalised ambient backgrounds for relaxation and meditation. Such music is typically devoid of strong melodic content and leads us towards a state of consciousness expansion while also remaining gentle and reflective in quality. This is music which literally enhances our inner journey of the spirit.

## A SELECTION OF MUSIC FOR
## MEDITATION AND RELAXATION

**Music for *Spirit*:**
  Aeoliah, *Inner Sanctum* (Oreade)
  Aeoliah and Mike Rowland, 'Twin Flames Rising' and 'We are One
    Light', from *The Reiki Effect* (Oreade)

# Appendix

Ash Ra, 'Ocean of Tenderness' from *New Age of Earth* (Virgin)
Harold Budd and Brian Eno, *The Pearl* (EG/Polygram)
*Ambient One: Music for Airports* (EG/Polygram)
*Ambient Two: The Plateaux of Mirror* (EG/Polygram)
Robert Haig Coxon, *The Silent Path* (RHC Productions)
Deuter, *Garden of the Gods* (New Earth)
Brian Eno, *Thursday Afternoon* (EG/Polygram)
Steven Halpern, *Eventide* (Halpern Sounds)
*Zodiac Suite* (Halpern Sounds)
Nancy Hennings and Henry Wolff, *Tibetan Bells* and *Tibetan Bells II*
    (Celestial Harmonies)
Iasos, *Angelic Music* (Bluestar Communications)
Japetus, *The Radiant Self* (Listen Music)
Gyorgy Ligeti, 'Requiem'and 'Lux Aeterna' from the *2001* soundtrack
    (MGM)
Ray Lynch, *The Sky of Mind* (Windham Hill)

## A SELECTION OF MUSIC FOR MAGICAL VISUALIZATION

### Music for *Earth*:
Chaitanya Hari Deuter, *Ecstasy* (Kuckuk)
Brian Eno, *Ambient Four: On Land* (EG/Polygram)
Steven Halpern, *Déjà Blues* (Halpern Sounds)
Kitaro, *Oasis* (Kuckuk)

### Music for *Water*:
Brian Eno and Harold Budd, *Ambient Two: The Plateaux of Mirror*
    (EG/Polygram)
Brian Eno and Harold Budd, *The Pearl* (EG/Polygram)
Larkin, *O'cean* (Wind Sung Sounds)
Pink Floyd, 'Echoes' from *Meddle* (Harvest/EMI)
Fripp and Eno, *Evening Star* (Island)
Edgar Froese, *Aqua* (Virgin)
Klaus Schulze, 'Crystal Lake' from *Mirage* (Island)

**Music for *Fire*:**
    Ash Ra, 'Sun Rain' from *New Age of Earth* (Virgin)
    Philip Glass, 'The Grid' from *Koyaanisqatsi* (Island)
    Laraaji, *Ambient Three: Day of Radiance* (EG/Polygram)

**Music for *Air*:**
    Brian Eno, 'Under Stars' and 'Weightless' from *Apollo* (EG/Polygram)
    Fripp and Eno, 'Wind on Water' and 'Wind on Wind' from *Evening Star* (Island)
    Edgar Froese, *Epsilon in Malaysian Pale* (Virgin)
    Paul Horn, *Inside the Great Pyramid* (Mushroom)

# SHAMANIC AND MAGICAL ORGANIZATIONS

The Foundation
    for Shamanic Studies
PO Box 1939
Mill Valley
California 94942, USA
Tel: (415) 380 8282
www.shamanism.org

Seven Circles Foundation
PO Box 559
Lagunitas
California 94938, USA
Tel: (510) 236 3512
www.sevencircles.org

D.O.M.E: The Inner Guide
    Meditation Center
PO Box 46146
Los Angeles
California 90046, USA
Tel: (323)851 9333
www.dome-igm.com/whatis.htm

Servants of the Light (SOL)
PO Box 215
St Helier, Jersey
The Channel Islands, UK
JE4 9SD
www.servantsofthelight.org

Readers may also contact the author via email: nevilldrury@hotmail.com

# BIBLIOGRAPHY

Andrews, T., *More Simplified Magic: Pathworkings and the Tree of Life*, Dragonhawk Publishing, Jackson, Tennessee 1998

Ashcroft-Nowicki, D., *Highways of the Mind: the Art and History of Pathworking*, Aquarian Press, Wellingborough 1987; *The Shining Paths: An Experiential Journey through the Tree of Life*, Aquarian Press, Wellingborough 1983; *First Steps in Ritual*, Aquarian Press, Wellingborough 1982

Balikci, A., 'Shamanistic behavior among the Netsilik Eskimos' in J. Middleton (ed.) *Magic, Witchcraft and Curing*, Natural History Press/Doubleday, New York 1967

Bardon, F., *Initiation into Hermetics*, Osiris Verlag, Koblenz 1962
*The Practice of Magical Evocation*, Rudolf Pravica, Graz-Puntigam, Austria 1967 (both titles republished by Merkur Publishing, Wuppertal)

Bharati, A., (ed.) *The Realm of the Extra-Human*, Mouton, The Hague 1976

Blacker, C., *The Catalpa Bow*, Allen & Unwin, London 1975

Bogoras, W., *The Chukchee*, Memoirs of the American Museum of Natural History, vol. XL, New York and Leiden n.d.

Bonner, J., *Qabalah*, Skoob Books, London 1995

Breuil. H., 'The Paleolithic Age', in Rene Huyghe (ed.) *Larousse Encyclopedia of Prehistoric and Ancient Art*, Hamlyn, London 1962

Budge, E. A. (ed.), *Lefefa Sedek: The Bandlet of Righteousness*, Luzac, London 1929

Butler, W. E., *The Magician: His Training and Work*, Aquarian Press, London 1959

Campbell. J., *The Inner Reaches of Outer Space: Metaphor as Myth and as Religion*, Harper & Row, New York 1988; *Myths to Live By*, Viking Press, New York 1972; *The Hero with a Thousand Faces*, Pantheon, New York 1949

Case, P. F., *The Tarot*, Macoy Publishing Co., New York 1948

Castaneda, C., *The Teachings of Don Juan*, University of California Press, Berkeley, California 1968; *A Separate Reality*, Simon & Schuster, New York 1971; *Journey to Ixtlan*, Simon & Schuster, New York 1972; *Tales of Power*, Simon & Schuster, New York, 1974; *The Art of Dreaming*, HarperCollins, New York 1993; *The Active Side of Infinity*, HarperCollins, New York 1999;

Cavendish, R., *The Tarot*, Michael Joseph, London 1973

Cohen, K., 'Taoist Shamanism', *The Laughing Man*, vol.2 no.4, p.49

Colquhoun, I., *Sword of Wisdom*, Spearman, London 1975

Cook, A. S., and Hawk, G. A., *Shamanism and the Esoteric Tradition*, Llewellyn, St Paul, Minnesota 1992

Court de Gébelin, A., *Le Monde Primitif*, Paris 1775-84 (nine volumes)

Crowley, A., *Magick in Theory and Practice*, privately published, Paris 1929 (republished by Dover and Castle Books, New York, various editions) *Book Four*, Sangreal Foundation, Dallas 1972; *The Vision and the Voice*, Sangreal Foundation, Dallas 1972

Das, P., 'Initiation by a Huichol Shaman', *The Laughing Man*, vol.2 no.4

De Mille, R., *Castaneda's Journey*, Capra Press, Santa Barbara, California 1976 *The Don Juan Papers*, Ross-Erikson, Santa Barbara, California 1980

Drury, N., *Everyday Magic*, Robert Hale, London 2002; *The Shaman's Quest*, Brandl & Schlesinger, Sydney 2001; *The History of Magic in the Modern Age*, Constable, London 2000; *Exploring the Labyrinth: Making Sense of New Spirituality*, Continuum, New York 1999; *The Elements of Shamanism*, Element, Dorset 1989; *Music for Inner Space*, Prism Press, Dorset 1985; *Inner Visions: Explorations in Magical Consciousness*, Routledge & Kegan Paul, London 1979

Drury, N., and Tillett, G., *Other Temples, Other Gods*, Methuen, Sydney 1980

Eason, C., *A Complete Guide to Magic and Ritual*, Piatkus, London 1999

Edinger, E., *Ego and Archetype*, Penguin, London 1973

Edsman, C. M.(ed.) *Studies in Shamanism*, Almquist & Wiksell, Stockholm, 1967

Eliade, M., *Shamanism*, Princeton University Press, New Jersey 1972; *Birth and Rebirth*, Harper and Row, New York 1964

Elkin, A. P., *Aboriginal Men of High Degree*, University of Queensland Press, 1977 (republished by Inner Traditions International)

Estrada, A., *Maria Sabina: Her Life and Chants*, Ross-Erikson, Santa Barbara, California 1981

Feinstein, D., and Krippner, S., *Personal Mythology*, Tarcher, Los Angeles 1988

Feldman, D. H., *Qabalah: The Mystical Heritage of the Children of Abraham*, Work of the Chariot, Santa Cruz, California 2001

Fisdel, S.A., *The Practice of Kabbalah*, Jason Aronson Inc., Northvale, New Jersey 1996

Fortune, D., *The Mystical Qabalah*, Ernest Benn, London 1957 (republished by Weiser) *Applied Magic*, Aquarian Press, London 1962

Freeman, D., 'Shaman and Incubus', vol 4. Psychoanalytic Study of Society, London 1964

Furst, P., (ed.) *Flesh of the Gods*, Allen and Unwin, London 1972 *Hallucinogens and Culture*, Chandler & Sharp, San Francisco 1972

Gettings, F., *The Book of Tarot*, Tribune Books, London 1973

Gilbert, R. A., *Revelations of the Golden Dawn*, Quantum/Foulsham, London 1997

Grant, K., *The Magical Revival*, Muller, London 1972; *Images and Oracles of Austin Osman Spare*, Muller, London 1975

Gray, E., *A Complete Guide to the Tarot*, Crown, New York 1973

Gray, W. G., *Inner Traditions of Magic*, Weiser, Maine 1984

# Bibliography

Green, C., *Out-of-the-Body Experiences*, Ballantine, New York 1973

Grof, S., *Realms of the Human Unconscious*, Dutton, New York 1976; *The Adventure of Self-Discovery*, State University of New York Press, Albany 1985

Halifax, J., (ed.) *Shamanic Voices*, Arkana, New York 1991; *Shaman: The Wounded Healer*, Crossroad, New York 1982

Harner, M., *The Way of the Shaman*, Harper & Row, San Francisco 1980; *The Jivaro*, University of California Press, Berkeley 1984
(ed.) *Hallucinogens and Shamanism*, Oxford University Press, New York 1973

Houston, J., *A Passion for the Possible*, HarperCollins, San Francisco 1997; *The Hero and the Goddess*, Ballantine, New York 1992

Howe, E., *The Magicians of the Golden Dawn*, Routledge & Kegan Paul, London 1972

Ingram, S., 'Structures of Shamanism in Indonesia and Malaysia', University of Sydney anthropology thesis (unpublished), 1972

Jamal, M., *Shape Shifters*, Arkana, New York and London 1987

Jung, C. G., *Man and his Symbols*, Dell, New York 1968; *Septem Sermones ad Mortuos*, Stuart & Watkins, London 1967; *Symbols of Transformation*, Bollingen Foundation, New Jersey 1956

Kalweit, H., *Dreamtime and Inner Space*, Shambhala, Boston 1988

Kaplan, A., *Meditation and Kabbalah*, Weiser, New York 1982

King, F., (ed.) *Astral Projection, Magic and Alchemy*, Spearman, London 1971

King, F., and Skinner, S., *Techniques of High Magic: A Manual of Self-Initiation*, C. W. Daniel, London 1977 (republished by Inner Traditions International)

Knight, G., *A Practical Guide to Qabalistic Symbolism* (vols.1 and 2), Helios, Cheltenham 1965; *A History of White Magic*, Mowbray, London and Oxford 1978

La Barre, W., *The Ghost Dance*, Allen & Unwin, London 1972

Larsen, S., *The Shaman's Doorway*, Harper & Row, New York 1976

Lessa, W., and Vogt, E., (ed.) *Reader in Comparative Religion,* 3rd edition, Harper and Row, New York, 1972

Lévi, E., *The Key of the Mysteries,* Rider, London 1959

Lewis, I., *Ecstatic Religion,* Penguin, Harmondsworth, London 1971

Lilly, J.C., *The Scientist,* Lippincott, Philadelphia 1980; *Simulations of God,* Simon & Schuster, New York 1975

Linton, R., *Culture and Mental Disorders,* Charles C. Thomas, Springfield, Illinois 1956

Masters, R., and Houston, J., *Mind Games,* Turnstone, London 1973; *The Varieties of Psychedelic Experience,* Holt, Rinehart & Winston, New York 1966; *Psychedelic Art,* Grove, New York 1968

Masters, R., 'The Way of the Five Bodies', *Dromenon*, vol. III, no.2, Spring 1981; *The Goddess Sekhmet*, Llewellyn, St Paul, Minnesota 1991

Mathers, S. L., *The Greater Key of Solomon*, De Laurence, Chicago 1914; *The Lesser Key of Solomon*, De Laurence, Chicago 1916 *The Grimoire of Armadel*, Routledge & Kegan Paul, London, 1980

Matt, D. C., *The Essential Kabbalah*, HarperCollins, New York 1995

Matthews, C., and J., *The Western Way,* Arkana, London 1994

Metzner, R., *The Unfolding Self: Varieties of Transformative Experience,* Origin Press, Novato, California 1998; *Maps of Consciousness,* Collier-Macmillan, New York 1971

Michael, H.N., (ed.) *Studies in Siberian Shamanism,* University of Toronto Press, Toronto 1963

Middleton, J., (ed.) *Magic, Witchcraft and Curing,* Natural History Press/Doubleday, New York 1967

Moore, R., and Gillette, D., *King, Warrior, Magician, Lover,* HarperCollins, San Francisco 1990

Nicholson, S., (ed.) *Shamanism,* Quest Books, Wheaton, Illinois 1987

Noffke, W., 'Living in a Sacred Way', *Shaman's Drum,* Fall 1985

Pagels, E., *The Gnostic Gospels,* Weidenfeld & Nicolson, London 1980

Pearson, C. S., *Awakening the Heroes Within,* HarperCollins, San Francisco 1991; *The Hero Within,* HarperCollins, San Francisco 1989

Peters, L., 'The Tamang Shamanism of Nepal,' in S. Nicholson (ed.) *Shamanism,* 1987

Regardie, I., (ed.), *The Golden Dawn,* vols. 1–4, Aries Press, Chicago 1937-40; *The Middle Pillar,* Aries Press, Chicago 1945; *The Tree of Life: A Study in Magic,* Rider, London 1932

Richardson, A., *Priestess: The Life and Magic of Dion Fortune,* Aquarian Press, Wellingborough 1987; *Dancers to the Gods,* Aquarian Press, Wellingborough 1985

Robinson, J. M., *The Nag Hammadi Library,* Harper and Row, San Francisco 1977

Roth., H. L., The Natives of Sarawak and British North Borneo, (2 vols.), University of Malaya, Singapore 1968

Scholem, G., *On the Mystical Shape of the Godhead,* Schocken, New York 1997; *Origins of the Kabbalah,* Princeton University Press, New Jersey 1990; *Major Trends in Jewish Mysticism,* Schocken, New York 1961

Schultes, R. E., and Hofmann, A., *Plants of the Gods,* Hutchinson, London 1979

Semple, G. W., *Zos Kia,* Fulgur, London 1995

Spare, A. O., *The Focus of Life,* Askin Publishers, London 1976; *The Book of Pleasure,* 93 Publishing, Montreal 1975

Steinbrecher, E., *The Guide Meditation,* D.O.M.E. Foundation, Santa Fe, New Mexico 1977 (republished in revised form by Weiser as *The Inner Guide Meditation,* 1994)

Tart, C., (ed.) *Transpersonal Psychologies,* Harper & Row, New York 1975 (ed.) *Altered States of Consciousness,* Wiley, New York 1969

Vasilevich, G. M., 'Early Concepts About the Universe Among the Evenks', in Michael, H. N. (ed.) *Studies in Siberian Shamanism,* University of Toronto Press, 1963

Waite, A. E., *The Holy Kabbalah,* University Books, New York 1960; *The Pictorial Key to the Tarot,* Weiser, New York 1973

Wasson, R. G., *Soma: Divine Mushroom of Immortality,* Harcourt Brace Jovanovich, New York 1968; *The Wondrous Mushroom,* McGraw-Hill, New York 1980

Wilby, B., *New Dimensions Red Book,* Helios, Cheltenham 1968

# INDEX

# Index